Evaluation as policymaking

Introducing evaluation into a national decentralised educational system

Books of related interest

The Use of Performance Indicators in Higher Education: A Critical Analysis of Developing Practice 2nd edition
Martin Cave, Stephen Hanney, and Maurice Kogan
ISBN 1 85302 518 6

Evaluating Higher Education
Edited by Maurice Kogan
ISBN 1 85302 510 0

Directors of Education - Facing Reform
Tony Bush, Maurice Kogan and Tony Lenney
ISBN 1 85302 506 2

Teacher Appraisal
A Nationwide Approach
Edited by Alan Evans and John Tomlinson
ISBN 1 85302 509 7

Evaluation 2nd edition
Edited by Joyce Lishman
ISBN 1 85302 006 0

Evaluation as policymaking

Introducing evaluation into a national decentralised educational system

Edited by Marit Granheim, Maurice Kogan and Ulf P. Lundgren

Jessica Kingsley Publishers
London

First published in Great Britain by
Jessica Kingsley Publishers
118 Pentonville Road
London N1 9JN

British Library Cataloguing in Publication Data
Evaluation as policymaking : introducing evaluation into a
national decentralised education system.
1. Education, Administration
I. Granheim, Marit II. Kogan, Maurice III. Lundgren, Ulf
379.15

ISBN 1-85302-515-1

Contents

Preface

This book originates from an initiative taken by the Royal Norwegian Ministry of Church and Education, following the 1988 Report of the OECD examiners on educational policy in Norway. The objective is to develop a model of evaluation for the Norwegian educational system. The result was a project, called EMIL, which is being administered by the Norwegian Council for Applied Social Sciences on behalf of the Ministry.

As part of the development of the project, but also to extend the argument to change visible in educational systems, it was decided to convene an international seminar of experts who met in Oslo in May 1989. Their contributions are now made available to the widest possible Norwegian and international audience. This book includes theoretical and critical perspectives of the nature of evaluation within a context of decentralisation. Other essays directly propose normative and operational schemes for implementation based on perceptions of Norwegian needs and the experiences of other systems. In presenting such a wide range of views they help emphasise the wide choice of patterns of evaluation which are and should remain available for use. Evaluation should lead to the continuous growth of practice and ideas and not to conformity and immobility.

In proposing that evaluation should become a key element in the improvement of Norwegian education, the government was concerned that all working in and for the schools, at all levels of practice and management, should be able to work out for themselves the potential and the dangers of a strong evaluative system.

Evaluation can be a constructive process leading to stronger professionalism, but only if teachers grasp the opportunity for reflection and growth that it presents. At the same time, evaluation can provide knowledge which will flow into the public discussion about education as well lend reality to policy-making.

It is hoped that this book will contribute usefully to the tasks of individual and institutional self-development.

Chapter 1

Introduction

Marit Granheim, Maurice Kogan and Ulf P. Lundgren

In this Introduction we draw attention to the themes of the expert contributions which form the content of this book.

After sketching in the Norwegian context in Marit Granheim's chapter we embark on the theoretical foundations of evaluation within its setting of government and its legitimation. We then turn attention to some of the technical and operational issues surrounding the use of evaluation as an instrument for the improvement of policy and practice. Finally, we look to examples of evaluation in the USA and Sweden before considering how it might beneficially be introduced in the decentralised Norwegian educational system.

In tackling these issues our contributors were invited to structure their papers in terms of the thematics conveyed in four sets of questions which concerned, first, the demands on evaluation made by decentralised school systems given specific national values and goals; second, responsibility and accountability for evaluation at different levels; third, the impact of evaluation on the governance of schools; and, fourth, how knowledge of education can be renewed and disseminated throughout society.

The aim and scope of this book are thus universal but grounded, nevertheless, in current Norwegian policy perspectives. It is with these that Granheim begins in describing the Norwegian system and the values to which it aspires; this account serves to remind us that evaluation should be and is context-specific and not a set of abstractions to be imposed from above or outside.

Part II, *Decentralisation and Evaluation*, contains four chapters. Lundgren reviews the crowded arena of policy-formation in which politicians have sought simultaneously to use decentralisation as a way of shedding central responsibilities which have become too heavy for the national authorities to carry and to give more freedom to the localities. In this, evaluation becomes a method of reconstructing the role of the centre in a more benign and liberal mode while endorsing a stronger part to be played by the local authorities.

Weiler analyses current educational reforms as demonstrating the problem of legitimacy faced by the modern state: 'Decentralising the making and the implementation of educational policy affects in very important ways the nature and interests of the state, particularly its ability to cope with the dual problems of policy conflict and the erosion of its own legitimacy'.

By contrast, Lauglo introduces the distribution of power to explain the surges towards decentralisation. This enables him to address directly the specific problems of Norway and thereby provides the groundwork for the issues deployed in several other articles that follow.

Eide's analysis refers to the problems of the Welfare State in coping with client demands while making tradeoffs between political authority and professional power. Decentralisation of decision making in a sector of public activity usually reflects a decline in political priority, and a wish to reduce public spending.

Logically, genuine decentralisation should imply a reduced need for data at the central level. When more data are demanded, it may reflect a wish for steering activities without being held responsible for the results. The greatest current problem is probably not a shortage of information, but a lack of capacity at the central level for processing and analysing available information. A simplistic system of indicators could serve as an excuse for not developing such a capacity.

Part III, *Evaluation and Knowledge Production*, introduces, with Popkewitz's chapter, the concept of evaluation as part of the public discourse about education and thus actively engaged in the production of ideology. He connects state planning with evaluation, which, through a process of 'enlightenment', will recruit more social actors to the state's causes. It thus becomes necessary to guard against discourse controlled and ordered by the power structure. In this context he notes how in the transformation of ideas and methods of evaluation from one national context to another that which is represented as technical and objective introduces contaminative values and power constructs. 'The problem of evaluation', he maintains, 'is not merely that of school improvement or decision-making, but of the *conditions* under which and the manner in which knowledge is produced in schools'.

Kvale, too, is concerned with evaluation as an exercise of power. Evaluation is to be regarded as a factor in the constitution and the censorship of knowledge; the decentralisation of administration is tested to see whether it necessarily implies decentralisation of power to define the nature of the knowledge transmitted through the educational system.

Wedman outlines different approaches to assessment models and techniques starting from the national assessment program in Sweden. At this point, our contributions move from the general considerations discussed in some of the previous chapters to more specific issues of evaluation and measurement. It thus links more general social and epistemological themes to the experiences of different systems, discussed in Part IV, *The State of the Art: Creating Evaluative Systems*, as they move from direct prescription into evaluative modes.

In Part IV three chapters introduce reflections drawn from the Swedish and US experience. Franke-Wikberg takes an external view of the public debate in the USA about school standards and what she considers to be harmful developments in evaluation, particularly when they are imported uncritically into another country, as has been the case of Sweden. Sykes presents the view of an actor in the US evaluation scene. He acknowledges the necessity for public evaluation but also its risks, which ultimately are worth taking. Wallin argues that the risk can be mitigated by the use of social scientific theory which can help practitioners and policy-makers to be more aware of the potential narrowness of particular approaches.

In Vislie's contribution we come closer to a particular educational zone and work through a programme area, that of the integration of children with special needs into the common provision, within the larger system. In her discussion we are offered specific proposals for a national system for evaluation.

House, too, offers a schema based on American experience which advances the case for an eclecticism which will include peer evaluation, based upon professional knowledge and concern, but well anchored into the local context. Tiller responds to the same theme in exploring the Norwegian experience at the school level.

Finally, Kogan attempts to complete the circle by linking some of the theoretical considerations to a schema for action and the distribution of responsibility at different levels of the decentralised system. In specifying detailed actions and relationships the final chapter offers a normative model which attempts to respond to the needs of policy-makers and practitioners, to be used in the light of all of the cautions and reservations that can be found in many of the other contributions.

Evaluation and decentralisation are major phenomena of educational governance in many countries at the approach of the 1990s. In this volume our contributors have sought to connect the enduring themes of control and freedom, and the use of knowledge in an action frame to the practicalities of school life and administration within democratic societies.

Chapter 2

The education system in Norway: the need for evaluation

Marit Granheim

The country and people

Geographically, Norway is unique. Few other places in the world have four million people living so far north, in a country that is mostly mountain and barren land. Almost half the country lies to the north of the Arctic Circle. People can live so far north in Norway because of the Gulf Stream and the westerly winds which ensure a mild climate all the year round. For most of the country the July temperature is 15-17°, and the average annual temperature 3-6°.

Norway is a sparsely populated country with about 70 per cent of all Norwegians living in densely populated localities, i.e. towns and cities. Some 20,000 Norwegians of Sami extraction live in Norway, mostly in the far north - 10 per cent or so of these are reindeer breeders. There is complete religious freedom in Norway, but about 90 per cent of the population belong to the Evangelical Lutheran Church of Norway.

Form of government

Norway is a fairly new nation. Her constitution, a constitutional monarchy with a parliamentary system, came into being 17th May 1814, even though true independence did not come until the final break with Sweden in 1905. Executive power is formally vested in the King, but it is exercised through the Council of State (the Cabinet), which is dependent on the confidence of a majority in the National Assembly, the Storting. Norway is divided into 19 counties and 454 municipalities. There is an extensive system of local government on both the county and the municipal level, based on elections every fourth year, held midway between the national elections.

Foreign policy and economy

The Nordic countries share a comprehensive community of language and culture and co-operate closely. Norway participates in all the specialised agencies of the United Nations, has a trade agreement with the European Economic Community (EEC) and is a member of the Organisation for

Economic Cooperation and Development (OECD). The country's security policy is linked to NATO.

Like other western European countries, Norway has seen her economy undergo radical changes since World War II. The primary industries have shown a marked decline, whereas industry's share of the national product has increased. The service trades' increasing share of manpower and of the national product is particularly striking. The oil and the electronic intelligence sectors are growing and expanding at a brisk rate.

The oil and gas fields on the continental shelf in the North Sea constitute one of the country's most important natural resources. The availability of cheap hydraulic power has been of decisive significance for the country's economic development. Other important natural resources are forests, fish and ores. The principle trades are agriculture, fishing, shipping, oil service and other industries.

Taxes and duties are high in Norway but must be seen in context of social welfare and egalitarian policy.

Recreation

In Norway there is almost unlimited access to open country and forest land. Only cultivated land may be fenced in. Norwegians are enthusiastic about outdoor life - for instance cross-country trekking, angling, swimming, camping and boating in summer and skiing and skating in winter. Skiing has been called the Norwegian national sport, crosscountry skiing in the woods and mountains being especially popular.

The educational system

The Norwegian educational system is predominantly a public one. Schools and universities are run by the public authorities, and education is free at all levels. About 850,000 people receive their education in schools, universities and other educational institutions every year. Of these roughly 550,000 are students in the compulsory elementary schools. The teaching personnel number about 50,000. In addition to ordinary school attendance, there are approximately one million people involved in adult education. The National Assembly determines the basic pattern of education by laying down the aims, structure and contents of educational provision by legislation. The Ministry of Education acts in professional and pedagogical matters on advice from expert bodies, for instance the National Advisory Council for Primary and Lower Secondary Education.

Basic school education

The municipalities are responsible for building and running the nine-year basic school. In every municipality there is a local school board, assisted by a chief education officer.

The basic school is divided into a six-year lower stage (primary), and a three-year upper stage (lower secondary). Basic school attendance is compulsory for all from the age of seven. The school is completely comprehensive, with very little organised differentiation outside the classroom. A fundamental principle is to integrate, as far as possible, all handicapped children into normal basic schools to ensure they receive the education to which they are entitled. The structure of compulsory schooling in Norway is rather decentralised, and there is a relatively large number of small school units. The number of schools where there are no separate classes for all age grades amounts to about 1000, and about 250 of these schools are ungraded, that is to say that all students are brought together in one classroom. All students with a Sami background who live in the central Sami districts are entitled to be educated in their mother tongue in all subjects.

Upper secondary education

The counties are responsible for building and running the upper secondary schools. Upper secondary education, which is also relatively decentralised, includes almost all education facilities between the compulsory school and higher education. This comprises education for students from the tenth to the twelfth school year, or students mainly from 16 to 19 years of age.

Upper secondary education is regulated by one particular act which aims to co-ordinate all training in general and vocational subjects in a comprehensive upper secondary school system. One of the fundamental objectives of the act is to give equal status to practical and theoretical education. Thus, general and vocational studies exist side by side at the same school, and can even be combined within the same course.

Since handicapped students in Norway have a right to receive adapted training according to their skills and qualifications, priority is given to the handicapped when admitting students to upper secondary education.

Education for all

A basic concept of educational policy in Norway is that education is for all. The aim throughout this century has been to raise the level of education by

- extending the length of schooling
- providing equal opportunities for all

- providing teaching adapted to each individual

Today, around a quarter of the population work in the educational sector, either as students or teachers. A large proportion of public spending goes to education and the idea of life-long learning is a governing principle. Education has been essential in transforming Norway into a modern and dynamic society. In this process efforts to stimulate greater freedom, equality, personal growth and tolerance have been of vital importance. This set of values is an integral part of the broader concept of education. Recently ecological awareness has come into focus.

Efforts have also been concentrated on improving teacher training and educational facilities. In recent years special initiatives have been taken to break down stereotypes concerning sex roles and to stimulate girls and women to choose untraditional careers.

More than 90 per cent of the students now continue to upper secondary level, the 16-19 age group. In addition, there has been a substantial growth in higher educational institutions. This is particularly true for the regional colleges, and the student body at this level has increased considerably.

Public education is free. Pupils in compulsory schools, living more than four kilometers from the nearest school, are entitled to free transport. Those who cannot live at home are accommodated free of charge. Scholarships and state loans are available for students in upper secondary education and in higher education. Increased knowledge and competence are guiding principles in educational planning at all levels in the 1990s. The present school-system is a result of several far-reaching reforms in the postwar period. Until the mid-1960s the main task was to expand the system in order to make education available to all. Then came a period of new expansion and structural reforms in the educational system. In the past decade the main emphasis has been on the content of education, which to a great extent boils down to the question of who controls education.

Current priorities

Today, attention is focused on the content and quality of education. All programmes and activities reflect that education must be concerned with the needs and demands of society. Special emphasis is now being placed on preparing the young for the information society and the new technologies.

Environmental education is growing rapidly and will be an area of primary concern in the 1990s. The question of 'sustainable development' is a new challenge of paramount importance. This applies to all levels of education. Computer technology is among the areas given high priority in recent years. The demand for qualified personnel in this field is increasing year by year.

In our internationally oriented society, characterised by rapid changes and huge inflow of information from all sources, some of the basic functions of education will be:

- to develop the students' ability to think and evaluate in a constructive and creative manner
- to teach effective work habits and self-discipline
- to develop intellectual curiosity and desire for life-long learning
- to develop the awareness of relationships with the rest of the world community and to foster international understanding.

In a period involving internationalisation and freer movement of people, knowledge of foreign languages and culture is essential. Therefore, it has been important to strengthen the provision for foreign language teaching and learning.

Attention has also been focused on school administration and educational leadership. Better leadership in school is one of the important tasks for educational research and school development. Training schemes in this field are being carried out in the various sectors of education. The intention is that development and innovative work should primarily be initiated locally. But initiatives have also been taken at national level.

In order to provide possibilities for life-long learning a broad spectrum of training and study possibilities are accessible to adults. High priority is also given to research, recruitment of research workers and post-secondary studies of long duration. This is considered necessary to improve quality and maintain a solid basis of knowledge.

The strengthening of the university sector is of particular importance in this respect. In addition to technological studies, high priority areas are economic and administrative studies, health education and social work and pre-school training. The educational system has in many ways been the domain of the teachers. Their professional ideas have to a large extent formed the attitude of the students at the classroom level. Modifications in recent years have tended to strengthen the position of the individual school and teacher. At the same time, interests outside the school have demonstrated a stronger interest in school affairs. Economic organisations are developing views on educational policies, as do professional pressure groups and ideological organisations.

Parents have also become more active in school affairs, and the students want to have more influence. Local politicians want to come in between the central government and the schools, and political parties seem less prone to leave educational matters to the professional educators.

The number of students in compulsory schools is on the decline. However, the reduction is not expected to be as pronounced as in many other western countries. Increased time of instruction and improved stand-

ards have so far made it impossible to reduce the number of teachers. On the contrary, the number of teaching posts have increased significantly over the past few years.

Decentralisation

Efforts to decentralise the system have increased the professional autonomy of the individual schools and institutions. A major step in this direction was taken in 1985. At that time a system of detailed earmarking of grants was replaced by a lump sum grant covering all central government transfers to local authorities. The intention is to give local and regional authorities more autonomy and make local priorities as to the use of resources in various sectors. It remains to be seen whether the new system will affect the quality of education and the principle of equal opportunities for all.

The old system was based on strong 'positive discrimination'. This made it possible to transfer much larger funds to rural and peripheral areas. Consequently, differences in the quality of schooling offered have been avoided. Curriculum plans are developed centrally for primary and secondary education. The plans usually define a core curriculum, but offer considerable leeway for local adaptions. The main trend is towards more local autonomy in the development of the curriculum.

Norway has no inspectorate, but a system of support functions for the schools is operating at the regional and local level. Development work and school experiments are encouraged, especially in the form of local initiatives.

Central research efforts have been reduced in recent years, but are now gradually being reinforced. There is now a heavy trend towards more emphasis on research and evaluation in order to improve the quality of education. Increased external control under the label of 'accountability' has not yet been widely accepted.

Legal instruments play an important role in central government policies for education. Regulations on work environment, safety, buildings and other facilities also apply to education.

Salaries for teachers at all levels are centrally negotiated within the framework of general salary regulations for public employees. It is now being considered whether this should be decentralised to lower levels.

The class size, the length of the school year, the minimum number of lessons and teaching obligations are centrally determined. The size and location of schools, the hiring of teachers and the daily running of schools are locally determined. The main trend is toward more local autonomy in the development of curriculum.

There is a fairly widespread agreement that the main structural features of the educational system should be maintained for a considerable time into the future. Lowering the age at which primary education should start is a point for debate at present.

There is also a broad agreement that we need to strengthen the international aspects of the curriculum. This is considered necessary for a small country in an increasingly integrated world. However, a small country needs to fight for its own cultural identity. Therefore, the Norwegian language and the transmission of our cultural heritage need strengthening. Furthermore, mathematics and natural sciences are important as well as civics and basic technological understanding.

In addition to this, the school is supposed to introduce the youngsters to adult life with all the problems and challenges it involves. This includes peace and international understanding, environmental issues and the fight against drugs, racism, alcohol and tobacco, sexual behaviour, hygiene, traffic rules, etc.

Admittedly, teachers feel somewhat overburdened by all these demands. Many of them argue that they are not appropriately paid, and some have left school to find other jobs.

Need for evaluation

When it comes to school evaluation, little work has been done. However, two different projects are now in operation. One project, called EMIL, tries to develop a model for national evaluation of the educational system. The other project works on international and school-based evaluation in the upper secondary school. The main objective in these projects is to improve the quality of education.

There is widespread agreement that a model for evaluation must be developed. This was also the conclusion in a report published by The Organisation for Economic Cooperation and Development (OECD) in 1988 that raised the following question: How can central authorities form an opinion of and influence the level of quality in a school system so strongly decentralised as the Norwegian one? The answer is to evaluate and monitor the system at different levels.

As a result the Royal Ministry of Church and Education initiated work on evaluation. At this stage it is important to find the right balance between school-based evaluation and externally based evaluation.

How can the Ministry verify that the decentralised school-system is working? First, it needs a far more secure quantitative data base enabling it to find out how the resources are being used. Second, and more difficult, it seems essential that both the local authorities and the Ministry have qualitative knowledge of how schools work, the OECD report concludes.

In this context Norway's high level of computerisation can be exploited. This can be done through the use of on-line networks between central, regional and local authorities and schools.

This will make it easier to evaluate and monitor the schools. Some of the monitoring might be in the form of tests, if used cautiously. Shallow samples testing could easily give the Ministry information on the state of knowledge in the schools and be a valuable diagnostic tool, the OECD experts argue. At the same time they hope that the schools will develop a strong practice of self-evaluation seeking help from external evaluation when necessary.

Why is it necessary to establish these new procedures? Simply because the state authorities must retain control over the distribution of resources. They also have to maintain standards in schools and uphold important national values, the experts say. This has proved necessary on the basis of experience in several countries that have adopted a system of general grants. Sooner or later they realise that some form of systematic evaluation must be developed and implemented to see to what extent national objectives can be met.

The main aim is not to reintroduce national controls through the back door. The idea is to find ways in which acceptable norms of educational practice can be established and better disseminated.

This view is shared by the Norwegian authorities and forms a vital element in the present evaluation work. In this process it is important to develop a satisfactory concept of quality and accumulate sufficient knowledge of what the level of quality actually is.

Evaluation is important to find out how scarce resources can be used to produce the best results possible. A prerequisite is that people in the educational sector should actively take part in the development of methods, models and the practical implementation of evaluation.

References

OECD (1988), *Reviews of National Policies for Educating Norway*, Department of the Examiners.

Part I

DECENTRALISATION AND EVALUATION

Chapter 3

Educational policymaking, decentralisation and evaluation

Ulf P. Lundgren

After the World War II, educational systems all over the world expanded to an extent that has no precedent in history (cf. Coombs, 1968). Educational systems in the Western world have only partly been able to cope with this expansion. Traditional methods have delayed the adaptation of the educational systems to the new demands and challenges.

During the last two centuries it has become increasingly important that the individual should have basic practical knowledge and should be adequately prepares for citizenship. Education has developed in such a way that it has been an investment for the individual as well as for society. And this development of a linking of education to the labour market and to the world of work has increased the demands on education.

As well as the obvious fact of population growth, there are two basic changes in society that have been of decisive importance. One is ideological and the other is economic in nature. The ideological aspect refers to ideas and patterns of thinking, which identify education as an instrument for changing the social structure of education and is perceived as something valuable in itself and a democratic right to receive. These ideas are expressed by those that demand education as well as by those that decide about the dimension and direction of education. The economic aspect refers to the relationship between a given structure and progress of production and changes of education.

After the World War II the economic aspect was given increasing importance in planning and expanding educational systems. The rationale behind this approach has been the economic-political goal of rapid economic progress. During the 1950s and 1960s several economists could show correlations between investments in education and economic growth (cf. Blaug, 1966). The OECD played an important role in developing these theories and promoting governments to consider and use them in national educational planning.

Of course, these two basic factors are related to each other, even though our knowledge about the relationship is limited. It can be assumed that the ideological aspect, in the last instance, is understood to be shaped by economic circumstances (cf. Correa, 1968).

In the field of economics of education two main theories were formulated. The first one is the theory of human capital, which was formulated during the 1950s and 1960s, and became one of the foundations for educational expansion. Or to quote one of its founders: 'Truly, the most distinctive feature of our economic system is the growth in human capital. Without it there would be only hard, manual work, and poverty except for those who have income of property. There is an early morning scene in Faulkner's *Intruder in the Dust*, of a poor, solitary cultivator at work in a field. Let me paraphrase that line, 'The without skills and knowledge leaning terrifically against nothing' (Schultz, 1961, p.17).

The other theory can be labelled the filter - or sorting - theory. According to this the aim of education is not in the main to refine manpower but to sort subjects. At the risk of oversimplifying, this theory can be expressed in the following way: education aims to sort the students according to their ability. An educational system is, then, a 'filter' for sorting and an information system for those who receive the products (cf. Arrow, 1974).

The first of these two theories can be seen as an important tool that had an influence on the planning of education during the expansion period. And perhaps even more of importance during the 1960s when the expansion was coming to an end, and it therefore became important to find ways of rationalising education. The expansion was an effect of new demands and new expectations voiced about education. Economic development in the postwar period allowed for rapid expansion. To some extent we can see today a renewal of theories on the economics of education as a consequence of changed economic conditions for education. However, these ideas are not now linked to human capital and sorting functions, but to the concept of markets.

During the expansion period political administration of reforms was relatively straightforward. Decision-makers ascribed the systems well-articulated goals, defined according to priority and provided resources that, it was assumed, would guarantee their attainment. The various sectors appeared as possible instruments for reaching political goals. If the administration failed, the blame was often ascribed to shortcomings in the original plan. These problems, it was felt, could be solved at the next stage. Moreover, by systematic use of research, an accumulation of knowledge was assumed to prevent such failures. Planning was possible to do in a rational way, or to use the words of Wildavsky 'The method called the "rational paradigm" (order objectives, compare alternatives, choose the highest ranking)' (Wildavsky, 1979, p. 8).

This rational paradigm called for centrally administered reforms and plans seemed to be possible not only to make but also to fulfil. It can be, as Wildavsky argues, that this rational paradigm 'is mistaken as describing either how decisions are or ought to be made' (Wildavsky, 1979, p. 8).

During the expansion and as a consequence of the rational paradigm central policy-making became important. The administrative structure of the Norwegian school system with the various staff units (Councils) illustrates this development. The centre made the plans, even controlled the development work, and was, by being central, capable of meeting various and often contradictory demands by negotiation.

In the 1970s we can see a change in educational policy. Evaluations as well as pure statistics pointed out that the earlier and basic intentions of the reforms had not been fulfilled. Centrally administered and controlled reforms had not been implemented as intended. The distribution of welfare had not followed the plans, and, specifically, education as an instrument for social change seemed to be a rather blunt instrument and not that easy to control from the centre. These statements can of course be disputed. The case of Norway gives perhaps another picture. The reforms were successful and gave another distribution of education socially and geographically. On the other hand it can always be discussed how well intentions are fulfilled. What we could see on the international scene was a renewed interest in how education contributed to the welfare of the society it nurtured (cf. Karabel and Halsey, 1978).

In many countries the arguments for decentralisation were renewed (during the reform period decentralisation could be called a frozen ideology that now has melted) and in the first instance realised by local development work - school improvement projects, school evaluation and a change in the role of headmasters from being given rules and directives to becoming policy-makers and managers in a process of school development.

This is one of the aspects discernible in the changes in educational policy of the 1970s. However, from a broad international standpoint the picture is not that clear. In the US as well as in the UK, changes in educational policy seem more to be directed towards centralisation than towards decentralisation.

> 'The changes towards decentralisation are not only limited to education. There has been for some time an important and much more encompassing debate on the possibilities and modalities of decentralising political and economic systems (Sharpe, 1979), with particularly interesting foci on the issue of decentralisation and planning (Himmelstrand, 1981; Rucht 1982) and on decentralisation in the context of development policies (Cheema and Rondinelli, 1983; Conyers 1984; Rondinelli *et al.* 1984). It is certainly not an exaggeration when Nelson Polsby calls the issue of centralisation and decentralisation 'one of the

great, resonant themes of contemporary politics' (Sharpe 1979, p. 1)' (Weiler, 1988, p.1).

There are, however, irrespective of changes in the direction of policy-making towards or from the centre some basic changes in the relationship between the state and general education and in the relationship between society and general education that is vital for a discussion of how central control is exercised. Before going into a specific discussion on the relation between decentralisation and evaluation I find it, thus, necessary to take up a brief discussion of these changed relationships.

Political governing

One important change concerns the relationship between national policy and the control of the national economy. With an increasing dependence on the international economy the possibilities to manage the national economy and the incentives for growth have decreased and changed in nature. This change has accentuated one basic problem for the modern state, to have a profound base for its legitimacy (cf. Habermas, 1973); a change in legitimation in a situation of diminished economic control as the impetus for moving state reforms from cost-taking initiatives to 'symbolic' reconstructions of existing institutions.

However, the international economic dependence is one of many factors involved. Another important change is the transformation from a labour market structured by industrial production to a labour market structured by service production, circulation of products and reproduction. It can be argued that the traditional organisations constructed to handle the economy and the political economy of a modern industrialised society are not suited for handling a post modern society. They cannot mobilise support for actions. Accordingly state institutions such as schools cannot attract and build on the interest of their clients. Reforms tend then to be directed towards increasing the influence of the clients (or users), but at the same time the basic organisation structure is not changed. Influence and control follows the same forms and are organised in the same way as before.

If we accept the thesis - at least in order to get a reference point - that problems are permanent and solutions bound to time and context (cf. Wildavsky, 1979), the changed relationship between economy and national policy-making calls for solutions that not only have economic consequences but will also renew existing human resources. Hence, the 'great, resonant themes of contemporary politics' - centralisation and decentralisation - are to be understood as a renewal of instruments for governing and the handling of permanent problems. Following such a line of argument it seems inevitable that the identification of what is the problem has to be renewed or refreshed. What has to be reformed has consequently to be identified as being in a crisis and, furthermore, that the crisis must be identified as caused by what has to be the solution; not due to lack of economic resources, but due to misuse of human resources. If the causes are identified as being human and as possible to control, then the solutions seem possible to implement by new or renewed instruments such as decentralisation, in-service training, professionalisation, etc.

The same could be discussed, as Goble does, as a crisis of purpose. Referring to the development of education in Europe he writes:

> The crisis of purpose is to a great extent a reflection of the painful adjustments which are taking place in the capitalist system within which the economy of Europe operates. Capitalism has had great difficulty in accommodating to the loss of balance resulting from decolonisation and the emergence of industries in formerly dependent countries. It has attempted to adjust by raising the scale of its operations to the supranational level. In doing so, it has taken much significant economic activity out of political control, since there is no such thing as a supranational political authority. This has raised difficult questions about the future of the nation-state, the possibility of real national sovereignty, and the feasibility of democratic control over those who hold real power. These issues find an echo in the current debate about the future structure and powers of the European Economic Community. When one considers that in Europe we find two thirds of the world's constitutional democracies, and when one observes how often bodies such as the Council of Europe and the European Communities affirm that education must maintain that democratic tradition, we must recognize that these developments have considerable significance for the educational system.
>
> The same trend to economic internationalism is changing the traditional roles of countries as producers and consumers, and therefore the life-styles and expectations of the people who live in those countries. In this, in fact, it is actually being reinforced by the reactions of governments, whose scramble to 'rationalise' the structures and interrelationships of their economies is simply an attempt to lessen the pain of convulsive changes over which they have no control. (Goble, 1986).

If we look at the political research carried out over recent years, we can find a certain degree of agreement among scientists about the predicaments of political governing or policy administration, although the starting point of their research may be quite different. Marxists and conservatives, together with researchers following a more traditional empirical line, seem to agree that political governing and policy administration has become more and more complicated (see, for example, Dror, 1981, p. 260).

What these researchers conclude is that rational decisions can seldom be taken; and if taken, they can rarely be implemented (cf. Lindensjö and Lundgren, 1986).

Of course, this consensus does not exist when the problems of policy administration and the implementation of reform programmes are to be explained. Some researchers question the possibility of governing according to existing strategies. Other researchers use concepts such as failing governing capacity in their analyses. The latter take as a point of departure the fact that political instruments can be renewed and these argue for new strategies. It is, of course, important in any discussion claiming that there are problems in political governing and policy administration to be able to specify the basic concepts of governing. In the discussion within political science about the problems of political governing and policy administration in welfare societies, the use of concepts varies. Discussions tend therefore to be rather abstract. In spite of these problems parts of this discussion are of importance in this context and have to be recognised.

One set of explanations as to why there are problems in political governing and policy administration focuses on the governing subject. What this means is not always clear. Here the discussion will be limited to two possible interpretations, namely the political leadership and the organisation in particular.

In the analysis of the problems of policy administration, the political government - the parliamentary majority and the government (some times the whole state apparatus) - are described as the governing subject. This subject is characterised as becoming weaker and sometimes incapable of governing. One explanation for this is the splitting up into small party factions which has taken place, thereby forcing the forming of fragile coalitions (cf. Crozier, 1977). It is argued that the classical ability of a government to be strong, to be able to reject demands, has been lost. This has had as a consequence an increasing 'sensitivity' to lobbying and power pressure, which in its turn has led to an overload of demands on decision-makers.

The political authority of a government and its administration is a consequence of two elements: its effectiveness and public consent (Rose, 1980). It is obvious that effectiveness and consent are related, but they can also conflict. In order to guarantee the consent of the electors more and more interest groups and associations have been formed. This strategy can in its turn create new problems. The more organisations that are formed, the more negotiations are necessary in order to gain support for one line of action or for a reform. A cooperative negotiation context is formed. In its turn this can result in indifference with respect to participation: the citizens become demotivated (cf. Rose, 1980).

These problems seem to occur quite frequently in modern educational administrations and sometimes result in governing documents becoming more 'abstract' to allow for various interpretations. It can also lead to compromises that are difficult to interpret for the 'street-level bureaucrats', i.e. the teachers.

The initiative for reforms seems to have moved partly from political bodies to other groups. Small margins between political blocks can lead the opposition to make too many promises, whereas the government is limited by economic constraints. The so-called 'power-study' in Norway that started in 1972 - was a study of the power relations in Norwegian society aimed at finding out about not only the real power relations in Norway and also to see how political governing was structured and implemented (NOU, 1982:3, p. 1; my translation; cf. Lindensjö, 1984) - the cooperative powers in Norway are clearly highlighted as important in assessing the constraints on governing. Specifically, the labour and employers' organisations have a decisive importance; they have close associations with political parties and well developed links to international networks. They are linked to the public decision-process through more or less formalised orders for representation (NOU, 1982:3, p. 7; my translation).

At the same time, many of the changes indicated here are only a part of more complex changes in the conditions of political leadership. There are reasons - in this context - for drawing attention to the differentiation within the state apparatus itself. To be able to control the development towards politically defined goals, the educational administration organisation must be capable of ranking goals, making priorities and identifying alternative actions that are best adjusted to given economic conditions. The strong specialisation and division of labour has to rely on this basis for a rational decision-making. This specialisation has as a consequence the splitting up of the organisation itself, with the risk of losing the overall perspective that is necessary for rational decision-making. The construction of the various advisory boards in Norway could be interpreted in this perspective as well as the rather poorly defined borders within state administration between the central state administration and the county offices.

It also seems that earlier planning models, developed during the educational expansion, cannot be used during a period of economic constraints. During the period of expansion, specialisation of the administration was a practical solution. Faced with the need to take new types of decisions, the existing organisation seems unable to act rationally.

The administration seems to be a conglomerate, a mixture of various interests - various sectors with different and sometimes contradictory interests. This provides the framework for more long-term and comprehensive planning. In a declining economy various sectors are forced to compete with each other. A consequence of this competition can be that goals for education are broadened in order to make the educational sector look as important and as competitive as other sectors. This broadening of goals is reinforced by the necessity to satisfy various demands. In a situation where demands on education cannot be met by expansion - by 'buying out' demands - the goals are forced to be abstractly formulated. They become products of a negotiation process. This tendency, therefore, contradicts the demands on goal governing that are supposed to be the governing vehicle in a decentralised system.

What is pointed out by many political scientists (cf. Wildavsky, 1979) is, thus, that the governing subject - the political leadership - has problems in taking the initiative for an active reform policy. We can see examples of a fragmentation of the educational administration, thereby creating problems concerning overall planning and the ability to master complex groups of interrelated problems. We can also see tendencies towards more policy-making being carried out by the administration itself.

The movements towards decentralisation can be interpreted as one way of solving the problems indicated above. At the same time, the motives for decentralisation do not indicate directly the problems of governing. Indirectly, however, the problems of governing may be seen to be there. Weiler (1988) describes three models or arguments for decentralisation behind various decentralisation movements. His classification gives a good analytical starting point:

- a) the 'redistribution' model, which is predicated on the sharing of power,
- b) the 'efficiency' model, which is geared to enhancing the cost-effectiveness calculus of the educational system through a more efficient deployment and management of available resources, and
- c) the 'cultures of learning' model, which emphasizes the decentralisation of educational content, (Weiler, 1988, p. 2).

However, a decentralisation of the educational system, irrespective of motives, puts in focus the balance between political and professional power over education. The governing or steering of an educational system can be described in two dimensions. On one hand it is a question of where the power is. On the other hand it is a question of who has the power. These two dimensions can be illustrated, in a graphic scheme, in the following way:

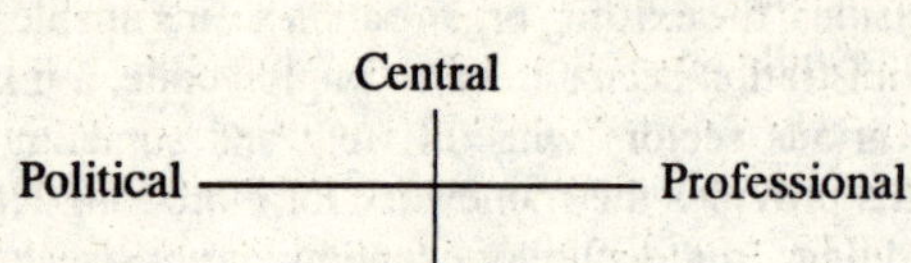

This distinction points out four main models for the steering or governing of education:

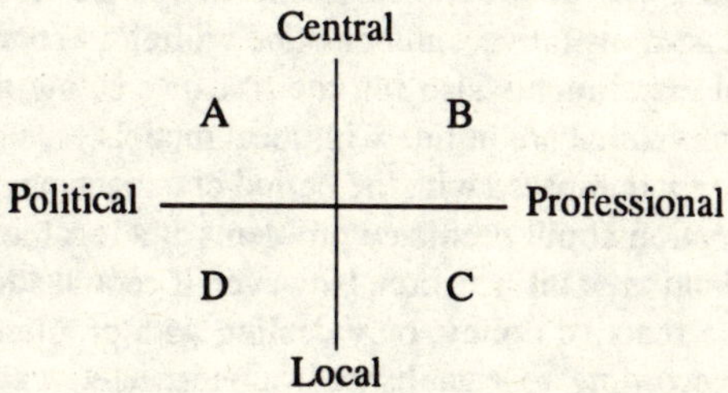

The direction of ongoing changes could be characterised in these four models. In moving from central steering or government towards more local steering or government it seems that the question of who has the responsibility is sharpened. Thus a movement towards decentralisation focuses questions around the professional ability of teachers and the professional responsibility of teachers. These questions, in their turn, seem to be directed towards teacher training - initial and in-service training - and its content. The decentralisation reforms in Norway can - following the three types of arguments pointed out by Weiler - be said to embrace all three. Placing these reforms in the models described in the scheme above it can be described as a move in the first step from A to B (ministry → governing boards) and in the next step from AB to DC. This diffuse borderline between political and professional responsibility represents a major problem. One major question to address in the conference is, therefore, 'How can a national evaluation system operate by defining the various areas of responsibility?'

Turbulent societies, undergoing technical, cultural and social upheaval as a result of rapid development, place heavy demands on economic resources for the public sector. In a declining economy much of the resources are used for anti-cyclic political measures. At the same time resources are needed for reforms. To combine these two demands calls for a high degree of political and administrative innovation (see, for example, Mayntz and Scharpf, 1975).

As the state is economically dependent on taxes or loans it must rely on political strength in order to boost the economy. Traditional policy means that acute problems can be solved and that articulated demands can be responded to either by following them or rejecting them. Such a reactive policy is sufficient where economic, technical and social change is slow, economic development rather stable and the political demands are modest. The increasing pace of change in contemporary societies seems to require an ability to master problems before they are articulated. This, however, assumes information resources of a new type.

One way of renewing information resources is, of course, decentralisation, moving decision-taking from the centre to the periphery. On a local level one can test solutions and devise models. At the same time this means that central administrative units must be willing to concede power positions. Local experiments also run the risk of creating new demands for central solutions that are in line with local models.

What is new compared with the period of expansion is the necessity to have information about predicted problems at a local level and this calls for a coordination of information. However, if central administrative units still follow a reactive policy, only dealing with problems when they are acute and according to established routines, decentralisation is not an adequate solution. Active political governing and policy administration must master the problems that arise from lack of coordination, resulting from the fragmentation within administration itself. The problems go over and beyond individual sectors but are handled by an administration whose sectors are clearly defined.

In this perspective evaluations can be seen as more than data-gathering and valuations of education; they can fulfil the function of coordinating various areas of knowledge within social, political and professional fields.

The legitimacy of public education

A modern educational system is always evaluated through the legitimacy it enjoys in society. Educational systems of the kind we now have cannot be evaluated entirely and fairly. Public evaluation of education is not simply related to evaluation studies of education. As long as an educational system is perceived as fulfilling its functions in society it has a legitimacy. Whether the educational system produces what it is supposed to produce (or reproduce) is subordinate to the fact that it is perceived as fulfilling its basic functions.

One obvious factor behind the expansion of education after the Second World War was the expansion of the economy. Changes in the labour market, with an increased demand for educated workers, appeared at the same time, and was, of course, linked to the expansion of education. Investment in education provided a value on the labour market both for the individual and for society at large.

This meant, also, that education for the individual was perceived as necessary in order to gain access to the labour market. Level of education was linked to level of income. It was through this relationship that modern education was given its legitimacy. The majority of parents trusted in the pragmatic value of education.

With changes in the labour market, with increasing and perhaps permanent youth unemployment, this trust in education started to decrease. During the 1970s we can observe in Western societies a growing criticism of education and the quality of education. This growing criticism was also related to economic cutbacks, or as Otto Mihaly writes: 'Budget cut-down can only be legitimized by ideologies devaluating the significance of education - in this or other way - playing down its momentum, casting doubts on its possible efficiency' (Mihaly, 1986. p. 38). At the same time as demands for a return to traditional methods are advanced in public discussion about education and schooling - 'more talk and more chalk' - demands are also articulated concerning the renewal of education and its adaptation to new challenges from society and from the labour market. The analysis of what these demands stand for is often poor. The criticism that the schools do not produce what they used to is, of course, true, because curricula have changed.

Two things are of particular interest in the debate on the knowledge level of education made evident in the debate on declining marks. One is the place it occupies in the public discourse about education and its consequences for the governing of education. For educational policy, when education itself is the subject of dwindling trust and diminished legitimacy, the interplay between political groups and various interest groups can create a mistrust in education conjuring up Doomsday. Criticism of education, even if incorrectly founded, can lead to sharpened demands on education, with few or no resources to respond to these demands. The initiative for reforms can be seen as swinging from the politically elected bodies to various other groups in society. As was pointed out briefly before, in a stagnating economy reforms are implemented with a view to increased efficiency. These demands for efficiency must be understood in relation to a decreasing trust in education. Decreasing trust in education is evaluated the more problems are found.

The other is that the public debate on declining standards in particular focuses just parts of the goals for modern education. In limiting the responsibility of schools to outcomes that are possible to measure in tests the very concept of evaluation is limited, and this limited concept seems to be synonymous with evaluation. Making testing and evaluation interchangeable means to bypass the development of models for programme evaluation and the development of methods for evaluation that have occurred since the late 1960s (cf. Dahllöf, 1970, House, 1978). By that jump a 'sleeping' tradition is awakened and 'sleepers' are activated. Up to the mid 1960s evaluation and testing were more or less one and the same (cf. Thorndike and Hagen, 1955).

At the same time the goals for education are defined to an ever increasing extent through negotiations with different interest groups, thus resulting in a more cooperative political system around the governing of education, giving rise to abstract goals. This means that the number of evaluations carried out has increased and they are now more difficult to interpret. Claims that there is a falling standard of education can partly be seen as a consequence of this situation. In many of the ongoing public debates on the quality of education, in which it is claimed that the test marks are falling, actual comparisons are in fact very difficult to make (Dahllöf, 1970). These claims seem to reflect the interest various groups have in assigning goals to education, goals that evaluation shows have not been achieved.

Criticism of education and the quality of education, based among other things on assessment, has reinforced the belief in the possibility of a rational planned educational system. The possibility of such a rational system is rarely called into question. Instead, the acquired rationality, from the period of expansion, seems now to have taken the form of an ideology.

The classical rationality, built on the relation between goals and measures, seems to have been replaced by an ideology of rationality. Perhaps an *idola fori* - to use a category from Francis Bacon. Or to quote Jurgen Habermas: 'The progressive "rationalisation" of society is linked to the institutionalization of scientific and technical development. To the extent that technology and science permeate social institutions and thus transform them, old legitimations are destroyed. The secularization and "disenchantment" of action-orienting world views, of cultural tradition as a whole, is the obverse of the growing "rationality" of social action' (Habermas, 1968; 1971, p. 81). Criticism of the feasibility of planning and implementing reforms rationally has been countered by the trust placed in new educational technologies and new methods for assessment. Rationality is guaranteed by the use of proper instruments and techniques.

Thus - even if it is only a rough sketch - we can see how various factors have come to form a basis for criticism of education: a decline in public expenditure, problems in administering and implementing state reforms and the claims and demands on education. This criticism in turn influences and complicates the problems of formulating and implementing changes in education. At the same time as the problems of governing education are complicated and diffused evaluations are getting a more and more central place on the agenda. Evaluations are ascribed close to mythological capabilities and preserve the belief in a rational paradigm for policy-making. However, any idea of evaluation has to be transformed to a concrete method, to a concrete instrument, and every concrete method will bring a specific set of data. The relationship between the demands on the arena of formulation (on which demands on evaluations are formed) and the arena of realisation (on which evaluations are carried out) has been more and more diffuse (Lundgren, 1982). To some degree the demands for reforms to increase the quality of education stem from the actual constraints of change.

Decentralisation and educational policy

The concept of decentralisation is rather difficult to define in a precise way.

> In the national and international glossaries of educational policy, 'decentralisation' has been a principal try for some time now, right next to such other favorites as 'participation', autonomy', and 'reform'. For a variety of reasons, the notion of decentralizing systems of education that, in most countries, tend to have rather heavily centralized structures of governance, seems to command a great deal of attention (see, for example, Lauglo and McLean 1985; Bray 1984; Périé 1987; Baumert and Goldschmidt 1980, Kogan 1979, pp. 37-42). This is so in spite of considerable difficulties in agreeing on what exactly 'Decentralisation' means in practice, and in spite of a less than overwhelming record of success in those attempts at decentralisation that actually have been undertaken. (Weiler, 1988, p. 1).

How a decentralisation in reality is taking 'gestalt' reflects administrative, budgetary and legal traditions. Decentralisation in the Norwegian context is on one level rhetoric, but on another level is a concrete process involving a rather drastic change of the entire educational system.

An educational system is governed mainly by three sets of instruments or governing systems (Lundgren, 1977):

(1) the legal steering system,

(2) the economic steering system,

(3) the ideological steering system (goals and content).

As a fourth steering system we can see the evaluation system. The more the first three steering systems are loosened up and become diffuse and thus gives space for various interpretations the more the evaluation will govern by giving interpretations in an operationally way.

The dilemma we are facing, therefore, is that the intention to increase decentralisation - in a system where central governing becomes complicated - demands coordination and a renewal of information resources and this will be interpreted as a demand that can be satisfied by a national evaluation system - as it has been pointed out in the OECD review. At the same time a national evaluation system can replace the earlier central systems for governing. What on one side turns out to be a change in steering systems directed towards a distribution of policy-making from the centre to the periphery, will on the other side be a strengthening of a central steering system.

Evaluation and monitoring

The discussion around political governing, I admit, has been rather abstract and partly impressionistic. The main point in the story is, however, to underline three important issues in the educational change from centralised governing to decentralised governing.

First, decentralisation is a reform strategy that has to be related to political currents embedded in the specific history of Norway. It is a response to demands that are essential part of the local society. In terms of reform strategies it can be seen as the melting of an ideology that was frozen during a period of major central reforms as part of the building of the welfare society. From this point of view the decentralisation has been a decentralisation of political responsibility from the centre to the periphery and a decentralisation of the control over curriculum content opening up the possibility to adjust the curriculum to the local cultural context.

Decentralisation as a reform strategy has also to be related to the economical situation in which the change in the overall economy together with changes in the demographic structure challenge the possibilities for the centre to act. Priorities for the distribution of welfare has moved out to the local communities.

Second, this decentralisation is taking place within a context for political governing that is complex and in which the demands for the renewal of instruments for governing seems to be necessity. The influences from the cooperative organizations have increased and the political decision processes are found more and more as heavy negotiation processes in an overcrowded arena. At the same time - if the national goals for education are indispensable - the implementation of them has to be centrally directed and evaluated. In a decentralisation of the educational system, in which there are common goals and values the decentralisation has limits and needs to be clearly clarified concerning the relations between the responsibilities at the different levels. Decentralisation creates demands on how information is channelled and how experiences are shared. A national evaluation has then to fulfil the double task of both delivering information horizontally and vertically within the system.

Third, decentralisation as a reform strategy can be understood, as linked to how education is perceived in the public eye. The public discourse on education has been focusing the traditional outcomes of education. As it has been discussed here this public debate can be seen as both a deep concern for educational quality and as designing a problem adjusted to an existing solution on how the welfare is to be distributed. Behind this discourse about quality of education there are solutions presented in terms of mechanisms for market adjustments. The productivity and the efficiency of education becomes then the legitimation for political governing of education.

These points taken together form the structure for a changed context for programme evaluation. Evaluation on a national level seems to give modes by which coordination within and between levels are possible to make. The instruments used can be guarantees for the control of central aims and values and form models for evaluations within the system. The problem here seems to be the public discourse about education in which evaluations are assigned omnipotent possibilities at the same time as the ideas of what a concrete evaluation is, is narrowed to simple tests and criteria of what is productivity and efficiency.

To clarify this I have to go back to the distinction between the arena of policy formulation and the arena of policy realisation (cf Lundgren, 1982). In the arena of policy formulation the conditions and the rules are different from the ones in the arena of policy realisation - on the level of the 'street-bureaucrats'.

Evaluation as an instrument for control and development in the arena of formulation appears as a solution for the demands for a more efficient educational system and at the same time is an instrument for handling the problems constituted by a decentralisation. On this level, in this arena evaluation there is a general instrument that reinforces the rational paradigm. Even if abstractly formulated the goals are products of concrete negotiations and appear here as solid concrete products.

In the arena of realisation, however, the goals will operate in quite another context, in which there already exists concrete goals. In this context central given goals and directions will be the subject of new negotiations. Also in this arena evaluations have to be transformed to concrete techniques and methods. Evaluation instruments brought in from above will enter a concrete educational process and have an impact on the direction and structure of this process.

The transformation of evaluation to a concrete 'gestalt' is then the key issue to how evaluations can be used and how it will respond to what is expected in the arena of policy formulation.

The concept of evaluation

The concept of evaluation is hard to define in a delineated way. Basically, it is defined as the valuation of the correspondence between goals and outcome. The classic problem is then how goals and outcomes are made comparable.

How the concepts of evaluation has developed can in brief be described from three aspects:

(1) the aspect of legitimation,

(2) the aspect of methods,

(3) the aspect of function.

In the Nordic countries at least valuations of education had its legitimacy in the authority of the state or the church, and the methods were linked to subjects (inspectors, etc.) and the function was to control the system. With modernisation as Berge (1974) has formulated it, as a shift from giveness to choice, evaluation has been, as House (1980) expresses it, 'an aid in making choices' (*op. cit.*, p. 16). But, furthermore, the modernisation of education was a shift both for changing society and for the individual to make a career. To evaluate the modern educational system the legitimation of evaluation must be linked to objective measures. The concept of evaluation became a part of the rational paradigm and the methods had to be perceived as objective. Its function became not only to control quality but also to develop education as well.

This demand on objectivity linked educational evaluation to the development of techniques for measurement and statistics within psychology and education; to simplify it can be described as a development of quantitative methods for measuring educational outcomes.

With the broadening of the functions of education in the post war period the established instruments for evaluation came under attack. And with the general epistemological debate within behavioural and social sciences in the 1960s new methods for evaluation were developed. The Cambridge manifesto of 1970, signed by a number of prominent scholars in the field, pleaded for broadening of evaluation models and methods. The legitimacy was still objective methods, but the concept of objectivity was enlarged and not identified with tests alone. The functions of evaluation were broadened including the responsibility of evaluators not only to respond to the formal political demands but also to the demands of the users (cf. Stake, 1976). With this change the traditional definition of evaluation as the valuation of the correspondence between goals and outcome was blurred, and even the concept of goal-free evaluation was coined (cf Scriven, 1973).

Even if the methods and models for evaluation today present a rather rich picture and the knowledge about evaluation both practically and theoretically are well documented in the public discussion expectations on what educational evaluation should be is, as said earlier, rather well related to the use of tests. With demands on accountability (cf. Kogan, 1986) the pressure on having 'objective' evaluations force back a rather simplistic notion on evaluation. The same is true with the demands created by a decentralisation of education. The development of a national assessment system in Sweden provides an excellent example.

Of course, tests will have a role in any broad national evaluation. The problem is the role it is given and the role it acquires. One problem lies embedded in the traditions of test construction. We can here talk about two paradigms. One paradigm is related to the development of tests assigned for selection. The other paradigm related to test assigned to measure a given body of knowledge. The theory behind these two paradigms are different. In the first case the test theory is built on constructing items that are discriminating between individuals, i.e. on a scale. Here we can identify two types of tests, aptitude tests and achievement tests. However, within this tradition achievement tests are constructed from the idea that tests are to discriminate between individuals. In the second case the test theory is built on constructing items that are discriminating not primarily between individuals but in relation to the structure of the content tested. In other words the first tradition of achievement testing can be likened with second tradition can be likened with a map on which individuals are placed. At least within the Nordic countries the first paradigm has dominated up to the 1970s. The first type of tests are not as time-consuming to construct as the latter type of tests. The second type of test will also demand test-constructors that are not only skilled in knowledge in test theory but also knowledgeable in the structure and content that is being measured. Elaborating on the concept of frozen ideologies we can say that there are now sleepers in the educational system that will be awakened - not at least of economic reasons - when evaluation is delimited to a narrow idea of evaluation as equal to testing.

In realising a national evaluation system in which these sleepers are and where the public pressure on evaluations reinforce a narrow idea about evaluation will then give consequence problems. To follow the first test paradigm will involve delivering evaluations that are more or less impossible to use in order to govern the system as the results will not tell how well a knowledge structure is covered, but how the students differentiate in relation to knowledge. It will thus provide the relative relation between the individual students within the system and leaving the system, but not how the content has been transmitted and the goals achieved, neither will it give a basis for decisions for change linked to political means such as resource allocation and in-service training.

In addition to the movement towards decentralisation having to be understood in an historical context and also how an evaluation policy is formulated, the history of educational evaluation must be evaluated in relation to the conditions in the arena of policy realisation.

References

Arrow, 'Higher education as a filter'. In I. Lumsden, (ed.), *Efficiency in Universities*. Elsevier, 1974.

Berger, P.L. (1974), 'Policy and the calculus of meaning'. In *Pyramids of Sacrifice*. New York: Basic Books.

Bergersen, A. and Tjeldvall, A. (1983), *Skole uten rektor*, Oslo: Nash Vorlag.

Blaug, M. (1966), *Economics of Education: A Selected Annotated Bibliography*, London: Pergamon Press.

Coombs, P.H. (1968), *The World Educational Crisis*, London: Oxford University Press.

Correa, (1968), *The Economics of Human Resources*, Amsterdam: North-Holland Publishing Company.

Crozier, M. (1977), *The Governability of West European Society*, University of Essex.

Dahllöf, U. (1970), 'Curriculum process analysis and comparative evaluation of school systems', *Paedagogica Europea, 1970/71*, Braunschweig: G. Wetsermann Verlag, 21-36.

Dror, Y. (1981), 'Social policy in a period of decrement: a perspective'. In OECD, *The Welfare State in Crisis*. Paris: OECD.

Goble, N.M. (1986), 'New challenges for teachers and teacher education', Opening address to the WCOTP, Council of Europe Seminar in Strasbourg, 28-30 April.

Habermas, J. (1973), *Legitimationsprobleme in Spätkapitalismus*, Frankfurt: Suhrkampf Verlag.

Habermas, J. (1968), *Technik und Wissenschaft als 'Ideologie'*. Frankfurt: Suhrkampf Verlag.

Habermas, J. (1971), *Toward a Rational Society*, London: Heinemann.

Hauge, P. and Saetr, P.K. (1988), *Pedagogik som vitskap, og utdanningspolitik*, Stockholm: HLS förlag.

House, E.R. (ed.) (1973), *School Evaluation*, London: Sage.

House, E.R. (1978), 'Assumptions underlying evaluation models', *Educational Researcher*, 7, 4-12.

House, E.R. (1980), *Evaluating with validity*. London: Sage.

Karabel, J. and Halsey, A.H. (1978), 'Educational research: a review and an interpretation'. In Karabel, J. and Halsey, A.H. (ed), *Power and Ideology in Education*, London: Oxford University Press, pp. 1-86.

Kogan, M. (1986), *Education Accountability: An Analytic Overview*, London: Hutchinson.

Lindensjö, B. (1984), 'Den dolda kompromissen: En studie av Maktutredningen'. In Broady, D. and Lundgren, U.P. *Skeptron, No1*, pp. 82-107.

Lindensjö, B. and Lundgren, U.P. (1986), *Politisk styrning och utbildningsreformer*, (Political governing and educational reforms.), Stockholm: Liber.

Lundgren, U.P. (1977), *Model Analysis of Pedagogical Processes*, Lund: Liber.

Lundgren, U.P. (1982), 'Between schooling and education'. Invited address to the annual meeting of the American Education Research Association, New York, March, 1982. Washington: Educational Research Information Centre. Ed. 218 193.

Mayntz, R. and Scharpf, F. (1975), *Policy Making in the German Federal Bureaucracy*. Amsterdam: Elsevier.

Mayntz, K. and Scharpf, F. (1978), *Interorganizational Policy-Making*, London: Sage.

Metcalf, L. (1978), 'Policy making in turbulent environments'. In Mayntz, K. and Scharpf, F., *Interorganizational Policy-Making*. London: Sage.

Mihaly, O. (1986), *New Challenges for the School and for Teachers: An Attempt for Interpretations of Problems*. Budapest: Centre for School Research and School Development, The National Institute of Education, p. 38.

NOU 1982:3, *Maktutredningen*, Sluttrapport. Oslo: Forvaltningstjenestene.

NOU 1988:28, *Med viten og vilje*. Oslo: Forvaltningstjenestene.

OECD (1974), *Reviews of National Policies for Education, Norway*, Paris: OECD, Education Committee.

OECD (1988), *Review of Educational Policy in Norway: Examiners Report and Questions*, Paris: OECD, Education Committee, May.

Peretti, A. (1986), *What Is in Question? The Teacher, The School or Culture Itself?*, Strasburg: The Council of Europe, AS/Cult (38) 11, 29 April.

Rose, R. (ed.) (1980), *Challenge to Governance: Studies in Overloaded Politics*, London: Sage.

Rose, R. (1980), 'The nature of challenge'. In Rose, R. (ed.), *Challenge to Governance: Studies in Overloaded Politics*. London: Sage. pp. 9-10.

Royal Ministry of Culture and Science, Royal Ministry of Church and Education (1987), *OECD Review of National Policies for Education: Background Report on Norway*, Oslo: Royal Ministry of Culture and Science, Royal Ministry of Church and Education, November.

Scharpf, F. (1973), *Planung als Politische Prozess*, Frankfurt am Mainz: Suhrkamp.

Scharpf, F. (1977), 'Public organization and the weaning of the welfare state', *European Journal of Political Research*, 6.

Schultz, T.W. (1961), 'Investment in human capital', *American Economic Review*, 51., 1-17.

Scriven, M. (1973), 'Goal free evaluation'. In House, E.R. (ed.), *School Evaluation*, London: Sage.

Stake, R.E. (1976), *Evaluating Educational Programmes: The Need and the Response*, Washington: OECD Publication Centre.

Thorndike, R.L. and Hagen, E. (1955), *Measurement and Evaluation in Psychology and Education*, New York: John Wiley.

Tiller, T. (1988), *Den tenkende skolen*, Oslo: Universitetsforlaget.

Weiler, H. (1988), *Education and Power: The Politics of Educational Decentralization in Comparative Perspective*, Stanford, unpublished manuscript.

Wildavsky, A. (1976), *Speaking Truth to Power: The Art and Craft of Policy Analysis*, Boston: Little, Brown and Company.

Chapter 4

Decentralisation in educational governance: an exercise in contradiction?[1]

Hans N. Weiler[2]

The principal thesis of this chapter is that policies of decentralising the governance of educational systems, whereas popular and compelling in the abstract, carry the seeds of their own contradictions. In particular, and with reference to some of the recent discussions about Norwegian education (Royal Ministry, 1987; OECD, 1988; Lundgren, 1989), I argue that there is a basic tension between decentralisation, on the one hand, and the tendency to reassert centralised control over the system, on the other. This tension reveals itself particularly where the relationship between decentralisation and evaluation is concerned.

This argument is being developed against the background of reviewing some of the more widely advocated rationales for decentralisation, and of showing how and why they are susceptible to important contradictions. These contradictions are not easily resolved. However, in dealing with them, it would be useful if we understood better the kinds of political dynamics of decentralisation policies that are discussed in the second part of the chapter. I will return explicitly to the precarious nature of the relationship between decentralisation and evaluation in a final part of the chapter.[3]

The appeal of decentralisation

In the national and international vocabulary of educational policy, 'decentralisation' has been a principal entry for some time now, right next to such other favourites as 'participation', 'equality of opportunity', 'autonomy', and 'reform'. For a variety of reasons, the notion of decentralising systems of education that have developed rather heavily centralised structures of governance seems to command a great deal of attention in a wide range of settings (cf. Baumert and Goldschmidt, 1980; Bray, 1984; Kogan, 1979; Lauglo and McLean, 1985; McGinn and Street, 1986; Pri, 1987; etc.). This is so in part as a reflection of a certain international 'periodicity' in educational policy priorities, where - for example - greater emphasis on equity and redistribution yields in time to greater preoccupation with quality and excellence, and where periods of stronger beliefs in centralisation are succeeded by heavy leanings towards decentralised modes of governance (cf. Lundgren, 1989, p. 12). The current emphasis on decentralisation seems to be particularly resilient, however, in spite of considerable difficulties in agreeing on what exactly 'decentralisation' means in practice, and notwithstanding a less than overwhelming record of success in those attempts at decentralisation that have actually been undertaken.

This preoccupation with decentralisation is by no means limited to education. There has been for some time now an important debate on the possibilities and modalities of decentralising political and economic systems more generally (Sharpe, 1979). Some of the particularly interesting parts of the literature focus on the issue of decentralisation and planning (Himmelstrand, 1981; Rucht, 1982) and on decentralisation in the context of development policies (Cheema and Rondinelli, 1983; Conyers, 1984; Rondinelli *et al.*, 1984). Considering this wealth of attention and analysis, it is certainly not an exaggeration when Nelson Polsby calls the issue of centralisation and decentralisation 'one of the great, resonant themes of contemporary politics' (1979, p. 1).

A good part of the literature on decentralisation is taken up by exercises in definition. As there seems to be little point in adding to this body of work, the present chapter takes a relatively broad view of decentralisation as 'a means to ensure wider representation of legitimate interests in education' (Lauglo and McLean, 1985, p. 5). There is some virtue in the distinction proposed by Conyers and others between 'territorial' decentralisation (to subnational units of smaller size) and 'functional' decentralisation (to para-statal, non-governmental, or private agencies) (1984, p. 187). In the argument that this chapter pursues, this distinction becomes slightly blurred, but the emphasis remains on the territorial dimension of decentralisation, or on what Polsby describes as 'movements, impulses, demands, rationalisations, constitutional injunctions or governmental arrangements tending to take power from national entities and vest them in smaller entities, more territorially restricted in their responsibilities' (1979, p. 2).

Within this broad definition, the chapter first reviews a number of propositions that are ordinarily used to both conceptualize and rationalise the idea of decentralisation. Concluding that none of these propositions appears adequately to capture and analyse the political dynamics surrounding the issue of centralisation and decentralisation, a second part of the chapter develops a more adequate framework for considering decentralisation around the notions of conflict management and compensatory legitimation. Against this background, the final part of the chapter returns to the issue of decentralisation and evaluation and shows why this is a particularly precarious and, quite possibly, contradictory relationship.

Decentralisation in educational policy: the prevailing arguments

Where decentralisation in educational governance is discussed, one normally encounters one of three models or arguments: (a) the 'redistribution' model, which has to do with the sharing of power, (b) the 'efficiency' model, which is geared to enhancing the cost-effectiveness of the educational system through a more efficient deployment and management of available resources, and (c) the 'cultures of learning' model, which emphasises the decentralisation of educational content. There are a number of variants of these three models both in the literature and in the educational policies of different countries (e.g. Lauglo and McLean, 1985, pp. 9-16; Rondinelli *et al.* 1984, pp. 9-26). Occasionally, the three also become intertwined, at least at the level of policy rhetoric. Essentially, however, they are predicated on three different rationalisations for decentralising the governance of educational systems; they are meant to respond to different political and social dynamics, and to have different effects on both the educational system and its environment.

I propose to review these three models and the ways in which they have been used to guide educational policies in different settings. This review will confirm both the existence and the utility of one or another of these three models. It will also show, however, that each of them, although for different reasons, has serious shortcomings where the adequate description and understanding of the profound tension between centralisation and decentralisation in educational governance is concerned. This conclusion will lead to the search for alternative models that should provide better explanations for the appeal of decentralisation policies in education.

Decentralisation and the redistribution of authority

In education as in other policy areas, authority is effectively exercised in two ways: through the regulation of (institutional and individual) behaviour, and through the allocation of resources - human, material and financial. Typically, and important exceptions and variations notwithstanding, this authority is exercised by the state and its agencies. Predominantly, and again with some significant exceptions, it is exercised in rather centralised ways. It is ordinarily the state that sets standards of qualification for students at different levels, often both at the point of entry into, and exit from, the educational institution, and for teachers and other educational personnel. These standards are set either in the form of curricular prescriptions, examination requirements, or certification and accreditation rules; in addition, although sometimes in less tangible ways, standards for educational qualifications are enforced by skill and competence criteria for entry into different parts of the labour market, including the public service.

Similarly, the state effectively exercises its authority over the allocation of resources at least to that part of the educational system that is 'public', but often at least partially to 'private' institutions as well. Through its budgetary authority, the state deals with the educational system's need for financial resources, but tends to control and regulate as well the supply of duly qualified human resources and of material resources such as land, space, equipment, teaching materials, etc. Part of the authority of the state over the allocation of resources consists of setting the terms for the contributions made to education by other entities such as students, families, local and regional authorities, philanthropic organisations, etc. Whereas there is less direct control by the state over the resources of private educational institutions (as in the large private sector of secondary and higher education in the United States), there is a great deal of indirect, but rather effective influence by the state over the resource conditions of private education through such measures as rules on taxation, inheritance, trusts, indirect cost recovery, student loan eligibility, etc.

Both the state's regulatory and allocative functions tend to be exercised in rather centralised ways; this does not always imply one single centre of authority (as at the national level in France or Sweden or in most state socialist systems in Eastern Europe), but may involve 'multiple centres', as in federal systems like the Federal Republic of Germany, the United States, Switzerland, or Nigeria.[4] While the organisational principle of centralisation is moderated in federal systems, that principle still applies in much the same way to the subnational unit (the Länd, Canton, etc.), and with the same rationale.

The rationale for centralised forms of decision-making in education seems to be remarkably similar across different systems. As far as the regulatory function is concerned, the principal rationale advanced is the need for standardisation: Curricula, qualifications, and examinations need to be reasonably similar across the national or subnational unit in order to facilitate mobility, the exchange of personnel, the mutual recognition of diplomas across different regions, etc. Even where, as in the 'cooperative federalism' system of the Federal Republic of Germany, educational policy is in the hands of the second level of political organisation (the *Länder*), a major effort is made (through the 'Permanent Conference of State Ministers of Education' ['Kultusministerkonferenz', KMK]) to standardise the main parameters of educational regulation across the *Länder* in order to achieve considerable homogeneity for the country as a whole (Baumert and Goldschmidt, 1980, pp. 1047-50).

Where the state's allocative authority is concerned, the argument for centralisation appears in two forms. Centralisation in the allocation of resources is supposed (a) to enhance equity by reducing or eliminating whatever disparities exist between different parts of the country in terms of resources, and (b) to increase effectiveness by utilising economies of scale and allowing greater mobility of resources to where they are most needed. When the responsibility for educational financing in California and a number of other states in the US shifted quite dramatically from the local to the state level in the 1970s (Elmore and McLaughlin, 1982), one of the key arguments for this shift was that it would reduce the effect of the disparities in the local property-tax base from which local school districts had traditionally derived their main income.

Against the background of this strong tradition of, and ostensibly cogent rationalisation for, centralised forms of educational decision-making, attempts to redistribute the exercise of regulatory and allocative authority in more decentralised arrangements have been conspicuous for their frequency, but not necessarily for their success. In some cases, there even is, as the example of the United States suggests, a tendency in the opposite direction, i.e. to move away from more decentralised and localised decision structures toward higher degrees of centralisation at least at an intermediate (state) level; in the US, this tendency has coincided with a further significant retreat of the federal government from the realm of active education policy under the Reagan administration. On the other hand, there are, as Norway and other cases have shown, serious and tangible instances of decentralising at least some of the centre's functions (cf. Bray 1984; McGinn and Street 1986; OECD, 1988). Even where that is the case, however, it is common to find mixed appraisals of the experience. The second OECD review of Norwegian educational policy, while impressed with the boldness and determination of the 1987 reforms, sees 'potential difficulties' in decentralisation with regard to both equity and standards (1988, pp. 40-1); McGinn and Street, after reviewing three instances of decentralisation efforts in Latin America (Peru, Chile, Mexico), reaffirm the central role of the state's political 'project' as the main determinant of whether decentralisation does or does not move beyond the level of rhetoric (1986, pp. 489-90).

Major reform proposals in such matters as curriculum development have on occasion brought out strongly held positions among groups of parents or local communities, as in the case of the debate over the curricular guidelines ('Rahmenrichtlinien') for different subject areas in some of the West German states (Hameyer, 1978). The ambitious plans of the West German *Bildungsrat* in the early 1970s for a major decentralisation of educational governance, however, ran into insurmountable political difficulties (Deutscher Bildungsrat, 1973; Weiler, 1989c), and have not had any lasting impact on the structural arrangements for the governance of the West German educational system. There has been, in the Federal Republic of Germany as elsewhere, a great deal of local initiative in launching major reform projects in the 1960s and early 1970s (some of the early experiments with the '*Gesamtschule*' model of comprehensive secondary schooling are a case in point [Weiler, 1983a; 1983b]). There again, however, most of this initiative has subsequently been absorbed into the existing centralised and semi-centralised structure of educational governance.

Why this should be so is really not too difficult to explain within the context of our theoretical understanding of the nature of the modern state (Carnoy, 1984; Offe, 1984; Scase, 1980; Weiler, 1983a). The proposition of a genuine sharing of the state's power to allocate and regulate seriously affects two key conditions for the maintenance of state authority, especially in advanced capitalist societies: (a) The need to maintain control under conditions of increasing and multiplying 'centrifugal' and control-avoidance tendencies, and (b) the need to assure as effectively as possible the reproduction of existing social relations with the help of the educational system. Both of these preoccupations contrast rather sharply with the sharing-of-power notion of decentralisation: Almost by definition, a wider and more diffuse distribution of the authority to regulate and allocate multiplies both the levels and the sources of control over the educational system (McGinn and Street, 1986, p. 489); similarly, a decentralised system of governance tends to introduce into the processes of regulation and allocation interests (such as those of parents and local communities) that disturb the relatively smooth and privileged interaction between the state and the agencies of capital accumulation (Naschold, 1974; Preua, 1975).

Considering this basic incompatibility between the power-sharing logic of decentralisation and the interest of the modern state in maintaining control, it is not surprising that forms of decentralisation that involve a genuine redistribution of authority remain rather scarce in today's world. Wherever they are attempted, they tend to raise concerns over the loss of control or lead to questions whether, in the words of the OECD examiners of Norwegian educational policy, 'the central authorities are satisfied that, given the ambitious drive towards decentralisation, . . . they have retained sufficient involvement in the shaping of policy' (1988, p. 51).

Decentralisation and efficiency

A second rationale for introducing more decentralised structures of governance is based on the claim that decentralisation may yield considerable efficiencies in the management of educational systems (e.g. World Bank, 1988, pp. 10-11). This claim involves two sets of expectations: (a) That greater decentralisation will mobilise and generate resources that are not available under more centralised conditions; and (b) that decentralised systems can utilise available resources more efficiently.

The first of these expectations has to do with the possibility of bringing hitherto untapped local and private resources into the overall resource pool available to education. Whereas there are traces of this strategy in the industrialised world, it has become a particularly prominent feature of the educational policy debate in developing countries, largely under the influence of the World Bank (World Bank, 1980, pp. 71-2). The reasoning goes like this: To the extent that decentralised systems of educational governance do actively involve a broader range of societal institutions and groups, these same institutions and groups could be expected to contribute resources that had previously, under more centralised forms of governance, not been available or been used for other purposes. This expectation is directed particularly at the local community, which, in return for a greater role in the making of educational decisions, is expected to express a stronger sense of commitment to the overall educational enterprise by generating added resources for school construction and maintenance, teacher salaries, etc. Similar, but somewhat more diffuse expectations are associated with a greater involvement of the private sector in educational decision-making and governance, which also is expected to lead to a commitment of more private resources to covering the overall cost of education.

The second expectation that links decentralisation with the notion of greater efficiency has less to do with how resources are raised, and more with how they are used. The argument recognises that, in the short term, decentralisation may involve a certain loss of efficiency as a result of diminished economies of scale - a concern with which the Norwegian government in its discussion of the financial aspects of decentralisation does not seem to be overly impressed anyway (Royal Ministry, 1987, pp. 143); over the medium and the long term, however, the expectation is that decentralised systems of governance will use available resources more wisely and efficiently. This is based on the assumption that decentralised governance will increase familiarity with local conditions and needs, which in turn will lead to a better match between demand and supply and thus to a more economical utilisation of limited resources (Cheema and Rondinelli, 1983, pp. 14-17).

The assessment of this argument rests very much on whether there is going to be a favourable tradeoff between the loss of economies of scale, on the one hand, and the enhanced efficiency in the use of resources, on the other. Whereas there is some evidence that the balance does, indeed, come out in favour of a more decentralised generation and utilisation of resources (Rondinelli *et al.* 1989, pp. 69-72), the overall picture is as yet too sketchy to allow a firm assessment. In the context of the poorer countries of the Third World, the dramatic erosion of the resource base of national governments may more than preempt whatever economies are being effected at the local or regional levels through decentralisation (Bray 1984, pp. 12-13; Cheema and Rondinelli, 1983, p. 16). In the more affluent countries of the world, the argument about a more efficient use of resources under conditions of decentralisation may well carry more weight. Whether it actually does, however, depends very much on a critical examination of the first argument on decentralisation and efficiency that I had advanced above.

This other argument, which had focused on the possibility of raising added resources through decentralisation, contains a very important and, as I have shown in a previous section, somewhat precarious premise. The premise is that additional resources would be provided by local and private institutions in return for their greater involvement in the process of making and implementing educational policy. The expectation of mobilising new resources is, in other words and quite realistically, contingent on a real sharing of power in the decision process: It is unlikely that local communities or private firms will make added resources available to an educational system over which they have just as little influence as they had before. This linkage brings the matter of resource mobilisation back to the issue of the redistribution of authority, on which I have already expressed a good deal of scepticism. Even though the reality of the linkage between decentralisation and resource mobilisation is more complex, it is reasonable to conclude that without any real transfer of influence away from the central authority of the state, it is unlikely that significant new resources will be forthcoming from either the local level or the private sector.

Decentralisation and the cultures of learning

A third and rather different argument for the decentralisation of educational systems has to do with the nature and the determinants of the learning process. This line of reasoning focuses on the decentralisation of educational content, and argues that decentralisation 'can provide greater sensitivity to local variations' (Bray, 1984, p. 9) or, in the words of the Norwegian report to OECD, '(adapt) the educational efforts to local conditions, both in terms of local economic activities, and in terms of knowledge and understanding of the special characteristics of the local region' (Royal Ministry, 1987, p. 124). In this view, centralisation tends to produce a mismatch between a student's and a school's specific learning environment (which tends to reflect local and regional cultures and traditions), on the one hand, and a centrally defined learning agenda or curriculum, on the other. A specific variant of the same argument has to do with the language of instruction in multilingual societies, where initial instruction in the students' mother tongue, which is likely to be a local or subnational language, is seen as providing a more functional bridge between learning at home and learning in school (Bamgbose, 1976).

As a diagnostic matter, the point seems well taken. Except in very small or culturally very homogeneous societies, most countries have considerable variation across regions, communities and language groups in terms of cultural and social frameworks of learning. The frames of reference for the study of history, botany, social studies and other fields vary obviously and significantly between Southern and Northern Italy, the state of Alabama and the state of California, Bavaria and Berlin, Northern and Southern Nigeria, Paris and the Provence, and Oslo and the Finnmark. It is differences like these that have, in countries like the Federal Republic of Germany and the United States, historically sustained the argument for a federal structure of educational governance, and for at least a modest amount of cross-regional differentiation as far as the content of education is concerned.

Here again, however, competing priorities seem to get in each other's way. On the one hand, the importance of culturally specific learning environments and learning media (such as language) is recognised; on the other hand, the demands of modern labor markets and communication systems seem to require more generalized and uniform competencies, skills and certifications at the national, and indeed, international level (cf. Royal Ministry, 1987, pp. 144-5). The linkage between culture and learning tends to get replaced by the linkage between learning and technology; the former linkage - that between culture and learning - tends to benefit from a more decentralised, disaggregated notion of learning and educational content; by contrast, the linkage between learning and technology tends to require more homogeneity and uniformity as far as the content of education is concerned (Nandy, 1978/79).

Decentralisation in education: an interim assessment

In reviewing the three rationales or arguments that are most commonly advanced in advocating greater decentralisation in educational governance, we have thus far found a rather equivocal picture. Whereas all three rationales do seem to make a certain amount of sense in the abstract, it turns out on closer inspection that all of them, to varying degrees, encounter substantial difficulties on either theoretical grounds or in the context of implementation, or both.

(a) The notion of decentralisation as redistribution of power seems largely incompatible with the manifest interests of the modern state in maintaining effective control and in discharging some of its key functions with regard to the system of economic production and capital accumulation.

(b) Decentralisation as a means to enhance the efficiency of educational governance by both generating additional resources and using available resources more effectively seems to have some potential in the abstract (especially where the utilisation of resources is concerned), but also appears to depend on premises, which, when studied more closely, are rather precarious.

(c) Lastly, the notion of decentralising the contexts and contents of learning so as to recognise the diversity and importance of different cultural environments in one society is generally considered meaningful and valid. At the same time, however, it encounters the conflicting claims for a kind of learning that is less oriented to the specifics of cultural contexts, and more to the national and international universalities of dealing with modern systems of technology and communication.

The question thus remains why, if decentralisation is such a precarious and problematic proposition, it continues to loom so large on the agenda of educational policies and reforms. The next section of this chapter will suggest an answer. The answer has to do with the fact that, largely independent of the kinds of considerations we have discussed so far, an overt commitment to decentralisation in educational governance has its important political utilities. Decentralisation in this sense becomes an important vehicle for both the management of social conflict and for what I have called 'compensatory legitimation'. I argue that it is this kind of political utility that tends to keep the notion of decentralisation on the agenda of educational policy, notwithstanding the contradictions and difficulties involved in implementing it.

Alternative conceptions of decentralisation

As the preceding section has shown, some of the more widely used rationales for decentralisation in education seem to be not only of limited effectiveness as policy tools, but also not very adequate as theoretical constructs for analysing what is going on in educational policy. This next section will argue that there are two other conceptions of decentralisation which describe more adequately the political dynamics of the argument over how much centralisation or decentralisation there should be in educational governance. These alternative conceptions have to do with two of the more serious challenges with which the modern state has to cope: The increase in conflict and the loss of legitimacy.

Decentralisation as conflict management

There is nothing dramatically new and revealing about the observation that conflict is endemic in modern societies (Dahrendorf, 1959; Offe, 1984). Theorists of politics argue over the sources of conflict and the possibility and the modes of conflict resolution, but there is no serious disagreement with the thesis of the ubiquity of conflict in contemporary society.

Beyond this general observation, however, educational policy has shown a particular propensity for conflict. Few policy issues - besides nuclear energy and questions of national and international security - have generated as much controversy in as wide a variety of settings as education, especially in situations where major changes in educational policy were proposed: The bitter debate over the introduction of comprehensive schools in Britain and West Germany, the succession of confrontations over university reform in France from 1968 to the Winter of 1986/87, the earlier conflicts over desegregation, and the more recent conflicts over religion in schools in the US, the tension between universalising primary education and expanding secondary and higher education in many developing countries - these and many other examples provide ample evidence for the potential of educational policy to generate conflict.

Nor is it surprising that this should be so. After all, education is closely interwoven with the social fabric in at least two important ways: It plays a key role in allocating social roles and statuses, and thus in determining and sustaining social hierarchies; and it is the principal instrument through which societies transmit their values and norms and inculcate them in successive generations of their citizens. The combined weight of these functions make education a central issue in any society, and make it particularly susceptible to controversy and conflict, especially where, as in most modern societies, there is substantial and profound disagreement over both the desired nature of social relations and the normative bases of human and social behaviour.

Conflict is thus a fairly constant element in the pursuit of educational policy in most countries, and tends to become particularly intense when it comes to plans to reform the educational system in some major way (Weiler, 1985). Few such controversies can really be resolved by decree; they will not simply disappear just because someone, no matter how authoritatively, says that they should. This being so, the exercise of central control does not normally qualify as a particularly promising tool for handling such conflicts. On the contrary: The more tenaciously different and conflicting positions on key educational policy issues are held, the more the exercise of central control is likely to generate enough resistance to further jeopardise the viability of the policy system; the 1984 explosion of public protest over the control of private schools in France serves as a reminder (Weiler, 1988a). Thus, where the resolution and elimination of conflict by central fiat proves unrealistic, the *management* of conflict becomes a critically important challenge in educational policy. If policy conflicts in education tend to be such that they can only be managed rather than resolved, the ability to manage conflict becomes an important prerequisite for 'successful' policy. By 'success' in this context I mean maintaining an open and reasonably peaceful coexistence between different policy objectives, keeping the system from getting mired in constant confrontations and upheavals, and at the same time maximising the utility of conflict for maintaining and enhancing the vitality and vigour of the educational system.

It is in this context that decentralisation in educational policy becomes potentially a very significant strategy for coping with highly conflictual situations. The overt advantage of decentralisation from the point of view of conflict management is that it allows the state to diffuse the sources of conflict, and to provide additional layers of insulation between them and the rest of the system. A classic (and disarmingly obvious) example for the use of this strategy was the reorganisation of the University of Paris after the disruptive 'events' of the May 1968 student protests. By breaking up the once unified mega-University of Paris into a dozen or more separate entities, and by doing this in such a way that the major elements of insurgence and dissent were concentrated and isolated in two of those entities - Vincennes (later Vincennes-Saint Denis) and Nanterre - the thrust of the protest movement was effectively deflected and channelled into parallel structures that could more easily be contained and monitored (Prost, 1981, pp. 272-319).

The modest degree of decentralisation that is inherent in the federal system of educational governance in the Federal Republic of Germany has served a similar role in the conflict over the introduction of comprehensive schools (*'Gesamtschulen'*) in the late 1960s and 1970s. Even with this element of diffusion, there was still a good deal of conflict, but one can easily imagine how much more intense the conflict over this particularly sensitive issue would have been if it had been played out in a unitary, centralised system of educational policy. As it was, the fact that *Länder* of different political persuasions were largely free to go their own way as far as introducing or not introducing comprehensive schools was concerned served both to diffuse and to defuse the issue sufficiently to keep it from being the political dynamite that it had the potential of becoming. In retrospect, one also has to note, however, that this diffusion of the reform effort contributed in no small measure to the ultimate defeat of the comprehensive school reform; to judge at least by the German case, decentralisation does not always and necessarily work to the advantage of implementing controversial reforms (Eliason and Weiler, 1989).

The ability either to create new forms of decentralised governance (as in the Paris case) or to use existing ones (as in West Germany) adds measurably to the state's capability for managing and containing the kind of conflict that tends to arise around educational policy issues. The examples also highlight, however, the substantial cost involved in the use of decentralisation in highly conflictual situations. Whereas decentralisation can and does contain and isolate the sources of conflict, it also tends to fragment reform movements and deprives the system as a whole of the full innovative stimulus of proposals for reform and change; the *Gesamt-*

schule reform in West Germany serves once again as a case in point. Decentralisation as an instrument of conflict management, in other words, also tends to serve inherently, and perhaps unintentionally, as a device to reduce innovation and change to localised phenomena of limited impact.

Decentralisation as compensatory legitimation

The previous section has dealt with the interest of the state in developing its capability for the management of conflict. This next section starts from a different, but related premise, namely, that the modern state faces a particularly severe challenge in terms of the erosion of its own legitimacy. The theoretical basis of this argument has a rich and complex history, which goes back to the work of Max Weber and the more recent contributions of the author (1983a; 1985; 1988a), Crozier *et al.* (1975), Habermas (1975), Offe (1984), Wolfe (1977), and others. For purposes of our argument here, it will suffice to restate the basic premise that derives from this theoretical ancestry: The modern state, for reasons having to do both with the volume and the nature of the demands placed upon it, faces an increasingly serious 'delegitimation of authority' (Crozier *et al.*, 1975, pp. 162-3) and rather basic challenges to its 'worthiness of recognition' (Habermas, 1979, p. 178). The normative basis of the state's authority, in other words, has become increasingly precarious.

In addition to this premise about the precariousness of the state's legitimacy and credibility, I assume further that those who act on behalf of the state - politicians, legislators, policy-makers, senior administrators - are very much aware of this erosion of the state's legitimacy, and have an interest in preserving or recapturing as much as possible of this rather precious commodity upon which rests, after all, the credibility of their own actions. This assumption has led me to suggest in some of my earlier work that an important consideration for those who design policies is not only what outcomes these policies will achieve (greater equity, more efficient schools, more employment of graduates, etc.), but also how these policies will affect the search for added legitimacy. I have elsewhere reviewed a number of different policy strategies in an attempt to further develop this notion of 'compensatory legitimation'. It turns out that, among the strategies that have (or are perceived as having) a particular affinity with the issue of legitimacy, the utilisation of expertise and research, the use or at least the invocation of rational planning procedures, and the involvement of legal institutions and norms loom particularly large (Weiler, 1983a; 1983b).

In this array of policy strategies that could serve as putative sources of compensatory legitimation, decentralisation may well play a particularly important role. This is so for two reasons. First, the problem with the legitimacy of the modern state seems at least in part to lie in its (real or perceived) over-centralised nature, its distance from the 'basis' of the political system, its monolithic quality, its structural inability to attend to important variations within the society, and the often 'impersonal, coercive, and dehumanising' quality of its administrative bureaucracy (Freedman, 1978, p. 262). If this assessment is correct, then anything that can make the state appear less centralised and monolithic, and more attentive to internal variations of needs and conditions, could well be seen as a potential source of added legitimacy.

The second point is more directly related to education. For reasons already mentioned in the first part of this chapter, there is a particular preoccupation in many modern societies with the adverse effects of overly centralised educational systems. The resurgence of cultural regionalism, of local languages, dialects and cultural and folkloric traditions, and of subnational alternatives to national conceptions of cultural identity have led to more emphasis on the limits of centralisation in education. These developments have further reinforced (and been reinforced by) the perception that centralised state structures tend to be a greater obstacle to democratic expression than decentralised structures.

There is thus a dual utility in the notion of decentralisation that makes it particularly attractive from the point of view of compensatory legitimation, and that may well explain the strong commitment to the idea of decentralisation in many countries. The dilemma arises, of course, when it comes to assessing the tradeoff between the benefits of enhanced legitimacy and the cost of losing control. As I have argued above, all real decentralisation (in the sense of genuinely shared regulatory and allocative power among levels of governance) does imply a loss of control. If it is true that decentralisation also holds out the attractive prospect of compensatory legitimation at a time when legitimacy is in short supply, a major challenge for the modern state lies in reconciling these two conflicting objectives: Retaining as much (centralised) control over the system as is possible without a severe loss in legitimacy, while at the same time at least appearing to be committed to decentralisation, and thus reaping the benefits in legitimation to be derived from that appearance. The frequent wavering between centralised and decentralised modes of policy behaviour - or, to be more exact, between decentralisation rhetoric and centralisation behaviour - may very well have its cause in this difficult task of walking the fine line between the conflicting imperatives of control and legitimacy.

Decentralisation and evaluation

It is against the background of this critical assessment of decentralisation policies that I would now like to examine the relationship between decentralisation and evaluation, which looms so large in the current policy debate in many countries, including Norway. I am arguing that this relationship is problematic for three different, but interrelated reasons, each of which goes back to some of my earlier points. These reasons are:

(a) Modern, pluralist societies face increasingly a lack of consensus on the objectives of education, and hence on the criteria for evaluating the performance of educational systems;[5]

(b) there is, protestations to the contrary notwithstanding, a very close and inevitable linkage between evaluation and control, which is difficult to reconcile with the basic premises of decentralisation; and

(c) evaluation tends to be seen and used as a means of 'compensatory legitimation' in its own right, i.e. for its legitimating rather than its informative capacity.

Evaluation and the lack of consensus

On the face of it, there should not be much of a problem. Should it not be possible to evaluate a decentralised system of education just as well as a centralised one? Could one not ascertain just as well under centralised as under decentralised conditions whether teachers teach what they are supposed to teach, whether students learn what they are supposed to learn, and whether the toilets are clean and the accounts properly kept?

On closer inspection, the answer is not that easy. There certainly are situations where one set of performance criteria is equally valid and acceptable in all the different parts and segments of a society, and can thus usefully serve as the basis for the system-wide evaluation of how education is doing. There is probably little disagreement over what to look for in assessing the physical quality of the school plant, or in determining the level of health of school children or the punctuality of the staff, even though there may well be variations in the relative importance attached to any of these measures.

Beyond this, however, things tend to get more problematic. Expectations about what educational systems should accomplish vary considerably not only from one society to another, but also across the different regions, groups, and classes of all but the most homogeneous societies. Multilingual societies face the dilemma of which language(s) to accord priority in the educational system; groups that are heavily involved in external commerce will consider proficiency in international languages (and in modern accounting and management methods) more important than the preservation of the country's cultural traditions and local languages. Those whose children grow up in more privileged and stimulus-rich circumstances will judge an educational system more by how well it cultivates outstanding talent and ability, whereas the parents of less privileged children will attach greater importance to the system's ability to foster more equitable learning opportunities for a larger number of people. Even something purportedly as universally valid and desirable as competence in dealing with technology turns out to be subject to profound disagreements once one moves beyond the rather simplistic premise that mathematical ability is important (Nandy, 1978/79). As the Norwegian government's report for the second OECD review states, there is not only tension between criteria of 'relevance and practical usefulness', on the one hand, and 'quality', on the other, but the very notion of 'quality' is 'open to widely different interpretations' (Royal Ministry, 1987, p. 145). This is an admission that is as rare (especially in official pronouncements on education) as it is insightful. More often, the deceptive facility of standardised testing seems to have lured many in the world of educational policy into some rather simplistic assumptions about how 'quality' in education should be conceived and measured. The fixation, in national as well as international circles, on cognitive achievement as the sole legitimate measure of educational outcomes has some of the same qualities of oversimplification (Weiler, 1988b).

The massive evaluation exercise that accompanied the experimental comprehensive school ('*Gesamtschule*') programme in the Federal Republic of Germany in the 1970s provides an instructive example for how the lack of consensus on educational objectives affects evaluation. The point of departure was the claim that a scientific basis was needed for arriving at a decision on whether to maintain the conventional three-tier system of post-elementary education or to introduce a comprehensive secondary school. On this basis, the evaluation programme was designed to compare the performance of the two types of school in an experimental fashion, using the conventional system as the 'control' group and the pilot comprehensive schools as the 'treatment' group (Weiler, 1983a; 1989b). The programme could not have been more thorough, rigorous, competently staffed and generously funded. And yet when all was said and done and when the findings on the comparative performance of the two types of schools became available, both sides in the policy dispute claimed, with some justification, that the data proved their point. Those who had all along advocated maintaining the existing system on the grounds that it functioned best in producing educational excellence found their views, by and large, confirmed by the data on the achievement of gifted children in the selective *Gymnasium*; at the same time, the advocates of the *Gesamtschule*, interested more in greater equality of educational opportunity and in raising the level of education for larger groups of less privileged children, found that the comprehensive school did rather well what they had expected it to do (Eliason and Weiler, 1989; Weiler, 1989b). In fact, the two frames of reference proved so utterly irreconcilable that the Federal-*Länder* commission set up to monitor the experimental programme, after submitting its findings on 767 pages of painstaking detail, declared itself unable to formulate an assessment of the findings that all of its members could accept (Bund-Länder-Kommission, 1982, pp. 19-20). The actual findings were a good deal more complex than this simplified description suggests, but the basic dilemma of evaluating educational systems under conditions of substantial disagreement on objectives is clear enough: Where there is a pluralism of non-reconcilable objectives, evaluation is likely to be inconclusive at best, and a source of further conflict at worst.

Decentralisation relates to this dilemma in a slightly ambivalent way. In one sense, a decentralised system of governance is likely to make the multitude of priorities about educational objectives more clearly transparent, forcing evaluation into a more complex and less standardised mode than it might adopt by its own leanings. In another sense, however, the very complexity and 'messiness' of a decentralised system may - as seems to be the case in the current Norwegian discussions - lead to the kinds of concerns that in turn prompt new demands for evaluation precisely for the sake of re-establishing a certain degree of homogeneity and of 'asserting the national norms' (OECD, 1988, p. 41).

Evaluation, information and control

The relationship between decentralisation and evaluation is problematic in another sense as well. Evaluation is rarely a disinterested activity, least of all in a domain like education where values and status play such critically important roles. While evaluation is about the gathering of knowledge, the gathering of knowledge is by no means all that evaluation is about. It is not at all surprising that a fundamental ambiguity on this issue permeates the discussion and the writings about decentralisation in Norway. The Government's report to the OECD is rather low-key on the issue of evaluation, noting that what little inspection there used to be was in the process of turning into 'pedagogical support services' (Royal Ministry, 1987, p. 101) and recording, without much apparent enthusiasm, 'political claims for more central control of a core curriculum and performance indicators' (*ibid*., p. 144). It is claims of that sort which, by contrast, loom conspicuously large in the report of the OECD examiners (OECD, 1988), which reflects a veritable preoccupation with the issue of evaluation. Notwithstanding their claim that 'we are concerned not with the reintroduction of national controls but with considering ways in which good norms of educational practice can be established and disseminated better in Norway' (*ibid*., p. 45), the examiners are quite obviously troubled by the 'lack of a clear ideological role for the ministry' (*ibid*., p. 43) and especially by the fact that 'there is no effective system for monitoring standards' (*ibid*., p. 40). This concern leads them to argue for a reappraisal of the role of the 'centre', i.e. the national government, which should 'establish its influence by asserting the national norms which should be expected of all local authorities and their schools, by creating means of monitoring and evaluating and by publishing their evaluations' (*ibid*., pp. 40-1). To be sure, they distinguish between the 'normative' power of the centre in a decentralised system and its 'prescriptive' power in more centralised settings (*ibid*., p. 44), but that distinction tends to get rather blurred. It seems clear that, in such critical matters as the allocation of resources and the determination of school curriculum, they see the centre as having the key role in setting nationally binding standards.

It is precisely this position that creates one of the critical dilemmas in the relationship between decentralisation and evaluation. To the extent that evaluation goes beyond the mere gathering of information about students, schools and teachers, and proceeds not only to publicising that information, but also to interpreting it authoritatively against certain standards - to that extent evaluation does become an obvious and major instrument of control and intervention. In the United States, we have nationally standardised 'Scholastic Achievement Tests' (SAT), which most high school students take as part of the competition for college entrance. When the local newspaper annually publishes the mean SAT scores for each high school in my part of California, that report is eagerly awaited by parents, teachers and students. What is more important is that it also sends a signal to both the 'winners' and the 'losers' in that competition - a signal and a message about what is important in education and about what directions to take if the winners want to stay on top and if the losers want to get to the top. And when then, from no less a place than the White House, international comparisons in mathematics and science achievement are prominently invoked as critical determinants of a nation's future, the message is not only made perfectly clear, but also endowed with a tremendous amount of both real and symbolic force. Here, 'evaluation' is not merely the gathering and dissemination of information. It also has something to do with the authoritative interpretation of standards, and is at least as effective a mechanism of control over educational objectives and practices as any I have seen a Ministry of Education use in a highly centralised country.

That may well be the way a given country may want it to be; what I am arguing here is that such a conception of evaluation inherently contradicts the notion and the practice of decentralisation as a genuine delegation of power. To the extent that the ultimate goal of evaluation is 'to assert the national norms' for the performance of schools, students and teachers, evaluation enters into a competitive relationship with the basic premises of decentralisation; against this background, one understands a little better the apprehension of the Norwegian authorities that 'stricter control measures may easily destroy the proper balance between the different aims of educational policy' (Royal Ministry, 1987, p. 105).

Evaluation as compensatory legitimation

My third observation on the problematic nature of evaluation goes back to my earlier argument about 'decentralisation as compensatory legitimation'. I propose here a similar argument about the role of evaluation. My point is that evaluation, as a result of the eminence of scientific rationality in our contemporary world view, enjoys a particularly high measure of prestige as an element in the policy process. It is this prestige, I would argue, that makes evaluation such a perfect and virtually irresistible target for those in search of added sources of legitimation for the policy process and its outcomes. I have little doubt that the phenomenal rise of evaluation as part of both the discourse and the practice of policy is in no small part due to its (real or perceived) capacity for conferring upon the policy process the added virtue of scientific respectability; for the policy process, in whatever field, to include explicit provisions for systematic and rigorous evaluation has become a mark of wholesomeness, and is seen as an effective way to provide added legitimation to a process that is often badly in need of remedial credibility. I would not follow Lundgren all the way in ascribing 'mythological capabilities' to evaluation, but he is certainly right in describing as one of the important functions of evaluation the preservation of 'the belief in a rational paradigm for policy making' (1989, p. 33). This relationship between evaluation and legitimation has become particularly pronounced for the field of curriculum policy, which has encountered special legitimation problems, especially in the context of major curriculum reforms, and has seen the device of systematic evaluation emerge as one of the ways for dealing with those problems (Hameyer *et al.*, 1976; Raschert, 1977; Weiler, 1989c; Wulf, 1975).

It is important to note that this line of argument moves the evaluation issue into an entirely different context. To the extent I am correct in suggesting that evaluation is being seen as a strategy of compensatory legitimation, the importance of evaluation lies not so much in the insights it generates and the improvements that become thereby possible, but at least as much in the connotation of scientific solidity and respectability that it confers on the policy process - almost regardless of its findings! This is not to suggest that the legitimating role of evaluation is uppermost in the mind of everybody who is talking about, or recommending, evaluation. What it does suggest, however, is the need for a much greater awareness of the multiple contexts in which the argument for evaluation can be, and is being, conducted. Evaluation, whether we like it or not, is a profoundly political process, and its potential for purposes of legitimating the authority of the evaluator (i.e. the state) is a key element in this process. 'All evaluation designs have the potential of realigning political power and redefining what is credible knowledge' (Noblit and Eaker, 1989, p. 127; cf. Palumbo, 1987). To do as if evaluation were a strictly technical, descriptive, and hence 'neutral' activity will make it either irrelevant or misleading.

Conclusion

Understanding the political dynamics of centralisation and decentralisation in educational policy requires going beyond the kinds of arguments that are typically advanced for advocating greater decentralisation. Decentralising the making and the implementation of educational policy affects in very important ways the nature and the interests of the state, particularly its ability to cope with the dual problems of policy conflict and the erosion of its own legitimacy. It is with regard to these two issues that the idea of decentralisation proves to be fundamentally ambivalent and precarious, and to present the state with one of its more profound and intractable dilemmas.

This dilemma becomes particularly acute in the attempt to reconcile the competing rationales of decentralisation and evaluation. For reasons having to do with the loss of consensus about the objectives of education, with the real or symbolic force with which the dissemination and interpretation of evaluation results affect an educational system, and with the profoundly political nature of evaluation, this reconciliation appears as a noble, but extraordinarily difficult task. In the final analysis, both decentralisation and evaluation have to do with the exercise of power, and there is always the possibility that the power that decentralisation gives away with one hand, evaluation may take back with the other. Reconciling the two may well turn out to be an exercise in contradiction.

Footnotes

1. This chapter is based on a paper prepared for discussion at an international conference on the Norwegian project 'EMIL - a national evaluation and the quality of education', organised by the Norwegian Research Council for Applied Social Science (NORAS) in Oslo, May 9-10, 1989. It encompasses and continues the argument of an earlier piece on 'Education and Power: The Politics of Educational Decentralization in Comparative Perspective', which was presented at an international seminar at the University of Luleå, Sweden, in June 1988, and was published in both the *Proceedings* of the seminar (Johansson et al. 1989, 117-27) and, in revised form, in *Educational Policy* (Weiler 1989a).

2. Work on this manuscript was undertaken while the author was a Fellow at the Center for Advanced Study in the Behavioral Sciences (CASBS) in 1988/89. The support of the Center and of the Spencer Foundation is gratefully acknowledged.

3. I should make it clear at the outset that it is not the purpose of this chapter to argue for or against decentralisation. What I am arguing for is the need to understand better the complex political dynamics that tend to affect decisions on centralisation and decentralisation.

4. In other words, a federal system is not necessarily 'decentralised' by virtue of being federal; it just has more than one 'centre'.

5. That difficulty is merely concealed, but not really resolved, by the establishment of a national evaluation system.

References

Bamgbose, Ayo (1976), *Mother Tongue Education: The West African Experience*, London: Hodder and Stoughton.

Baumert, Jürgen and Goldschmidt, Dietrich (1980), 'Centralisation and decentralisation as determinants of educational policy in the Federal Republic of Germany (FRG)', *Social Science Information*, 19, 6, 1029-98.

Bray, Mark (1984), *Educational Planning in a Decentralised System: The Papua New Guinean Experience*, Sidney University Press.

Bund-Länder-Kommission für Bildungsplanung und Forschungsfröderung (1982), *Modellversuche mit Gesamtschulen: Auswertungsbericht der Projektgruppe Gesamtschulen*, Bühl/Baden: Konkordia.

Carnoy, Martin (1984), *The State and Political Theory*, Princeton University Press.

Cheema, G. Shabbir and Rondinelli, Dennis A. (eds) (1983), *Decentralisation and Development: Policy Implementation in Developing Countries*, Beverly Hills: Sage.

Conyers, Diana (1984), *Decentralisation and Development: A Review of the Literature, Public Administration and Development*, 4, 187-197.

Crozier, Michael J., Huntington, Samuel P. and Watanuki, Joji (1975), *The Crisis of Democracy: Report on the Governability of Democracy to the Trilateral Commission*, New York University Press.

Dahrendorf, Ralf (1959), *Class and Class Conflict in Industrial Society*, Stanford University Press.

Deutscher Bildungsrat (1973), *Zur Reform von Organisation und Verwaltung im Bildungswesen. Teil I: Verstürkte Selbständigkeit der Schule und Partizipation der Lehrer, Schler und Eltern*, Bonn: Bildungsrat.

Eliason, Leslie C. and Weiler, Hans N. (1989), *The Politics of Educational Reform in Western Europe: Do Policy Systems Learn from Past Experience?* (paper prepared for the Annual Meeting of the Western Political Science Association, Salt Lake City, Utah, 30 March - 1 April).

Elmore, Richard F. and McLaughlin, Milbrey Wallin (1982), *Reform and Retrenchment: The Politics of California School Finance Reform*, Cambridge, Mass: Ballinger.

Freedman, James O. (1978), *Crisis and Legitimacy: The Administrative Process and American Government*, Cambridge University Press.

Habermas, Jürgen (1975), *Legitimation Crisis*, Boston: Beacon.

Habermas, Jürgen (1979), *Communication and the Evolution of Society*, Boston: Beacon.

Hameyer, Uwe (1978), *Innovationsprozesse: Analysemodell und Fallstudien zum sozialen Konflikt in der Curriculumrevision*, Weinheim, Basel: Beltz.

Hameyer, Uwe *et al.* (eds) (1976), *Bedingungen und Modelle der Curriculuminnovation*, Weinheim: Beltz.

Himmelstrand, Ulf (ed.) (1981), *Spontaneity and Planning in Social Development*, Beverly Hills, Calif: Sage.

Johansson, Henning, Lundgren, Ulf P. and Popkewitz, Thomas S. (eds) (1989), *Proceedings of the Symposium in Pedagogics, 12 - 15 June*, Lule, Sweden: *Challenge Future Through Your Culture*, Lule: CENTEK.

Kogan, Maurice (1979), *Education Policies in Perspective: An Appraisal*, Paris: OECD.

Lauglo, Jon and McLean, Martin (1985), *The Control of Education: International Perspectives on the Centralisation-Decentralisation Debate*, London: Heinemann.

Lundgren, Ulf (1989), *Educational Policy Making, Decentralisation and Evaluation: An Invitation to Papers*, Oslo: EMIL.

McGinn, Noel and Street, Susan (1986), 'Educational decentralisation: Weak state or strong state?', *Comparative Education Review*, 30, 4, November, 471-90.

Nandy, Ashis (1978/79), 'The traditions of technology', *Alternatives*, 4, 3, 371-85.

Naschold, Frieder (1974), *Schulreform als Gesellschaftskonflikt*, Frankfurt: Athenum.

Noblit, George W. and Eaker, Deborah J. (1989), 'Evaluation designs as political strategies'. In Hannaway, Jane and Crowson, Robert (eds), *The Politics of Reforming School Administration: The 1988 Yearbook of the Politics of Education Association*, New York: Falmer Press, pp. 127-38.

Offe, Claus (1984), *Contradictions of the Welfare State*, MIT Press.

Organisation for Economic Cooperation and Development (OECD), Education Committee (1988), *Review of Educational Policy in Norway: Examiner's Report and Questions* [ED (88) 2], Paris: OECD. (Cited as 'OECD 1988'.)

Palumbo, Dennis J. (ed.) (1987), *The Politics of Program Evaluation*, volume 15, *Sage Yearbooks in Politics and Public Policy*, Newbury Park: Sage.

Polsby, Nelson (1979), Preface. In Sharpe, L.J. (ed.), *Decentralist Trends in Western Democracies*, London: Sage, pp. 1-7.

Preuss, Ullrich K. (1975), *Bildung und Herrschaft: Beiträge zu einer politischen Theorie des Bildungswesens*, Frankfurt: Fischer.

Prié, René (1987), *L'Education nationale l'heure de la décentralisation: Changements et continuité*, Paris: La Documentation Française.

Prost, Antoine (1981), *Histoire Générale de l'Enseignement et de l'Education en France. Tome IV: L'Ecole et la Famille dans une société en mutation*, Paris: Nouvelle Librairie de France.

Raschert, Jürgen (1977), 'Problem der Legitimation von Lehrplänen und Richtlinien'. In Haller, Hans-Dieter and Lenzen, Dieter (eds), *Wissenschaft im Refomprozess: Aufklärung oder Alibi?*, Stuttgart: Klett-Cotta, pp. 21-27.

Rondinelli, Dennis, McCullough, James S. and Johnson, Ronald W. (1989), 'Analysing decentralisation policies in developing countries: A political-economy framework', *Development and Change*, 20, 57-87.

Rondinelli, Dennis A., Nellis, John R. and Cheema, G. Shabbir (1984), *Decentralisation in Developing Countries: A Review of Recent Experience*, World Bank Staff Working Papers Number 581, Washington: The World Bank.

Royal Ministry of Cultural and Scientific Affairs and Royal Ministry of Church and Education (1987), *Reviews of National Policies for Education: Norway*, Report to OECD, Oslo: Government of Norway. (Cited as 'Royal Ministry 1987'.)

Rucht, Dieter (1982), *Planung und Partizipation: Bürgerinitiativen als Reaktion und Herausforderung politisch-administrativer Planung*, München: TUDUV.

Scase, Richard (ed.) (1980), *The State in Western Europe*, New York: St. Martin's.

Sharpe, L. J. (ed.) (1979), *Decentralist Trends in Western Democracies*, London: Sage.

Weiler, Hans N. (1983a), 'Legalization, expertise, and participation: Strategies of compensatory legitimation in educational policy', *Comparative Education Review*, 27, 2, 259-77.

Weiler, Hans N. (1983), 'West Germany: Educational policy as compensatory legitimation'. In Thomas, Murray (ed.), *Politics and Education: Cases from Eleven Nations*, Oxford: Pergamon, pp. 33-54.

Weiler, Hans N. (1985), 'Politics of educational reform'. In Merritt, Richard L. and Merritt, Anna J. (eds), *Innovation in the Public Sector*, Beverly Hills, Calif: Sage, pp. 167-212.

Weiler, Hans N. (1988a) 'The politics of reform and non-reform in French education', *Comparative Education Review*, 32, 3, 251-65.

Weiler, Hans N. (1988b), 'Uncertainty and power: New paradigms of knowing and the knowledge base of educational planning', paper prepared for an international seminar on 'The Futures of Strategic Educational Planning' at the International Institute for Educational Planning, Paris, 28 November - 2 December.

Weiler, Hans N. (1989a), 'Education and power: The politics of educational decentralisation in comparative perspective', *Educational Policy*, 3, 1, 31-43.

Weiler, Hans N. 'Why reforms fail: The politics of education in France and the Federal Republic of Germany', *Journal of Curriculum Studies*, 1989b (in press).

Weiler, Hans N. (1989c), 'Curriculum reform and the legitimation of educational objectives: The case of the Federal Republic of Germany', paper prepared for the 1989 Meetings of the Comparative and International Education Society, Harvard University, 31 March - 2 April.

Wolfe, Alan (1977), *The Limits of Legitimacy: Political Contradictions of Contemporary Capitalism*, New York: The Free Press.

The World Bank (1980), *Education Sector Policy Paper*, (third edition) Washington, DC: The World Bank.

The World Bank (1988), *Education in Sub-Saharan Africa: Policies for Adjustment, Revitalization, and Expansion*, Washington, DC, The World Bank.

Wulf, Christoph (1975), 'Funktionen und Paradigmen der Evaluation'. In Frey, Karl (ed.), *Curriculum-Handbuch*, München: Piper, pp. 580-600.

Chapter 5

A comparative perspective with special reference to Norway

Jon Lauglo

In the spatial sense, decentralisation can be measured by distance from the centre. As for the spread of institutions, it is, of course, possible to measure their physical dispersion from a geographical centre or from a nation's capital. In this sense, hospital services or universities are decentralised when provisions are geographically diffused and made more accessible to a dispersed clientele. However, spatially dispersed institutions can be tightly controlled by a central authority. They can also be run in a regimented way by their institutional management. On the other hand, an institution in a single geographical location can have quite autonomous sub-units and allow much individual discretion. Universities exemplify this pattern. Thus, spatial dispersion and the distribution of authority are conceptually distinct. When decentralisation in education is discussed, it is usually the distribution of authority to which one refers. That is also the object of this chapter.

Nonetheless, in a system of geographically dispersed institutions, the chain of authority will have an associated spatial dimension. This spatial aspect of decentralisation can become quite important politically when levels of authority coincide with independently constituted governments that are not simply agents of the nation state but have their own legitimacy and power base: e.g. states in a federal system, regional assemblies, local councils. Further, the problem of communication with a 'centre', when an institution is geographically remote, is an argument for institutional autonomy. In fact, isolation breeds autonomy perforce whether intended or not. Thus, 'space' and geographical dispersion can be conditions that influence the distribution of authority.

A decision can be a process. Deciding on policy certainly is. When decisions are expected to have far-reaching consequences, they are more likely to become a process - 'decision making'. There is exploratory diagnosis; goals are set; information is sought and received. Representations are made; negotiations are undertaken; proposals are formulated and appraised, anticipating the reactions of groups affected. There can be new rounds of modifications until the decision is reached.

In discussion about the control of education, attention will naturally centre on the distribution of decision-making authority - legitimate power, and on officially recognised rights of access to that authority (rights to make representations, to be consulted, to participate in councils, etc.). Authority is indeed at the core of the control system of education. However, authority is subject to influence, which, in complex decisions, can be exerted at different stages in the process of deciding. This wider and far more elusive concept of influence, which is an even wider concept than power, also takes many forms: ranging from manipulative pressure and strings attached to offers of resources, to persuasion and supply of information. Influence is not always actively exerted, it can also be of a passive kind, serving as constraints on or opportunities for decisions.

The distribution of influence will differ from that of authority. Decisions made by the central political authorities can, of course, be strongly influenced by more broadly based aggregation of political interest. Opposition groups too, even in sharply polarised political systems, exert influence - as factors to take account of. Conversely, in some countries seemingly independent decisions by local government bodies can, through party discipline, be tightly controlled by a central party organisation that also controls the state, so that local autonomy is illusory - or even a means by which a party seeks to control local institutions more directly than it could through the state civil service. Decentralisation moves in post-Independence Tanzania, after initial tightening up of central control (Dodd, 1968), may be an example of the latter.

A wide variety of decisions are made in education systems - from the most general and far-sweeping to the minutiae of daily work. At one extreme: legal frameworks, the scale of financial resources and long-term policies; at the other: setting tomorrow's homework for a particular student. The variety defies any detailed typology. However, within a given structure of education, a first level in the listing could be by types of inputs (these will be reflected in the organisational structure): students, teachers, curriculum with related materials and assessment procedures, facilities, finance and management. Within each of these 'input areas', there is a hierarchy with 'higher-level' decisions (in terms of generality) setting the frames that direct and constrain the 'lower level' and the more specific decisions in various ways. Going 'down' in terms of generality, there are first stable and general rules: a constitution, laws; then policies setting goals, strategies and general resource frames; then more changeable and situation-specific regulations and directives; all the way to decisions only intended for an individual case - and routine implementation. A parallel and equally important hierarchy of decisions concerns the budget, with the volume of resources to spent on more specific items subsumed under more general categories.

Who decides and who exerts influence will depend on how far-reaching the decisions are. Some decisions will be more 'centralised', others will be taken further down the hierarchy. There will be a degree of correlation between organisational level and the scope of a decision (Lyons,1985), but this match will vary among countries; thus perhaps indicating systematic differences in degrees of centralisation.

In general, it is easier to define centralisation than decentralisation, for centralisation refers to the concentration of decision-making authority at the top of the organisational hierarchy. Of course, no education system can be entirely 'centralised'. Important parts of education - not only the transmission of values and attitudes - inherent in personalised interaction which no centrally imposed 'materials-methods' system could steer. These decisions will often be taken during the process of teaching itself. Much of the curriculum is inevitably made on the spot even when there is a manual to be followed - or it fails to be made at all! And teachers work in relative isolation from direct daily scrutiny by their superiors, who themselves liaise with authorities outside the school mainly by letters and telephone. As already noted, physical isolation creates a separate social space for each school.

The decision-makers in education - let alone the much greater number who exert influence - do not fit a 'centre-periphery' polarity. Insofar as education systems have a single chain of authority, there are many levels in it and, therefore, many alternatives to concentrating authority at the centre. More authority for an intermediate level will often make those one step down on the ladder more diffusely dependent on their superiors. Thus, teachers unions usually resist the kind of decentralisation that increases the local accountability of teachers. Rather than diffuse local dependence, it is better to have the autonomy to work within rules laid down by more distant masters.

In education, there is often a sense of common professional identity among teachers and institutional managers and officials who have risen from the ranks. This professional identity can blur a 'management-worker' divide, and make autonomy for the profession as a whole a shared concern. However, the strength of this shared identity varies. It is likely to be strong precisely when institutional managers and lower-level administrators have relatively little scope for decisions and function more as bureaucratic intermediaries so that few locally contentious decisions are theirs to make. The head teacher is then a *primus inter pares*, a teacher with some added administrative responsibility. Under such conditions, they can take the lead in interest advocacy for teachers. Involvement in a teachers' union can even be a stepping stone to becoming a head teacher - this has been the case in Norway - at least in the upper secondary schools in the 1960s (Lauglo, 1976). Ironically, the forms of decentralisation that strengthen institutional managers are likely to weaken their role as 'spokespersons for the profession', because their teachers will then become more like subordinates and less like colleagues. This is probably happening in England and Wales today under the Baker education reform. It may be a more general international trend, as increasing complexity of school management leads to professional separatism of managers.

It is really a distortion to think of education systems as a single hierarchy that is accountable only at the top to political masters.

First, there are private schools. They are not extensions of the state though they will be subject to its regulations. Is privatisation a form of decentralisation? Current World Bank promotion of 'decentralisation policies' assumes this to be so (World Bank, 1988). Private schools vary enormously in their control structures (and in quality): some are established as charitable foundations, others are profit-making private-venture schools. Some are community-based, others are local extensions of a nationally organised private system. In many countries, the Catholic Church runs its own large-scale education system, from nursery school to university. Autonomy from the state can coexist with high concentration of authority within them. Schools run by the Jesuit order are an historical example of concentration of authority both within the institution and in the larger system of private schools. Private-venture schools usually concentrate authority within the institution in the hands of the owner. As private schools usually depend on income from fees and donations, they will also tend to become more customer-oriented.

Within the public system, there is also divergence from a simple model of bureaucratic authority. Many countries have several levels of separately constituted political authority - each with some politically 'independent' responsibility for education. Certain institutions may be directly under the purview of higher levels; others may be owned and operated by local government but are subjected to rules and regulations (and receiving some resources) from regional or national government. One form of decentralisation is to give more authority to such local or regional government bodies, but this is very different from - and sometimes clashes with - augmenting the professional authority of educators close to the classroom.

The picture is further complicated by groups that are outside the political and administrative apparatus of government and that are not 'members' of the education system - they do not 'attend' or work there, but they have a vested interest in education and may become organised in pursuit of those interests. There are external 'user groups' (parents, the local community), which, for certain institutions, have special rights of representation outside the normal political channels, serving as a kind of quasi-constituency. The balance between such external groups who may feel it is 'their school', local government, and the insiders in the school (teachers, students, administrators) can be a contentious issue that decentralisation glosses over (Baron, 1981). There are other external groups that are not a quasi constituency for individual schools, but that have a vested interest in education and seek to exert influence at different levels in the authority structure. Cultural/ethnic and religious groups, in particular, will have an interest in the curriculum. Employers and labour unions will have a special interest in vocational training.

To conclude, rather than thinking in terms of a centralised-decentralised polarity, one should think in terms of the distribution of authority on a great many 'actors' within the school system and outside it. The term 'decentralisation' will, therefore, in different contexts refer to shifts in favour of rather different groups. These shifts are likely to vary greatly in their antecedents and consequences in different countries. Further, there are other dimensions to examine - notably the variety of types of decisions, and there is a need to bear in mind the wider concept of influence that will in its distribution differ from that of authority.

Factors behind decentralisation

The distribution of authority in an education system has great inertia. Thus, in order to understand that distribution it is necessary to examine the conditions that prevailed when a system of institutions was first established (Scotford Archer, 1979). In some countries schools were clearly established by state authority (e.g. the French system of 'secular' schools). In other countries local communities took the early lead (e.g. the United States). Or local patrons and voluntary organisations took the initiative (England), with government later moving in to fill the gaps. Thus, patterns were established of tight state control in some countries, local government (or even school district) control in others, and a high degree of institutional autonomy in yet others. It usually takes radical political change to alter fundamentally such established patterns of control.

In Norway, the spread of mass schooling was intimately connected with the initial *raison d'être* of locally elected government - with the Church to take initiative and supervise on behalf of the state. As the authority of the Church over local schools has receded, local operating responsibility has grown. In basic education we have no national inspectorate to replace the earlier roles of bishops, deans and parsons. The role of the state has been to legislate, provide rules and regulations, assist heavily with finance to compensate for inequalities in the local resource base, and to lay down curricula and syllabuses. Within these regulations, which have become less specific in recent decades, considerable local autonomy has evolved - more than in Sweden, but less than in Denmark (Lauglo, 1981). Looser regulations regarding curriculum will in practice increase the autonomy of local professionals because they are the natural experts, even when outside groups are pulled in through participatory mechanisms. This has been true in Norway too (Baarstad *et al.*, 1977). Conversely, looser central control over the use of resources - the change from earmarked central support to a block grant to local councils, will strengthen the control of local politicians. The growth of a local government education bureaucracy is an important third development. Are the local education bureaucracies means by which politicians control schools? Or are they more effective channels for professionals to claim resources for education at the same time as they providing the schools with a buffer against direct political intervention? Or, is the local school bureaucracy largely an independent third force, gaining in influence at the joint expense of teachers and politicians - some kind of managerial revolution? Recent Norwegian research has shown that there are few proposals by the local school bureaucracy that are overturned by politicians (Ånensen, 1987).

The distribution of authority is legitimated by political ideologies (McLean and Lauglo,1985). The Democratic Centralist variety of socialism clearly has been a force for central direction, both through the apparatus of the state and a parallel party organisation - notwithstanding Marx's vision of a post-revolutionary society with direct participation of the labouring masses (Lauglo, 1988). On the other hand, an 'anarchist' or syndicalist version of socialism that stresses the voluntary cooperation between work organisations that would have a high degree of internal democracy is the ideology of 'participatory democracy'. This would be collective control by those whose daily work lies within the school: the collective of teachers in particular. Students would be involved, as learners of democracy when young, and co-equals when old enough. It is this concept of decentralisation with an associated relativist notion of a negotiated curriculum that was espoused by the student movement of the 1960s. Neo-Marxist prescriptions for education (Young, 1971) bear its imprint: the curriculum is to be 'negotiated' among those directly involved - keeping the 'outside' local political authorities and employers at arm's length. It left traces in the Norwegian system in higher education - especially in new institutions conceived at the time. The reason why higher education was marked more by this 'anarchist' view of decentralisation is not only the strength of the student movement at universities. Internal - rather than external - control is the mainstream university tradition. And so is the notion of a community of scholars that embraces tutors and students alike in a field.

The liberal democratic tradition has also two main branches: one that stresses central control, and one that stresses institutional autonomy. The former is distinctly French, the latter is distinctly English. The centralist view sees a democratically constituted state as the crusading embodiment of the general will, against vested interests that are entrenched in the periphery that is still marked by the old social order. It is the city that is the source of progress and enlightenment - and rural areas that need to be protected from their own traditional oligarchy. State schools are then a source from which reason and light radiate. This view is a main legacy of the French Enlightenment for education in Europe. Condorcet plan for French education can stand as the prototype. The state is here seen as a democratising force, and schools are the tool. Teachers then become internal missionaries of progress, agents of democratic change and Rationalist modernity in the community (Clifford-Vaughan, 1963) - not agents of the community.

There is affinity between this Rationalist view and that of Democratic Centralism. But then Marxism owes much to the French Rationalist notion of unilinear progress in which urban, industrial society is the vanguard. Marxist appreciation of the school as a source of 'enlightenment' is not confined to education under socialism. Unlike Western Neo-Marxists of the 1968 generation who sought to relativise and debunk as 'bourgeois' much of academic high culture, Marx and Lenin valued the scientific and cultural achievement of the social order they sought to overturn (Partington, 1988). Similarly, Gramsci greatly valued academic disciplines and the tradition of the state-provided Italian primary school (Entwistle, 1979).

The other liberal democratic tradition - the 'English' one - has its roots in the defence of privilege ('liberties') against arbitrary rule. It is a tradition of institutional autonomy, thus encouraging the ideal that schools have their own individuality. It builds protective buffers around professional autonomy (though professions may have their own powerful controlling establishment). This restrains the directive influence of local political authority on the schools. However, local government is itself not merely an implementing agent of the state, it has its own buffers against state control - its own 'ancient liberties'. Thus, the pattern resists bureaucratic streamlining from the classroom to the Ministry along a single chain of authority. Rather, it encourages private foundations and 'quango's' - quasi autonomous government organisations. It tolerates and encourages private education - both private-venture schools and as charitable foundations. By this tradition, decentralisation in education means professionalism and institutional autonomy from 'political interference'. It is a tradition which is most clearly expressed in universities.

In addition to socialist and democratic ideologies, a third main strain is populism. Populism assumes a fundamental cleavage between the 'people' as a broadly defined and organic group - 'common folk', the 'common man'- and a narrowly defined upper class or elite whose legitimacy is challenged. The elite is seen as alien, effete or exploitative. The good sense and rights of ordinary people are stressed. They are the carriers of the national identity, they may even be perceived as the heirs of a golden age of long ago - Latin American campesinos as heirs of a pre-conquest civilisation; the American 'common man' as heir to the pioneer settlers of the West; Middle Eastern market-traders and peasants as guardians of Islamic beliefs and virtues in a secularised world; African village traditions of 'self-help' and mutual support that have survived from a harmonious pre-colonial past; and, of course, the Norwegian yeoman farmer as the heir of the culture of the Sagas, before centuries of foreign domination. The invocation of such myths helps sustain populism.

Populism owes much to the Romantic Movement with its naturalistic admiration of the peasant or 'noble savage', its rejection of industry and urban life, its stress on an organic *Gemeinschaft*. Social and geographic mobility - which is a liberating, horizon-widening experience in the Rationalist democratic view, is in the populist tradition at best a source of purely economic opportunity for the 'common man' (e.g. Midwestern populism). However, mobility is often perceived as a cause of alienation. In this view of the world, it is in the rural periphery, not in the urban industrial centre, that good sense and cultural authenticity is found; and the vision of human betterment is one that must be in keeping with the traditions of rural communities (Kitching, 1982). Mahatma Ghandi, Mao Zedong and Julius Nyerere all viewed development as something to be rooted in the collectivity of the village. Popular culture is celebrated. Language revival movements are the products of populism. There is also in populist movements sturdy confidence in what Philip Coombs coined as 'informal education': learning that occurs without much institutional differentiation from the flow of daily activity: on the farm or in the small workshop, and in everyday community life. As manual labour - or production of physically tangible output - distinguishes those who 'work' (the people) from those who do not (the elite), physical toil becomes a source of righteousness.

'Sitting on the school bench' is, therefore, a bit suspect as life that is unproductive and too easy. Good farmers and artisans are not made on the school bench! Book learning can even warp and enfeeble youth. An example from Norwegian fiction is the case of the young man Eleseus in Hamsun's *Markens Grøde*. The Norwegian-American social scientist Torstein Veblen's wry concept of 'trained incapacity' is arguably in the same tradition. Schools can still be wanted and respected - not as means of social mobility - but only when they do not undermine the high culture of ordinary people and then as a supplement to valued skills and knowledge acquired in the home, community and workplace. You work your way through college and study engineering or theology - not philosophy or anthropology. Conversely, esoteric knowledge that lies outside the experience of common folk is not much respected. Intellectuals are therefore easily resented (Hofstadter, 1963). There is no place for modern, abstract art in this tradition! Nor is there much respect for the bureaucrat. Both professional and bureaucratic expertise are suspect, unless tangible, useful results are shown.

The traits of populism imply that government must be 'close to the people'. First, the units of locally elected government must be so small in order to coincide with a local 'community'. When countries are compared, the size of local government units is by no means a mere function of geography and population density. Contrast the larger size of local authorities in the Scottish highlands with the municipalities (*kommuner*) of Western and Northern Norway. Second, populist patterns of control can by-pass elected councils, by means of referenda (Swiss democracy), or direct election of officials (Mid-Western election of judges, sheriffs), thus making officials directly accountable to the populace. In a populist political culture, schools are the property of the community, not only in a legal sense, but also culturally. And teachers are the servants of the community, but whether they become subservient to community leaders or themselves such leaders will depend on a variety of conditions as evinced in the contrast between Norway and the American Mid-West (Lauglo, 1982).

When Lundgren (1989) refers to decentralisation as a 'sleeper' - as an ideology which in Norway was 'frozen' during the period of centralist welfare state construction, it is populist decentralisation that was put on ice - when the Labour Party was using the state apparatus - schools included - for the purpose of egalitarian modernisation. But whether what now may be 'thawing' is really what was put on ice is not so clear, as will be discussed in the concluding section of this chapter.

To establish and run primary schools was right from the beginning a local responsibility in Norway. The growth of locally elective government was occasioned by it. The agrarian movement that combined with urban radicals into the Left party (Venstre) was consistently hostile to the state bureaucracy, seeking to curb its authority and cut its pay. For the leaders of this movement - many of whom were school teachers, the local councils were the training ground for national politics. The cultural and linguistic gap between the urban elite and the rural population was in fact not especially great in 19th-century Norway, compared to other Western European countries. However, in Norway this gap became politically important through populist politics. The high culture of the rather modest Norwegian upper class became suspect, its language was not authentic Norwegian but bore the trace of Danish origins, the 'national' credentials of the upper class were also questioned by populists because the political spokesmen of the upper class were allied with the king against the advent of parliamentary rule, and the king who was until 1905 shared with Sweden became identified both with upper class rule and Swedish overlordship.

By the end of the 19th century, when the populist wave was culminating, primary schools were operated by the local councils - often in municipalities with less than 1000 inhabitants. The councils also hired the teachers, could lay down the syllabus within central guidelines (not directives). Further, each school had its own 'supervisory committee' mainly of parent representatives. At a time when pupils in other parts of

Europe were punished if they used their vernacular at school, the teachers in Norway were by law required to adapt their speech to that of the children's dialect. A language revival movement was gaining momentum in the countryside, seeking to replace the official Norwegian of the upper class with a New Norse based on rural dialects.

Primary school teachers played the role of agitators and local leaders in these populist movements, as the most educated persons from popular origins, identifying with those origins, and active at work to 'revive' popular culture. They could play an active local role in politics because they were accountable to their allies, and because in large parts of rural Norway the yeoman-farmers who were active in local politics did not rank so much above the poorly paid teacher in economic status - it was in fact not unusual for the teacher to be a farmer on the side (Lauglo, 1982).

The rural populist tradition is closely identified with Norwegian nationalism and its democratic character ('hytter og hus men ingen borge!': cottages and homesteads but no castles!). It has, therefore, lingered as invocable ideals in the political culture - though society has, of course, changed greatly from the late 1800s: production has become differentiated from the household, local communities have become physically and culturally blurred by transport, mobility and by mass media; and most people now live in towns. Various aspects of the populist tradition (culture, religion and rural interest politics) have continued as the respective emphases of the centrist parties that are most clearly the descendants of the old 'Left' coalition. However, populist ideas extend far beyond these parties. The rural, thinly settled periphery has an influence that long has been much greater than the share of the population living in these areas. There is a widely supported political commitment to maintain the economic viability of remote districts and communities. Populist 'decentralist' ideas seem to have gained influence in the Labour Party and socialist Leftist politics since the early 1970s because the 'urban, industrial modernising' elements (the Conservatives and the Labour Party establishment) were then defeated in the referendum on whether Norway should join the Common Market. But the Norwegian Labour Party was right from its inception not only an industrial workers' party - but was also a party with a base in fishermen and rural workers and small-holders.

In close accord with the populist tradition there are very small population units of local government, ranging down to municipalities with only some 5000 inhabitants. There was deeply felt resistance from parties of the populist centre, when the then more centralist Labour government agglomerated smaller units some 30 years ago. Small schools are strongly favoured in Norway. It takes few pupils to keep a school going - at great unit cost. Parliament has declared that in primary and junior secondary education, a school unit above 450 pupils is 'too large'. Each school has a collaboration committee to involve 'concerned groups' in school governance - local politicians, parents, the head teacher, teachers and other staff, old pupils. The mix of insiders and outsiders could be construed as a blend of socialist 'participatory democracy' and centrist 'populist democracy' in the Norwegian context. As a mechanism for extensive consultation but without much formal authority, it seems to assume harmony of interests among insiders and 'outsiders close to the school'. The decision to 'localise' the curriculum, in the sense of gearing the content of basic school more to the character of the local community, agrees closely with the populist ethos.

Populism views schooling with mixed feeling. Admittedly, there are now high participation rates in Norwegian secondary school up to age 18 and 19, but primary school has a very late (age 7) and gentle start. Characteristically, until the mid-1950s, rural children attended school only every other day. In keeping with populist (and with Lutheran) views, the educative importance of the home is affirmed in the Education Act. Populist culture values useful knowledge and is sceptical of esoteric knowledge. Now even more so than earlier, short cycle 'applied' higher education has more competitive entry than long-cycle and more purely academic courses. In post-16 education, it is more difficult to enter vocational training than further general education of an academic kind. Needless to say, classics barely survive - they were nearly banished from the secondary schools in the late 1800s.

Political control

Regardless of ideologies and their implications, the views that political groups have on the distribution of authority will reflect their interest in gaining and securing power. Such interests can favour centralisation of control - as well as decentralisation. Politicians will only reluctantly concede greater authority to units or levels of government that are the bastions of their opponents. Rather, they will seek to curtail the authority of such units. Also, those in power nationally will defend the authority of the state, whereas those in opposition will tend to discover the virtue of autonomy for local government if that is where they have their strongest base. Those who fail to gain any substantial position in the political system, will discover the importance of 'direct action' of an extra-parliamentary kind. In general, the views of any political grouping on the distribution of authority will in part be shaped by its own distribution of influence in the authority structure of government.

Weiler (1989) claims that decentralisation policies are in general 'conflict management' strategies. However, extensive devolution of authority to member states or 'regions' is no guarantee of a stable settlement - as exemplified at present in Yugoslavia. Further, insofar as conflict management is the aim, it would seem that the direction of authority redistribution will depend on the strength of the various political 'players' and on how far there is common ground or conflict between them. However, when policies are response to conflict, the parties concerned are likely to be clearly political and independently constituted: national government, regional or 'local state' government, local government - or organise pressure groups.

It is common to distinguish between 'deconcentration', 'delegation' and 'devolution' of authority. Deconcentration transfers authority to the geographically dispersed agents of the central government, strengthening regional and local staffs of the State civil service. This is a means to increase - not weaken - the role of the state in decision-making, though locally placed civil servants may be better informed than central bureaucrats and can, therefore, take more account 'local views'. 'Delegation' is an easily revocable transfer of authority, usually to appointees at lower levels in the same hierarchy. 'Devolution' is transfer of authority by law, away from the state and to some regional or local (or private) authority that is not directly accountable to the centre. Deconcentration and delegation (or the revocation of such decentralisation) can be responses to conflicts internal to the state bureaucracy. However, because neither delegation nor deconcentration involves any redistribution of authority between a bureaucracy and 'outside' independently constituted groups, it is devolution (or its abrogation) that tends to be involved when authority shifts in response to conflict between the state and political groups outside its civil service. Further, in the 'politics of control' between levels of independently constituted government, education is usually only a part of the contested ground; and within education the concern will often be with finance and use of resources, school structure, location of provisions and appointments/patronage. In countries with sharp cultural divisions, curriculum contents and the medium of instruction can also be included.

Governments can transfer some authority to groups that have previously not been politically mobilised, in the hope that allegiance will follow in the train of their inclusion in the authority structure. Thus, Disraeli sought to widen the base for Conservative government by extending the franchise. Decentralisation policies by the military regime some years ago in Bangladesh is said to have been an attempt to 'win the sympathy of the villagers' by involving them in government - bypassing opposition politics organised at the national level (Rondinelli and Cheema, 1983). In the United Kingdom, at present, the policy of the Thatcher government to weaken the authority of the Local Education Authorities and the teaching profession, and to increase the authority of the central government, of institutional managers and of direct 'users' of schools (parents, employers), shifts power away from the government's opponents - the Labour-controlled large urban LEAs. The government probably expects that locally influential parents will sympathise with its 'hard' educational views.

Governments bent on radical change frequently seek to alter the distribution of authority in their favour, in order to use the schools for their control purposes and quash opposition. Usually this means tighter central control - as in the case of Tanzania after independence, or in an extreme form in Stalin's Russia (Lauglo, 1988). Similarly, governments that dig in to defend status quo conditions will tighten central control over schools too. Witness schools for Blacks in South Africa that are much more tightly controlled than schools for Whites.

If nationally dominant elites have close affinity with those that dominate locally, control by local government will carry no risks for national policy-makers. In England, rural school boards in the late 19th century were dominated by a local oligarchy that usually was in close affinity to the national political elite. However, the autonomy of school boards was curtailed when some radical urban boards had carried out changes that the national government disapproved of - introducing Science schools (Perraton, 1983). However, later, when the Conservative government feared loss of national power to Labour, it abolished the previously imposed provisions for their purposes (White, 1975). In the United States, the consolidation of small urban school districts (dominated by bossism and ward politics) into large 'centralised' urban school districts in the late 19th century, is another shift in authority designed to weaken the influence of certain groups (Katz, 1975). Thus, in the distribution of authority in education - as in the redrawing of constituency boundaries - political expedience can be important. Such manoeuvres to gain advantage and minimise disadvantage will be common in political systems where the main contending groups deeply distrust each other, so the consensus established between them about the rules of the game is weak.

Devolving power to regional political units can also be a needed concession in order to preserve national unity in some countries. Faced with strong regional identities and secessionist sentiments, governments may turn repressive to 'keep the lid on' - or they make concessions to defuse secession. Spain under Franco pursued the former strategy, but under democratic government, the latter course is followed. Papua New Guinea is an example of a country in which a high degree of autonomy for each member state over education, was part of the political settlement necessary to keep the country together at Independence (Bray,1984).

Under circumstances of extreme resource scarcity, it can also happen that responsibility for operating and financing education is devolved upon regions or communities. In many developing countries, community finance of education is now increasingly looked to simply because other sources are drying up (Bray, 1985). Devolution of operating responsibility without corresponding financial support from the centre, can be a means by which a national government seeks to wash its hands of responsibility for intractable problems. It has been claimed that such considerations motivated decentralisation policies of the military junta in Chile. In this case, devolution is not a means of maximising control over education but rather of evading the responsibility for its deteriorating condition.

In Norway, the clearest example of politics of educational control is probably the drive of the agrarian liberals in the late 19th century to clip the authority of the national civil service over the local schools. In the 1950s, the politics of the written medium of instruction also involved tactical considerations about control. Advocates of a written mode that would more closely approximate the vernacular, have looked to national and local politicians and sought to avoid direct votes by the parents of pupils concerned, believing that parents taking part in such referenda would be unduly swayed by the prestige of urbane upper class speech.

Theoretical perspectives on the curriculum differ in their control implications. Knowledge-centred approaches that stress either the importance of disciplines or of 'basic skills' are compatible with national curricula that spell out the contents to be covered for a given stage of education, regardless of the personal circumstances of the pupils, of the local community context, and the shifting social and political concerns of the day. The old Rationalist view of knowledge as 'enlightenment' accords with central formulation of what is to be taught. Modern discipline-centred curriculum theory will also support the authority of didactic subject expertise - inside or outside the education bureaucracy. 'Basic skills' emphases can imply that outside 'users' should exert influence (e.g. employers). However, in either case, expertise above the school - often at national level - will define in some detail the contents and sequence of the syllabuses.

The extent of such elaboration will also reflect the professional competence of teachers. In general, the more professionally competent teachers are, the less their task will be set out for them by their bureaucratic superiors, and the less teachers will accept - let alone request - detailed direction (Beeby, 1966). Thus, in the case of the German gymnasium, a highly knowledge-centred curriculum content can coexist with considerable teacher autonomy - also over assessment, probably because of the traditionally high professional standing of the *Studienrat* - a condition resembling university teachers.

However, the 'soft' process-oriented strain of the Pragmatist tradition of Progressive Education seems more clearly to require delegation of curriculum decisions to the school and classroom. This tradition stresses the importance of learning as an active process that is related to individual and local contexts. The ideal is that of a teacher who is a manager of learning situations, a 'facilitator' who is ever ready to capitalise on naturally occurring important events or issues in the life of pupils, in the community or in society. Centrally prescribed curricula can indeed hold up such methods as approved practice and provide illustrative examples, but 'activity methods' seem to be intrinsically incompatible with advance specification of contents - and especially sequence. This is because of the relativistic nature of the 'problems' and 'active interests' that should by this view be the point of departure for teaching. Thus, this vision of pedagogy implies great professional autonomy for the teacher. To be viable as a strategy it also seems to require highly professionalised teachers.

The twin factors of professionalism among teachers and the view of knowledge, do not suffice to explain Norwegian conditions. As noted earlier, Norway stands out as a country in which primary school teachers had unusually high status during the period from the late decades in the 19th century to the early 1970s. Teaching attracted the best and the brightest from 'popular origins' especially in rural areas. It is probably also true to say that knowledge-centred curriculum theories have been distinctly weak in Norway. There is the old Grundtvigian reaction against classics and 'bookish knowledge', followed by great openness to the ideals of activity methods in the pre-war curriculum for primary schools. Nonetheless, the Norwegian decentralisation pattern has never been one of local professional autonomy. Schools have worked to a fairly detailed curriculum in terms of timetable and syllabuses, and with central approval of textbooks. When since the early 1970s these specifications have been replaced by looser guidelines from the centre, authority has at least formally been transferred to local government and through that to participative committees connected with each school - though teachers and principals will naturally exert great influence in these local committees (Baarstad *et al.*, 1977).

Local professional autonomy over the curriculum has probably in Norway been constrained by populist concepts of control and knowledge, as discussed earlier. Another reason may be that individualist 'activity methods' never really became part of mainstream practice of Norwegian teachers. Collective definition of what should be taught can be important for other reasons than a discipline-centred notion of knowledge, e.g. because it accords with both old and new justifications that argue that school knowledge should be is shared by all. In that sense there is continuity from the Pietist starting point of preparation for Confirmation, to modern egalitarian views that a curriculum should as far as possible be the same and shared by all pupils. Thus, not only emphasis on shared culture, but also the important egalitarian goals of Norwegian education have reinforced a common school and a common curriculum within that school, regardless of the teacher responsible and regardless of location. Therefore, when greater variation between schools is now allowed, it is mainly in the name of adaptation to the local community outside the school. The intention is not to let some schools race ahead of others by covering more knowledge in key academic subjects.

'Efficiency' will here be used as an umbrella rubric to also include control issues related to innovation, professionalism, management by objectives and styles of evaluation. It is often argued that some degree of central coordination is necessary for the efficient working of education, to ensure that there is a 'national system' in some minimal sense. It is claimed that some uniformity of school structure, teacher training, timetable and syllabuses in the schools, and mode of examination is necessary in order to ensure equivalence of credentials and mobility among institutions as well as among the different parts of a country. One notes that the European Community, which remains looser than a confederation, is actively seeking to establish such equivalence of credentials, in order to facilitate free movement of labour. Nonetheless, countries differ widely in prevailing views about the degree of central coordination that is required within the country on efficiency grounds. Notions of efficiency requirements are in fact heavily conditioned by established patterns of legitimacy: Who should have the right to decide? Federal states often lack even basic central direction to ensure equivalence of credentials. In Switzerland, Germany, and the USA, it is the member states that certify teachers, the nation state does not have the authority to require equivalence.

The 'efficient' distribution of authority will also depend on the scale of a system. China and Malta could not be administered in the same way. Large systems cannot be so directly controlled from the top as small systems, even when those in power nationally seek to concentrate authority in their hands. Some deconcentration will be required perforce. Central control in large systems will probably need to rely more on rules and regulations, than in small systems, because the officials at different levels in a large system are less likely to be personally known to each other. Conversely, a very small systems might make more use of delegation (easily revocable transfers of authority) to suit the personal ability of office holders, and the scope of responsibility of officials will tend to be wider (Bacchus and Brock, 1987).

The distribution of authority will be conditioned by the confidence that politicians and officials have in their subordinates. This confidence will influence readiness to delegate, deconcentrate or devolve authority. Jobs will be simplified and more directly supervised when they are filled with poorly motivated persons of low competence. Conversely, controls are relaxed and autonomy is conceded when people are thought competent and highly motivated. Thus, the reputation of teachers and educational administrators will influence the autonomy that is accorded them and the definition of their task. If they are ill-trained and poorly motivated - true in many countries, their superiors will seek to simplify and standardise the task of subordinates, using highly directive supervision.

This is the case in many developing countries. However, low confidence, among policy-makers, in the teaching profession is also a feature of many industrialised countries today - with risks of spiralling demoralisation among teachers who already feel underpaid and undervalued, if the teachers' autonomy is further restricted.

A key consideration concerning an 'efficient' distribution of authority must be the nature of the task. It is a much repeated argument in organisation theory, that when tasks are highly stable and capable of being broken down into constituent components, little autonomy is needed for their performance. Even complex tasks (e.g. assembling a car) can then be broken down into a series of complementary simplified jobs, which can be carried out according to set instructions. This is the familiar logic of bureaucratic organisation. The more the task of each job can be simplified, the less training is required. On the other hand, the more a task has complex contingencies, the less possible it is to break it down into simplified jobs. People in such complex 'non-routine' jobs will then, therefore, need more training to develop depth and breadth of skill, and they need more autonomy - elbow-room to respond to contingencies (See, e.g. Perrow, 1970). Applied to schools, the recognition of complexity, of the non-routine in the educational task, becomes crucial (McLean and Lauglo, 1985). Schools can standardise the task of teaching (as a fixed body of knowledge to be transmitted to all, regardless of contingencies), or they can define knowledge as more open and evolving, with a need for varied methods and dialogue, thus requiring greater pedagogic sophistication.

Task simplification combined with tight supervision may well be cheaper than professionalisation. However, some tasks are by nature complex and non-routine. Innovation is an example. System-wide innovations probably do require concentration of authority at the centre; the Scandinavian experience may well exemplify this argument (Lauglo, 1977). However, innovation initiated locally will require autonomy for local staffs, for change in the process of education can only be brought about by teachers and school administrators themselves. Innovation requires creativity, exploration of alternatives, responses to unforeseen contingencies, and strong dedication. It is the opposite of routine, and one cannot innovate by following a manual. A high degree of autonomy may well be a necessary condition for such activity. However, it is not a sufficient condition. Without sufficient competence and commitment, autonomy can merely entrench inertia - in schools as well as in university departments or business subsidiaries. 'Decentralisation' is, therefore, no panacea for making those who gain greater autonomy more innovative (Hurst, 1985). Ability and strong professional socialisation (both before and during work) is needed in order for autonomy to be an 'efficient' response to complex non-routine tasks.

The demands on teaching and running schools have similarly become complex and non-routine. There is the rapid change of knowledge, the widening of the task of education into 'social' and pastoral functions, and a changing student clientele whose attention and respect are seemingly more difficult to command than in the past. In these circumstances it is probably not 'efficient' to impose on the schools detailed rules and syllabuses. Rather, autonomy is needed but this requires increased emphasis on professionalisation - beyond the traditional concern with selection and initial training for teaching. In any profession, much important training occurs on the job. Thus, staff development and 'institutional development' efforts that take seriously the concerns which teachers and managers themselves have, are needed.

However, under today's conditions of tight public finance, politicians are unwilling to devote large resources to staff development or to intensive institutional development schemes. Professionalism does not come on the cheap, and it is in any event difficult to achieve and sustain in a large occupation that cannot be highly selective at entry. Declining pay-relativities for teachers further compound problems of low morale. Under such conditions, it is tempting for policy-makers to strengthen the role of the much smaller group of institutional managers, combined with tighter monitoring of teaching performance. However, school principals and local education administrators then become by training and task increasingly differentiated from ordinary teachers. This seems to be the trend in Norway too - though research on this question seems lacking.

Management by objectives is yet another 'efficiency' response to non-routine tasks for which detailed rules are not appropriate. One can speculate that the political importance of this management strategy - and of the associated use of performance indicators, is a function of perceived task complexity, confidence in the teaching profession and of the general preoccupation with getting more value for money.

Management by objectives requires detailed elaboration of institutional goals. It also seeks to bind the efforts of staff to the purposes of the organisation by involving them in setting their own targets. Staff at all levels can more easily be made responsible for failing to reach targets when they themselves have helped to set these targets. The performance of individuals and units is laid more bare to scrutiny by this approach, and pressure is built up to work hard and produce in order to meet the targets. In industry, public administration, and education alike, management by objectives is in many respects a revival of the 'scientific management' approach that once was acclaimed as a recipe for efficient management not only by some capitalist captains of industry but also by Lenin.

Applied to education, it would seem that management by objectives - if pushed with determination, will reinforce tangibly measurable outcomes - especially such 'hard Pragmatist' learning goals as basic communication skills and employable skills. It could easily weaken 'soft pragmatist' process-oriented pedagogy as well as knowledge-centred curriculum goals that stress holistic understanding. Therefore, many educators and academics resent performance objectives as an undue narrowing of educational goals. Though the intention is to specify goals more clearly so as to give more discretion to professionals in their choice of means, an elaboration of goals will constrain the means. 'Production targets' are in any case necessarily means to realise higher-order goals.

Like 'materials-methods systems' of the 1960s, management by objectives will be resented by many teachers as a denial of professionalism. Whether used as a tool by central authorities, local government, or institutional management - management by objectives and the associated monitoring techniques are a tightening up of direction from above - but it need not be central control. The process of setting objectives and targets can be institutionally based. If so, it shifts more authority to institutional management while increasing the controls of which the classroom teacher is subjected. Privatisation of education - in public institutions introduced in the form of higher fees ('user charges') - is likely to have a similar effect: to strengthen the power of institutional management.

Contrasting styles of educational evaluation differ in their control connotations. Goal-based evaluation and the wider 'systems-approach' in which output value is compared to input, provide useful information for assessing both effectiveness (goal realisation) and efficiency (optimum use of resources), taking the stated goals and their derivatives as starting points for measuring value. This style fits a managerial-technocratic perspective on education and can serve as a means of managerial control. By way of contrast, 'illuminative evaluation' is more concerned with the process of education, and with the perceptions, experiences and goals of those who are directly involved in that process. This approach can be part of action research (e.g. 'the teacher as researcher') relating to the efforts that the school 'insiders' make to improve educational practice. In practice it is often a style of evaluation that seeks to tell the teachers' story, or sometimes the students'. Illuminative evaluation can also be used to focus attention on hidden or 'unofficial' motives or consequences - thus exposing the weaknesses of official designs. In that sense, it is potentially more 'anti-establishment' than goal-based evaluations or 'systems approaches'.

Decentralisation and evaluation in the Norwegian setting

As noted at some length in this chapter, there is a strong Norwegian tradition of decentralisation in education and it is mainly a populist one. Its golden age was in the late 1800s. Unlike their American colleagues, Norwegian teachers were not reduced to humble servants of the community by populist politics. Rather, they became themselves the local agitators and exponents of rural populism. The status of Norwegian teachers rested more on their role in public life, outside the school, than on any reverence for their role within the school. As rural populism has subsided, so has probably the status of school teaching. But an enduring legacy of populism - probably given new lease of life by the success in 1972 of the Movement opposed to Norway's entry to the Common Market - is the cult of the local community in Norwegian education, and the enshrinement in law of the home, as a partner to the school.

Along with the 'soft' side of populism - community, emphasis on the vernacular, on parental involvement, there is also a 'hard side': of utilitarianism, 'value for money' and distrust of esoteric expertise. Perhaps it is this strain that now is tapped in support of shifts in authority: away from both the central government and away from the teacher, but in favour of institutional managers and local government. When teachers no longer stand out as tribunes of the people - surrounded by the aura of high-minded idealism, suspicions about excessively long holidays are more easily aroused.

In general, the main thrust in current decentralisation policies in Norwegian education seems to be concerned with efficiency: with improved quality and with better use of resources. This differs sharply from the 'participatory democracy' trend of the late 1960s. It also curtails, rather than strengthens, individual professional autonomy. One example is the attempt to steer university activity - including research - by means of 'management by objectives' techniques. Similarly, in the Basic School, shifting from management by rules to management by elaboration of curriculum objectives can be construed as an attempt to tighten up schools which are widely perceived as 'too slack'. The climate of opinion behind these changes is dissatisfaction with the quality of education in Norway, and concern about the cost of public sector services at a time when economic austerity policies are pursued.

It is possible that Norwegian education needs this reorientation, and that there is insufficient respect for achievement - quite apart from the value and usefulness of what is learned. It could also be that the work ethic is too slack in the labour force, especially given the high pay levels, and that schools should - as preparation for work - do more to instill a general achievement orientation - drive, initiative, hard work. However, there is a need to go beyond 'widely shared impressions' and to address these questions in systematic research.

It is indeed poor logic to blame the schools of today for the economic ills of present-day society, rather than blaming the schools of some 20-40 years ago which helped shape the generation that is now in its productive prime. But this recognition should not be used to 'explain away' the problems of the schools of today. The complaints about inferior quality are long-standing; the present worries about the country's economic performance just adds political weight to these concerns. There is not only a desire to restore the work morale of an earlier generation. It can also be argued that Norway needs to become a more efficient society than in the past, in order to remain internationally competitive.

Further, the efficiency argument is not only about improving the quality of the output, but it is also about making better use of available resources. This concern will be strong under conditions of tight public finance. However, there is probably an inevitable long-term trend, regardless of business cycle effects, that greater efficiency will be demanded of education. This is because of rising costs, not because of any necessarily declining or insufficient quality. Education is very large-scale and labour-intensive. Real unit cost per student year is bound to go up, rather than down, as real salaries increase in the long run. Political attention will increasingly focus on efficient use of the large volume of public resources in all such labour-intensive public services. Management by objectives has appeal as a device to get more 'time-on-task' from professionals in return for increased pay. A related attempt is to define the teachers work day or work year to formally also include a set number of hours/days - rather than only specifying the periods in class. Both in Britain and Norway, the employers' side has pressed for such change in pay negotiations with teachers.

Different evaluation approaches can have contrasting control connotations: as a managerial tools of monitoring, or to tell the subordinates' 'unofficial' story. The evaluation practices in the years to come will reflect the distribution of authority in Norwegian education, not only by what they reveal but also by the methods used. The challenge is to combine the two approaches - the 'hard' and the 'soft', results and process. In a parallel manner, the challenge in improving the schools is to combine strategies that work from the bottom up with those that work from the top down.

References

Ånensen, M. (1987), *Styrer eller styres skolestyret?* (Does the municipal school board govern or is it governed?), Tromsø: MA dissertation, Institute of Social Science, University of Tromsoe.

Bacchus, K. & Brock, C. (1987), *The Challenge of Scale: Educational Development in the Small States of the Commonwealth*, London: Commonwealth Secretariat.

Baron, G. (ed.) (1981), *The Politics of School Government*, Oxford: Pergamon Press.

Beeby, C. (1966), *The Quality of Education in Developing Countries*, Cambridge, Mass.: Harvard University Press.

Bray, M. (1984), *Educational Planning in a Decentralised System: the Papua New Guinean Experience*, Sydney: University of Papua New Guinea Press/Sydney University Press.

Bray, M. (ed.) (1987), *Community Support for Education in Less Developed Countries: Issues and Policy Implications*, Oxford: Pergamon Press.

Baarstad, B., Endrerud, T. & Grondahl, S.E. (1977), *Samarbeidsutvalg i ungdomsskolen*, (Collaboration committees in the junior secondary school), Oslo: Pedagogisk forskningsinstitutt.

Clifford-Vaughan, M. (1963), 'Enlightenment and education'. *British Journal of Sociology*, 14.

Dodd, W. (1968), 'Centralisation in education in mainland Tanzania', *Comparative Education Review*, 12, October.

Entwistle, H. (1979), *Antonio Gramsci: Conservative Education for Radical Politics*, London: Routledge.

Hofstadter, R. (1963), *Anti-intellectualism in American Life*, New York: Knopf.

Hurst, P. (1985), 'Decentralisation - Panacea or red herring?' In Lauglo, J. & McLean, M., (eds), *The Control of Education: International Perspectives on the Centralisation-decentralisation Debate*. London: Heinemann.

Katz, M. (1975), *Class, Bureaucracy, and the Schools*, New York: Knopf.

Kitching, G. (1982), *Development and Underdevelopment in Historical Perspective: Populism, Nationalism and Industrialization*, London: Methuen.

Lauglo, J. (1976), 'Upper-secondary teachers in Norway: Organizational participation and its correlates', *Comparative Education*, 12.

Lauglo, J. (1977), 'Educational change and aspects of bureaucratic organization - The Scandinavian school reforms'. In Glatter, Ron (ed.), *Control of the Curriculum: Issues and Trends in Britain and Europe*, University of London Institute of Education/ National Foundation for Educational Research.

Lauglo, J. (1981), 'Participatory committees and contrasting administrative styles in Scandinavian school governance'. In Baron, George (ed.), *The Politics of School Government*, Oxford: Pergamon, 1981.

Lauglo, J. (1982), 'Rural primary school teachers as potential community leaders? - Contrasting historical cases in western countries', *Comparative Education*, 18, 3.

Lauglo, J. (1988), 'Soviet education policy 1917-1935: From ideology to bureaucratic control', *Oxford Review of Education*, 14, no. 3.

Lundgren, U. (1989), 'Educational policy making, decentralisation and evaluation', paper presented at Conference organised by the Norwegian Council for Applied Social Research on Evaluation and Decentralisation, Asker, Norway, May.

Lyons, R., (1985), 'Decentralised educational planning: Is it a contradiction?' In Lauglo, J. & McLean, M. (eds), *The Control of Education: International Perspectives on the Centralisation-decentralisation Debate*, London: Heinemann Educational/Institute of Education University of London.

McGinn, N. & Street, S. (1986), *Educational Decentralisation: Weak State or Strong State?*

McLean, M. & Lauglo, J. (1985), 'Introduction: Rationales for decentralisation and a perspective from organisation theory'. In Lauglo, J. & McLean, M. (eds), *The Control of Education: International Perspectives on the Centralisation-decentralisation Debate*, London: Heinemann Educational/Institute of Education University of London.

Partington, G. (1988), *The Concept of Progress in Marxist Educational Theories*,

Perraton, H. (1983), 'Local control of education: Lessons from English history for ourselves and others', paper presented to a conference on 'Central versus Decentralised Control in Education', University of London Institute of Education, February.

Perrow, C. (1970), *Organizational Analysis*, London: Tavistock.

Rondinelli, D. A, & Cheema, G. S. (1983), 'Implementing decentralisation policies'. In Cheema, G. S. & Rondinelli, D. A. (eds), *Decentralisation and Development Policy Implementation in Developing Countries*, London: Sage.

Rondinelli, D. A., Nellis, J. R. & Johnson, R. W. (1984), *Decentralisation in Developing Countries: A Review of Recent Experience*, Washington: The World Bank.

Scotford-Archer, M. (1979), *Social Origins of Educational Systems*, London: Sage.

Smith, B. C. (1985), *Decentralisation*, London: Allen & Unwin.

Weiler, H. (1989), 'Decentralisation in educational governance: An exercise in contradiction', paper presented at Conference organised by the Norwegian Council for Applied Social Research on Evaluation and Decentralisation. Asker, Norway, May.

White, J. (1975), The End of the Compulsory Curriculum. In The Curriculum, The Doris Lee Lectures, University of London Institute of Education.

World Bank (1988), *Education in Sub-Saharan Africa: Policies for Adjustment, Revitalization and Expansion*, Washington DC: World Bank.

Young, M. F. D.(ed.) (1971), *Knowledge and Control*. London: Collier Macmillan.

Chapter 6

The tradeoff between evaluation and autonomy: who cheats whom?

Kjell Eide

The running of a modern state - and especially a 'welfare state' - has as one of its foundations an implicit understanding between political authorities and various professional groups. The members of the professions are assumed to have specialised qualifications essential for the rendering of high quality welfare services - in schools, hospitals, social services, etc. Political authorities and top administrators do not have the qualifications needed for judging the quality of the professional work performed, and it thus seems rational to leave a considerable amount of authority to the professions in the performance of their tasks.

Such a delegation of authority is, however, based on certain conditions: the profession (or public certifying agencies) must strictly regulate access to the profession, according to agreed criteria of professional competence. The profession must exercise various forms of peer evaluation, a form of mutual control of the professional performance of colleagues, based on generally accepted rules of conduct. Finally, the profession must be trusted to act on behalf of its clients, and represent their interest.

As recently as the early 1900s, the professionals were few, had a high status and a relatively high income. However, over the years the professionals have become numerous, their expertise is no longer unique and their status somewhat reduced, and other, less educated groups have been able to reduce the difference in the level of income. The latter has been achieved through organisation and effective trade union activities. It seems logical enough that professional groups have resorted to similar organisational practice, in order to maintain at least some of their distinction.

This, however, inevitably raises doubt about the extent to which professional groups are really making claims on behalf of their clients, or perhaps rather on behalf of their own interests as a group. The more professional groups resort to trade union practices, the more they are treated by political and administrative authorities as trade unions. One bargains with such groups, accepting fully that they have their own legitimate group interests, but their claim to represent primarily the interests of their clients is looked upon with more and more scepticism. In a sense, the implicit understanding underlying the granting of professional autonomy has been broken, and external authorities find it necessary to establish stricter controls to ensure that resources spent on professional activities really benefit the clients.

This is probably the main reason why external evaluation of professional services, including education at various levels, has come much more in focus in recent years.

The rewarding attacks upon the school

There is, of course, much more behind the declining confidence in professional performance among authorities and clients in recent years, than increasing trade unionism among the professions. Especially in education, the youth unrest of the late 1960s and the early 1970s came as a shock to most parts of the established, adult society. The youngsters seemed to attack and show no respect for nearly all the established institutions in the society. Somehow, educational institutions must have failed in the task of socialising the young.

On this background, attacking the school proved a very profitable political platform. It aroused anxieties among parents for their children's future, and even provided a legitimate outlet for the natural aggression of parents towards their children, which is normally repressed in modern families in the Western world. Such attacks upon the school, which became a standard part of the political rhetoric of conservative parties all over the West, quite irrespective of the nature of the school system, served to legitimate cuts in education budgets, probably mainly aiming at general reductions in public spending, and they also served to justify stricter external control over education. Education policy could no longer be based on widespread trust in the professional competence of educators, their performance should be controlled and judged according to criteria established outside the profession.

The validity of the criticism launched against educational institutions is clearly doubtful in many respects. A suspicious fact is that a practically identical criticism appeared in the course of a few years in a wide variety of countries with quite different school systems. Even more telling are perhaps the figures from Gallup polls on attitudes towards education, as illustrated by the latest annual survey by the Gallup Institute in the US. Only a tiny fraction of the respondents found the American school system good or reasonably good, whereas the vast majority expressed strong dissatisfaction. However, 40 per cent of the respondents found the local school system good, and 70 per cent of the parents found the schools attended by their children quite good. We are obviously faced with two quite different conceptions of reality, the local school as experienced by individuals, and an image of the national school system created by the media, representing mainly specific political interests. This appears to be one of the increasing number of cases in which individuals have given up applying their own experience as a test to images of reality created by the media.

In some Western countries, there are signs recently that the platform of aggressive school criticism is now seen as politically less rewarding. This does not necessarily mean that the interest in evaluation diminishes, or that the traditional trust in professional groups returns. However, it may mean an increased effort to avoid forms of evaluation that may lead to a complete strangulation of professional autonomy.

Local autonomy

In most Western countries, the 1970s witnessed an increased interest in local decision-making, and as pointed out by Professor Lundgren in Chapter 3, there are tendencies in many countries towards more decentralised decisions in the education sector. As indicated by Lundgren, there may be several reasons for this, and particularly greater faith in the rationality of decisions taken by people who know the local circumstances well (or perhaps disillusion with inflexible central decisions), and also an acceptance that local communities might have interests and values deviating somewhat from those of national policies. The complex of problems related to national objectives, local autonomy and trust occurs again, in a different setting.

As in the case of the work of professional groups or institutions, the approach to this question usually follow some form of 'management by objectives'. Central political or administrative authorities state the goals to be achieved, whereas local authorities or professionals have the freedom to pursue the practice that they find most suitable to achieve the objectives. In the case of decentralisation to local political authorities, an additional element comes in: local objectives may also be pursued, provided they do not run counter to an acceptable standard in terms of national objectives.

Nearly 30 years ago, in a book on planning and organisation, I identified some basic principles for a genuine development towards autonomy for so called 'semi-autonomous' groups in industry. They seem to apply to decentralisation even in a wider context:

> Decentralisation of decision-making to local units must not make the unit too weak in relation to external interests. A school may find itself rather helpless standing up on its own against pressures from local interests, market forces or national professional organisations, and may feel that decentralised decision-making reduced its autonomy.

> The right of the local unit to make its own decisions must be sheltered towards the right of central authorities to make decisions concerning national goals. Spillover effects from the national authority may easily reduce the local autonomy to a mere formality, especially if its keenness on pursuing national objectives is subject to positive or negative sanctions from 'above'. The local autonomy must operate within well defined and well defended areas.
>
> Ideally, the local unit should have a high degree of autonomy in relation to other units at the same level. If the degree of autonomy is low in this respect, it should at least have a reasonable amount of bargaining power. An example would be the position of a local school in relation to a predominant employer of its graduates, or to strong educational institutions at the next higher level in the educational system.
>
> The purpose of local autonomy is that local clients should be better served. There is a need for guarantees that the interests of local clients are properly taken into consideration, for instance by active participation in decision-making by the clients themselves or their representatives (parents, local authorities).
>
> The activities of the local unit must be of sufficient interest to engage the participants, and the interplay of different interests should be expected to deviate somewhat from the corresponding interplay at the central level.

It seems to me that most of the efforts on decentralisation within education in Western countries break one or more of the rules set out above. There are certainly reasons to question the assumption that decentralisation efforts necessarily lead to a genuine increase in local autonomy. Furthermore, it is quite uncertain who at the local level obtains more autonomy - the headmaster, the teacher, the local school authorities, the parents or the real clients - the pupils?

The new management principles

The logic underlying the theory of management by objectives also seems rather shaky. The national curriculum plans for the Norwegian school system, for instance, abound with goal formulations. What these have in common is that they are quite impossible to put into practice, in the sense that they give very little direction for action. For goals to be operational, they need to be based on some assumptions about inputs into the process, and the way the process is performed. The final outcome of schooling, for instance, as measured by examination marks, tell us next to nothing about the performance of the school. The school's real performance is what the economists would call 'the value added' to the various inputs. We have, however, no valid production theory for education, explaining more than a fraction of the differences in individual pupil performance in terms of educational inputs. In other words, we have no basis from which 'value added' can be deduced. This is even more obvious if we take into account the many objectives of the school not measured by examination marks, and of the fact that what a pupil experiences from spending most his or her childhood and youth in school is probably far more important than the examination results.

The fact is, in education as well as in many other sectors of society, that the level of goal achievement cannot be meaningfully judged unless the evaluator also judges what has gone into the process, and the form of the process itself. This again means that, by necessity, the evaluator must form opinions on a wide range of issues that presumably should be within the discretion of local decision-making. It is, therefore, no surprise that local units often find that extensive external evaluation is a high price to pay for what may amount to a very limited range of decentralised decision-making power.

On the other hand, if central authorities accept that their ability to judge in any detail the appropriateness of local practices is lacking, and stick to more general, fairly inoperational goal formulations, they may find that their authority in educational policy matters is mainly of a symbolic nature. The school system runs its own course, whereas central decisions remain at the level of rhetoric. There are Western countries where this description comes close to reality.

Finally, and perhaps more typically, we may find central authorities clinging to a few quantitative indicators of the performance of the educational system as the basis for central policy measures. This could happen even when the indicators only vaguely reflect even the national goals of the educational system. If the central authorities still have access to strong policy instruments, local units may be forced to pursue such simplistic and partly irrelevant goals. In such a game, all parties will lose, and especially those whom the school is supposed to serve, the pupils and students.

Governance in the Norwegian school system

We turn now to the Norwegian school system, and the question of whether a meaningful and useful system of evaluation can be established, without the many harmful side-effects indicated above.

In doing so, we must take into account the peculiarities of the Norwegian educational system. Essential in this context is the decision some years ago to rearrange the financial relationship between central government on the one hand, and the communes and the counties, running compulsory schools and upper secondary schools respectively, on the other. The aim of this reform was the decentralisation of decision-making, but the approach was strange, in that neither the Royal Commission working on those matters, nor the Government or Parliament, faced the essential question: what responsibilities for educational policy-making should remain at the central level? instead, the decision was made to put a ban on the use by central authorities of financial instruments in its relations to local authorities.

The trouble in this case is, of course, that no responsible Norwegian politician, nor the public opinion, will defend the idea that the Government should have no responsibility for education. On the other hand, as no one has defined the limits to that responsibility, the Government is quite naturally blamed for all that is felt to be wrong with education. The change from previously is primarily that the central government now has a much more restricted set of policy instruments to implement any policy decided upon by Parliament in this field.

There are certainly legal regulations for the schools, and a reasonably well functioning administrative system of controlling that legal regulations are being followed. There are also detailed national curriculum guidelines, but they are mainly of an indicative nature, and even if they should be seen as prescriptive, there are hardly any means of controlling their implementation.

Traditional educational statistics are fairly well developed compared to other countries, although most statistics on the use of resources got lost when central government transfers to local authorities lost their relationship to actual local resource use. What else is needed as a basis for central government policy making in the field of education?

Some basic assumptions

The following discussion is based on the series of assumptions, described below.

In broad terms, the present system of legal regulations will be maintained, as well as the administrative machinery for ensuring that legal regulations are followed by local authorities and individual institutions. This applies, for instance, to such matters as teacher salaries and criteria for teacher qualifications, building space per pupil and other health-related regulations, class size, prescribed numbers of lessons in various subjects, etc.

Such legal control cannot be replaced by any set of statistics or other general indicators, it requires detailed local knowledge and must be performed by local controlling bodies (municipal school authorities, 'school directors' at the county level, county school authorities, etc.), as it is done today. I will not deny that this machinery needs reforming, but it is not a matter of new forms of evaluation.

Furthermore, it is assumed that central government has at its disposal roughly the same types of policy instruments as it has today. This means, for instance, that on issues where central government has no instruments for implementation, decisions will not be taken at the central level, and there is consequently no need for information at that level.

This simply means that I assume that the stated policy intentions of decentralised decision-making are to be taken seriously. This implies both that on a number of issues, local competence and insight is accepted as the best basis for decisions, and that to some extent, local authorities are free to pursue locally defined objectives.

Finally, I leave out the whole area of educational research. It is clearly a responsibility for central government to ensure that resources are available for extensive research efforts in the education field, in order to increase the understanding of the functioning of the school system. Extensive research activities, far beyond those found in Norway today, are clearly an essential part of any central policy for evaluation of the educational system. In this context, however, I refrain from trying to outline what such an extended research activity should look like, concentrating instead on the need for regular collection of data and information as a basis for central policy decisions. Assessing the need for information for local decisions should be left to the discretion of local authorities.

Possible national responsibilities

As mentioned before, there exist no formal decision or consensus-based agreement on the extent of, or the limits to, central government responsibilities in the field of education. As a substitute, I use some formulations in the most recent White Paper by the Ministry of Education on the educational policy of the present government.[1] According to the White Paper, the education system shall provide knowledge, as well as contribute to the personal development to those involved, and transfer to them values, norms and attitudes inherent in our culture. In addition, it shall

- provide the basis for effective work performance, and thereby contribute to employment and economic growth
- enhance cultural development
- strengthen awareness of environmental issues and the need for self-sustaining development
- offer equal educational opportunities for all
- promote equality between the sexes
- strengthen our democratic traditions
- contribute to the maintenance of the current geographical distribution of the population

- strengthen our capability of operating in an increasingly international society, and contribute to peaceful co-existence and international solidarity
- improve the utilisation of resources within the educational sector

Although such objectives are obviously meant to be valid for all levels within the educational system, one may perhaps assume that they also define concerns for which central government has some responsibility. If so, what would this imply in terms of information for central decisions?

Implications for evaluation

To take the last objective first, it is the pet objective of any Ministry of Finance. It may seem redundant, as commitment to the achievement of substantive objectives logically implies the effective use of available resources. But the formulation may serve as a general key, opening up any issue for central intervention, and it is frequently used that way. A friendly interpretation, however, may be that it could imply acceptance of the fact that in many cases effective use of resources is best secured when decisions are taken on the basis of detailed local knowledge.

For most of the other objectives, the central instruments of policy are obviously curriculum plans, regular updating of curricula, effective and recurrent teacher training, and improvement and updating of textbooks and other learning materials. Furthermore, the central government must ensure that appropriate professional expertise is involved in the development of curricula, for instance, in the various fields of vocational training. Extensive research is clearly needed in this context, but beyond legal control of curricular prescriptions, there is hardly much need for additional regular data collection. An exception may be statistics on the actual use of textbooks and other learning materials.

Traditional flow statistics on pupils, teachers and resource-use will supply most of the information needed. Probably, such statistics should be extended to include more detailed information on the behaviour of both sexes in various educational contexts. More data on the actual functioning of the current machinery for 'School democracy' and participation might also be useful.

The existing registration of local school research and developmental work, with open access to the data base, is a valuable contribution. It might be extended in order to provide more information on attempts by individual schools or local authorities to pursue locally defined objectives.

The educational performance of individual students or individual schools is no concern for central government. Under the present limitations on policy instruments used by central government, this also implies to the average performance within school districts. The information provided by traditional statistics on the flow of students through the various parts of the educational system should offer sufficient statistical information on geographical differences for possible government actions, although additional qualitative information through the administrative system is obviously needed.

Exams at the end of compulsory education and of upper secondary education provide information about the general level of performance by the pupils, although it does not in itself tell much about the performance of individual schools. Such information requires much more detailed qualitative knowledge in order to provide a basis for political actions, and such actions belong to the local level.

Consequently, I see no need for additional central information through specific achievement tests or other performance indicators. Assessing the state of teaching and learning in various fields would in any case require much more intensive qualitative studies. If such information is wanted, a more systematic use of sensor reports might be a useful source.

The idea that achievement tests in various fields could show the development of the average achievement level over longer time periods, is based on the assumption that curricula are static. If such comparisons were really meaningful, it just means that curriculum revisions have been lacking for a long time, and that a fundamental curriculum reform is needed.

An even more unsound idea is to use achievement tests to compare with the performance of students in other countries. There exist no supernational set of goals for education to be reflected in such tests, and the efforts that have been made in this direction are based solely on the ideas of self-appointed researchers about what education should be like. Such comparisons thus lack both political legitimacy and scientific validity. This is why responsible international organisations, such as UNESCO and the OECD, have refused to be involved in such exercises.

My conclusion is thus that the need for evaluation as a basis for policy decisions at the central political level in Norway can be satisfied with a relatively limited expansion of the present system of regular data collection. (However, a much more extensive research effort is needed, including more effective information on international research in this field.)

The system of traditional statistics will need some expansion, but probably the greatest problem in this context is the time-lag, which makes collection of data through administrative channels on short notice a necessary duplication. The administrative system within the school sector could be more effectively tapped for information that could relatively easily be collected locally if the necessary instructions are given.

The improvements of the existing information system will require some resources, although in view of their usefulness, they will certainly be more than paid for in terms of more efficient decisions. A main problem, however, is that much of the statistical data collection is undertaken by an agency outside the control of educational authorities, and is governed by priorities not easily influenced by such authorities. From experience it seems that the most effective way of influencing such priorities is for the sectorial authorities to develop their own statistical services. The threat of having their monopoly on official statistics broken has sometimes proved to have an effect upon the priorities of central statistical authorities.

The greatest current problem, however, is probably not shortage of information but the lacking capacity at the central level for processing and analysing available information, and for the consequent development of policy. There is a real risk that a simplistic system of indicators could serve as an excuse for not developing such a capacity.

More general information needs

Up till now, I have discussed the need for evaluation and information underlying central government decisions. It may be said, however, that the central government also has a responsibility for providing information for other levels of decision-making and for the public in general. Could this change the conclusions drawn above?

The present system of educational statistics does, to a great extent, serve such a purpose. The centralised data base on developmental work in individual schools and local areas clearly has a similar function. Research work, also research initiated by central authorities, functions in the same way.

Going much further than this, however, raises the question of safeguarding of the local political and professional insight is replaced by a limited set of crude national indicators, it may easily result in a serious decline in the quality of local decisions, as has been shown in some cases. The publication of national norms may easily threaten the reality of the assumed local and professional autonomy.

We have, for instance, had the practice of offering standardised tests to teachers who want to compare their judgement of their pupils' performance with some national average. Probably, this can do little harm when it is used by individual teachers as a check upon their own initiative. The compulsory use of such tests, and the availability of the results to school leadership and possibly to the whole community, implies, however, a strong intervention in the professional autonomy of the teacher and the school. Furthermore, as discussed earlier in this chapter, such results are regularly misinterpreted to reflect the performance of the teacher or the school.

A well-known effect of the use of standardised tests is the cumulative development of quality differences between schools, in terms of both the pupils and the teachers recruited. As long as our official policy is to provide education of equal quality to all, such a development would be disastrous, and it should certainly not be the responsibility of central government to contribute to it.

Finally, I should recall the underlying assumption for this discussion, that the current system of governance of the Norwegian educational system remains largely as it is. It could well be argued that rational decisions about changes in the system of governance require information beyond what has been sketched above. Again, I have difficulties in seeing that any simple indicator system could contribute significantly to such decisions, although well directed research programmes certainly could.

The most important contribution to more effective governance of the Norwegian educational system would, however, be a politically accepted delineation of the responsibilities of central government, and a corresponding, clear definition of the range of discretion for local authorities and professionals within the system. This would permit a rational discussion of effective policy instruments needed at the different levels, including the need for evaluation procedures and data collection. Without such clarification, a meaningful discussion of evaluation systems is hardly possible.

Part II

EVALUATION AND KNOWLEDGE PRODUCTION

Chapter 7

Some problems and problematics in the production of evaluation

Thomas S. Popkewitz

The Norwegian approach to school reform evaluation seeks to understand the diverse issues and complexities that underlie the processes of reform, and how the tasks of evaluation can contribute to a more informed policy-making. This focus is important to all who promote intellectual integrity and social equality in schooling. It has particular appeal to me because the Anglo-American context, in which evaluation tends to be instrumental, functions in a way that has not always been educationally progressive.

As the distinctions produced by evaluation schemes are both dispositional and cognitive, a major task of evaluation is to foster public consciousness about those issues around which policy will be constructed. In this chapter, I consider four themes that relate to the undertaking of evaluation. The first two themes are a cautionary tale about evaluation - its production in social fields and issues of power. The second set of themes concerns a problematic in the organisation of an evaluation.

The first two themes focus upon prior assumptions in evaluation. These themes are:

1. Evaluation is a state strategy that occurs as a part of the production of ideas in a social field. That production includes power relations. To export evaluation strategies to another social field (in this case, Norway) requires understanding the processes of production in the new social field.

2. Words that have currency in evaluation (e.g. measurement, assessment and professionalisation) also have social epistemologies. To consider the assumptions, implications and possible consequences of the strategies chosen, we must take these social meanings into account.

The second set of themes pursue a problematic in the construction of an evaluation. They are:

3. Evaluation has a policy 'clarification' purpose. It does not tell us what policy is most efficient or useful, but it can help to illuminate the tensions, contradictions and ambiguities that underlie the production of educational reform and its realisation in the current situation. Although this may seem obvious, reform programmes respond to perceived issues and problems that, at face value, are not clearly defined and do not have linear outcomes. Reforms are responses to structural relations that are in constant flux. Of the deepest value to the public debates around which schooling in a democracy is positioned (and of importance not only to policy makers) is an understanding of the strains and tensions found in the relations in school arenas.

4. In addition to giving a sharper delineation to the tensions of schooling in a changing society, evaluation should consider the relation of pedagogical practices to enlightenment issues embedded within the purposes of schooling. Social and political transformations contain certain general educative commitments of schooling that are beyond traditional notions of learning. As priority is given to labour markets, school efficiency and socialisation, these commitments are often lost.

Social production and social reception of ideas

At least two related issues are central in evaluation. One is the relation of evaluation to state planning; this is important even when efforts to include more social actors exist, such as in the current Norwegian decentralisation policy. Second, the epistemology of recent efforts to promote evaluations through international settings contains particular sets of ideas that are part of state formations. As a result, the 'borrowing' of evaluation strategies and procedures in new national sites maintain social values that should be scrutinised.

State policy policing and evaluation

Evaluation is a part of state regulation, monitoring and steering. In this sense, policy and policing are epistemologically related; policing, in the framework of the state, enables individuals to be useful to society (Foucault, 1988, p. 154). Older forms of evaluation involved political arithmetic or statistics, in which the state collected demographic and other data to steer reform policies during the formation of the modern state. More recently, evaluation is intended to provide public accountability for different and sometimes contradictory school reform strategies (such as to increase international competitiveness, to provide a humanism, to produce a nationalistic citizenry, or to monitor the impact of particular policies related to equity).

On the surface, the current situation in Norway has a particular historical character. Evaluation is considered necessary for the decentralisation of decision-making. However, to understand this situation, we need to think relationally about the state, local community and schooling. The commitment to local governance and school improvement occurs as part of state formations in which accountability and steering are of great importance.[1] Lundgren argues in his introduction that the problem of evaluation is not to disregard the societal purposes that are part of the normative construction of the state but to understand how these purposes are reconstituted through new, decentralised steering and mediating institutions. Thus, evaluation has a policing quality in the modern state, whether we see it as part of the noble intent and desire of those who seek to improve school or as part of the darker side of social regulation.

My reason for starting with this assertion is neither to demean the effort of state actions nor to pose an anarchist view of the social processes of schooling. Rather, my intention is to remind the reader that evaluation is not merely a strategy that places values upon school activities or a process that describes what occurs in schools. The problem of evaluation must be positioned within educational fields that include power relations, which, at root, contribute to the processes of social production, reproduction and the creation of human capabilities.[2]

To consider evaluation as an element of state practice, however, is not sufficient. Evaluation has occurred within certain sets of structured relations as in Western state planning, particularly during the expansion of state involvement in schooling in post-Second World War United States. This involvement contains a social epistemology which has a pragmatic, instrumental view of change, seeing progress as linear and evolutionary.[3] Thus, as US strategies for evaluation become a part of an international discourse about planning and school improvement, more often than not it is a particular discourse pattern drawn into a global pattern of clashing discourses through international agencies, such as OECD and the World Bank. This last observation is part of the irony of social history. The current Norwegian effort to develop an evaluation emerged from an OECD review; it involves, however, scepticism concerning the major framing devices that give organisation to national evaluations.

The social production of ideas and social fields

The problem of evaluation has the state as a central actor within particular social fields and power relations. The questions, conceptual schemes and 'tools' are often 'exported' without an awareness of the assumptions, debates and implications of what is borrowed. Here, I want to challenge the conventional logic about knowledge as the 'diffusion' of ideas from one national setting to another. The image is of rarefied ideas brought into another context and diffused, as a dye added to water. In place of a concept of diffusion, I want to consider evaluation as a problem of social production that includes social relations and power dimensions. The social/cultural imperatives embedded in any evaluation contain tensions. An attempt to 'adopt' or 'adapt' procedures, such as testing or notions of school based management approaches, demands consideration of the power relations and debates in the field where the procedures were produced.

The problem, then, is not that we cannot learn from others' experiences but that 'learning' itself entails elements of social fields and power relations. Let me provide some examples from the current discourse about school reform in the United States, not only because I am familiar with its history but also because its approaches have become an important commodity in the international fields of evaluation. Some general public claims about the current US reform movement, focusing upon its rhetoric form as a discourse strategy that can produce commitment or at least acquiescence to specific practices, will be discussed first. Then some assumptions and presuppositions of the practices will be explored. The discourse practices link, in my view, historically formed priorities and assumptions with the concrete actions and patterns of evaluation.

The public discussions in the United States give attention to the changing international character of economic relations, the redesigning of national priorities in schooling and the need to maintain greater cultural strength through the socialisation processes of schooling. This new nationalism stresses the country's international competitiveness while focusing upon local flexibility and semi-autonomy - with national standards by which to judge attainment. In contrast to the last major school reform effort in the United States, which made curriculum issues focal, the current reforms give attention to teacher quality, standards of work and professional education. Market metaphors are combined with those of outputs (accountability) in the current reforms, replacing attention from outcomes and giving an illusion of progress.

The impulse for reform is so powerful in the educational field that it is practically impossible to distinguish research from evaluation. The name of the current Anglo-American 'game' seems to be what can lead to improved school practice.

Teachers' work is a centerpiece in the evaluation processes and reform programmes. The discussions relates the quality of teaching to the limitations of the bureaucratic organisation of schooling. There is continual reference to the amount of time teachers spend doing administrative work and routine activities, such as collecting and grading papers or responding to central office requests. The language of reform seeks to produce a more professional teacher corps that has increased status, responsibility and financial reward.

The reform proposals about teachers' work are legitimated through a number of practices, including longitudinal studies of teachers. A number of indicators thought to influence teacher quality are identified; these include teacher efficacy, demographic information, career plans and the age characteristics of teachers.

More recently, the demographic data has been enhanced by categories designed to evaluate and alter the working conditions of teachers. Emphasis has been given to the cultural circumstances in which teachers work, focusing upon degree of collegiality (such as how often they communicate with each other), shared goals towards academic performance, participation in school decision-making, assistance in the induction of new teachers into the profession, and varied financial reward (such as merit pay). There are efforts to produce models of pedagogical reasoning that will introduce greater efficiency and effectiveness into teachers' tasks and conceptions of learning.

We can interpret the evaluations and reforms in two ways. First, there is a tendency to consider the behavioural conditions of reform: are teachers making decisions about curriculum, are parents participating in school forums, have performance indicators changed? Evaluations have also focused upon the conditions of teachers' work; do they, for example, have more time to share ideas and to attend professional conferences? Notions of standards, collegiality, professionalisation and community appear as ways to describe the reform and to evaluate the conditions of teachers work. In what seems to be a contradiction to collegiality, there is also a competitive emphasis that incorporates statistical data about children's achievement as a performance criterion of teachers within and across schools.[4]

If we use a second approach to evaluation, considering it part of a mental structure by which problems are defined and dispositions produced for action, we can enter the discussion at a different layer of analysis. Evaluative strategies 'carry' cultural and social interests not evident in their formal rationales and publicly defined purposes. The concern for achievement, participation, community, collegiality and professionalisation contain particular assumptions that may, in fact, reintroduce bureaucratic practices to schooling.

Drawing upon a positivist tradition that dominates US evaluation, teaching is thought of as a hierarchy of tasks and skills that can be ordered in a manner that defines what is most efficient. This is responsible for the evils of bureaucratic patterns found in schooling. But these categories do not have fixed and unyielding definitions. In fact, the words have taken on meanings that tie the regulatory values found in United States schools to the concept of bureaucracy that the new reforms were instituted to change. Teaching models subdivide the 'thought processes' of teaching into specific and discrete elements of reflection. Participation and community are formulated in relation to a pluralistic interest group theory that focuses upon procedural elements (for example, do teachers make curriculum decisions?) or the involvement of publicly defined role groups. Here, the essential ingredient of involvement is the representation of social groups in the production of a consensus about values and procedures. The notion of interest participation emerges from a liberal (Lockean) theory concerning the origins of society in the social contract and practices of *laissez-faire* in which standards of justice are presumed to flow from the pursuit self-interest (Billig, 1982).

When these views of teaching and participation are placed in the current context of evaluation, their assumptions about and categorisations of social phenomena contain a classical Weberian formulation of bureaucracy. Social reality becomes one-dimensional; its products are seen in relation to utilitarian values. Community consensus and participation are based upon administrative criteria; the conflict and debate about purposes are structured out of consideration. Teaching is orderly; elements can be placed into proper and, thereby, manageable places. Each component has a self-contained unit with a specific relationship to other elements. Action is seen in relation to an abstract frame of reference that is divorced from the specified, complex tasks of teaching. There is no sense of the history and the power relations involved in the formation of schooling.

The sense of community and participation and the indicators of teaching success contain particular notions of change and progress that are obscured in the rhetoric about schools. Change is seen in relation to existing patterns; each component is viewed as a unique entity. Change is evolutionary and cumulative; its stages are irreversible.

The discourse is based upon a form of positivism that emerged from the interaction of religious movements of US eastern Protestant dominations with social amelioration in urban areas, a political reconstitution of the state in the progressive era (1880-1920), and economic changes to a corporate economy. The modern social research organisation turned its attention to the problems of policy-makers. Knowledge was seen as directly useful; science built upon the accumulation of discrete and sequential information. A particular 'methodological individualism' was maintained that linked social contract ideologies to the organisation of social science and practices of reform.

This brings us to two issues that can be summarised and evaluation strategies. It is clear that the categories of research and evaluation do interrelate to provide boundaries that give structure to certain possibilities and legitimate others through the discourse that is constructed about school change. In addition, the discussion of teacher improvement in the United States carries certain historical assumptions about social relations and progress. To transfer these strategies into another national and cultural context requires that they be scrutinised in relation to patterns and relations of power.

The problematic quality of words

Part of developing an evaluation scheme is to understand the problematic quality of words often identified with school improvement. We cannot take the meanings of words for granted but need to develop a social epistemology of the categories and organising concepts that direct research. Let me take as examples the emphasis given to professions and to school improvement as a goal of policy in the current educational reforms. These words appear in various ways in the reforms of the United States, Iceland, Australia, Sweden, Spain and other nations. The words, however, do not have an absolute character that refers to basic ideas or conditions of schooling. Words do not represent reality, they are part of its creation, sustenance and renewal. Words refer to concepts that change in relation to their position with other words and in relation to the social conditions in which they are used.

Let me explore this by focusing upon the words 'professions' and 'professionalism'. I recently participated in a three-year international symposium on professions. It became apparent that there could be no understanding of profession in any universal manner. There are important differences between the Anglo-American and continental traditions of professions. In part, these differences have to do with the different forms of state developments in relation to certain middle class and elite occupations. In many European countries, there was no word similar to that of the Anglo-Saxon word 'profession'. In recent years, however, the word 'profession' has been brought into the language of many continental countries to describe the social formations of work within the middle class and increase importance of expertise in the process of production/reproduction.

To incorporate the Anglo-American conception of profession imposes an implicit interpretive 'lens' about knowledge, occupations and state. Much of the discussion about Anglo-American professions concerns ideal types of disinterested occupations that are separate from the state. Autonomy, technical knowledge, occupational control of entry, remuneration and high ethics dominate this recounting. The ideal types, however, have little basis in fact; they ignore the political struggles, debates and compromises involved in the formation of the professions. Nor do these types account for the ways in which modern professions of these ideal types is as legitimating strategies for maintaining cultural and social authority, not for analytical purposes.

The 'ideal type' of profession has assumed importance in the US as an issue of school improvement. As an ideological stance, it seems difficult to argue against; teachers should participate in their work with autonomy, integrity and responsibility. At this level, the slogan is important to a reconstruction of schooling. However, to talk about professionalism, integrity and responsibility without focusing upon the content of the participation and the structural relations that shape it is to lose sight of the historicity of our practices.

'Professionalism' has been an aspect of reform in US education since the early 19th century; it referred to two different layers in the formation of the occupation. Professionalism was a slogan for those 'at the top,' including administrators and university professors. This occurred with the specialisation in university training and the development of new disciplines of educational sciences (as part of the planning and evaluation of schooling). This strata of the occupation tended to be male-dominated and better paid than teachers (typically women); administrators and professors enjoyed degrees of responsibility in the conceptualisation and organisation of their work conditions. The organisation of higher education and research in education provided routes for the occupational mobility for men. Further, much of the research and evaluation schemes for schooling relegated teachers to an ancillary status and focused upon assessment of large groups of students and indicators of qualities of the entire school system. The administration also contained elements of social regulation for those at the bottom of the occupational ladder - usually in the name of school improvement or effectiveness.

At the bottom were teachers. Many of the reforms of the late 19th century made teaching more bureaucratic in the name of professionalisation. Standardised hiring practices, uniform curriculum policies and teacher evaluation practices eroded spheres of teacher autonomy and responsibility through an increased rationalisation of school organisation and didactics. At no time in the history of modern mass schooling have the working conditions of teachers in the US provided the opportunity to reflect about their situation in a sustained manner. Teacher education has been pragmatic, and fragmented; it devalues an intellectual focus.

These trends continue in current reform efforts, linking professionalism to school improvement. A recent study of three school districts (Popkewitz and Lind, 1989) involved in an effort to increase teachers' professionalism indicates this very clearly. The reform strategies increased the teachers' work load and the level of monitoring of teacher practices. Evaluation was to provide 'evidence' of teacher accountability and more rational approaches toward school improvement. It was the knowledge of evaluation and specific practices and actions. Teacher evaluations valued instrumental and procedural concerns and devalued the craft and emphatic elements of teaching - the elements that have gender implications.

Terms like school assessment, school improvement, professionalisation, local control, decentralisation, and teacher empowerment abound in the US discussions of reform. They are also found in the discourse about school reform in which the English language has played a role in the articulation of social and research agendas. These words need to be made problematic; writers must consider the historical conditions and power relations that these words predispose and antedate. If we focus more upon terms like 'professionalisation' or 'school based evaluation' than the content and conditions of teachers' work or more general purpose of schooling, we will lose sight of the historical conditions in which teaching emerges. This includes the gendered qualities of teaching. Also, it entails a consideration of the bureaucratic conditions and the differentiations in schooling that are part of the patterns of production and reproduction in schooling. The reception of words of reform and evaluation in other contexts, such as Norway, requires a clarification of the country's relations and social fields. It is the only way to construct ideologies and practices that appropriately express the purposes and goals of the education system. While professionalism and school-based improvement are slogans that appeal to many of our cherished beliefs and noblest hopes about schooling, the words have no intrinsic meaning. They exist in relation to other words in social patterns and institutional settings.

Tensions in the relation of state and schooling: a problematic for evaluation

The two previous themes focused upon the historical limitations and contradictions of evaluation; I would now like to focus upon a different element in the problematic raised in Ulf Lundgren's paper. I will argue that the promise of evaluation is not in foretelling what is to be done, but in understanding the tensions, dilemmas and ambiguities that underlie the current transformations. Reform is not an object that can be installed or that has essential properties to be discovered. The processes of reform are dynamic, not static or linear; therefore, evaluation requires a scrutiny of the relations that occur in its setting. Further, it will be argued that evaluation is inevitably about the past rather than the present or future. Its contribution to policy-making is through an illumination of the dilemmas, tensions, and contradictions of how things have worked.

In one way, the focus of evaluation upon the tensions that underlie the current reformulation of state regulation of Norwegian schools seems quite apparent. The current decentralised reforms respond to and are part of a process of reformulation of the state's decentralisation; we cannot make assumptions about the agencies and actors involved in the reform. Notions drawn from liberal theory define actors as social interest groups which compete in public affairs (parents, teachers, administrators or policymakers). These categories do not enable us to grasp the subtle reformulation of structural relations that are occurring. As policies are formulated and realised, evaluations should make problematic the mediating agencies. The decentralisation modifies state practices to expand the settings in which policy is articulated, mediated and realised. New mediating agencies, such as professionalised groups within education or local community coalitions that act in relation to central state agencies, may be created in the process. To proceed with the assumption that the problem of evaluation is to provide precise 'data' about school indicators or success of programmes misrecognises the dynamics of schooling.

In most countries, reforms are being produced in a context of increased demand for educational productivity, with little understanding of the constitutive cultural and economic elements that result in and define productivity. There is an increasing internationalisation of economy that weakens the older European conceptions of the nation-state. At the same time, there is a heightened awareness of cultural nationalism and social pluralism. Further, pressures of global commodifications of cultural elements (for example, those produced by such international corporations as Benetton's, McDonalds and Sky Cable television) have produced national debates, dislocation and reflection about the sagas that have unified nations. An increasingly educated population produces a different set of 'actors' in the discussion as teachers have decreased educational status and attainment.

In the Norwegian context, the new strategies of decentralisation have produced changes in the notion of expertise and a shift in central state law from detailed regulations to broader policy guidelines. The system of transformation that is occurring in education has multiple points of stress and tension, even at this early stage, including the mediations and tradeoffs between central government and local communities in establishing teacher salary, hiring policies and education.

If these examples are correct, evaluation is not a problem of school improvement as it is traditionally assumed. Nor is it a problem of 'testing' or 'verifying' state practices as though there is a consensus of values or a standard notion of progress. The problems are of a different order, one which evaluations will not solve but will help to illuminate.

Let me conclude this section by saying that I do not believe evaluation can provide a direct plan of the present or of the future. Evaluation is inevitably about the past. Epistemologically, evaluation and social science are dialects of language and involve descriptions of what has happened. There is also a political question here. When we adopt a belief that knowledge is about prediction and administration, we allow science and its relation to the empirical world to move into the realm of ideology and social control. The rituals of science and evaluation become a rhetorical form whose purpose is to convince others that what is being done to them is in their best interest.

I say this because I can find no evidence that social science and school evaluation have anything to say, *qua* science, about the future. They do offer methods for understanding the boundaries that exist in the past and the dilemmas that are embedded in those arrangements. This is not to say that science cannot help us in the choices we make, but it is often in a negative voice. To borrow partially from Karl Popper, science (and evaluation) do not verify but refute. They can help us understand what choices not to make, such as in eliminating fluorines, controlling the deforestation in the Amazon, or limiting the use of intelligence testing. But - in the policy arena - the findings of science are part of a public debate that rarely concerns evidence alone. The determination of futures is no longer reserved for particular elites and experts who claim a sacred knowledge.

Before ending this discussion about past, futures and evaluation, there is an important caveat. Evaluation is about the future in an indirect way. The categories of evaluation organise phenomena in a manner that sensitises us towards certain possibilities and, at the same time, filters out others. Implicit in practices, then, are ways in which people are to challenge the world and locate themselves in its ongoing relations. This is what Steiner Kvale has made clear in his discussion of evaluation as a knowledge and constituting practice that produces a censorship of meaning.[5] To focus upon the problem of tension and ambiguities is not to remove the necessity of collecting demographic or achievement data, but to make the collection of data responsive to the central issues posed in the evaluation. The role of evaluation and evaluators in the ongoing construction of the world is one of continual scrutiny.

The Enlightenment Project as a problematic for evaluation

Often the pedagogical problem of educational evaluation is placed in the context of the contribution of schooling to upbringing. (It was called Americanisation in the early years of the US mass schooling, but now with new minorities and changing times it is referred to as 'a new nation building.') There is also the matter of labour socialisation: are people being educated to compete successfully in the labour market? In either case, the emphasis upon large-scale data about school achievement and other indicators of school 'success' leads to a narrow view of evaluation in which what is directly measurable is what is important.

What I would like to propose here is a reconsideration of the Enlightenment Project in schools as a major purpose of evaluation. By the phrase 'enlightenment' I mean a view in which people have assumed responsibility for the governance of their own lives. Schools, in this context, are an important educative institution in the realisation of that goal. The major strands of 20th-century analytic philosophy, sociology of knowledge, cultural studies and discourse analysis refocuses the problem of the enlightenment on the boundaries to our existence, the ambiguity of knowledge and the fundamental relationship of social practices with knowledge. The task of the Enlightenment is bound with a recognition that there are multiple truth claims, that these truth claims are historically bound and emerge from the social struggles and tensions of a world in which we live, and that the production of human possibilities always contains contradiction.

The posing of a curriculum is an assertion that there are general and seemingly transcendent values that we wish to maintain in schooling. In the West, these values relate to notions of democracy and reason. Curriculum supposes philosophical assumptions about human 'nature,' political assumptions about the relation of people to their institutions, and cultural assumptions about the central values and patterns that should give direction to social affairs. Yet contemporary scholarship makes us aware that however noble our hopes, a curriculum is a socially constructed and politically bound practice. At all times, our language and social practices are precarious and limited. As we engage in the tasks of constructing and realising a curriculum, what are defined as possibilities are also prisons.

The problem of evaluation, then, is not merely that of school improvement or decision-making, but of the conditions under which and the manner in which knowledge is produced in schools. Evaluation needs to focus not only on fundamental assumptions about the purposes of schooling that underlie practice, but also, as significantly, on issues about the relation of individuals to society that exist in the constructions of pedagogy. Evaluation should promote a discourse about education that examines the ways schools illuminate or obscure the social conditions in which people live. Although I recognise the difficulty of conceptualising such assessments, I believe that attention should be continually directed to what is most important through conceptualisation as well as data collection.

The complex and profound problem of curriculum can be expressed as a conflict between the hope we place in schooling and what happens as people seek to create, sustain and renew the conditions of their world (see Lundgren, 1983). The history of curriculum is the manner in which they are intended. As theories are put into social practice, there are always unintended, unanticipated and unwilled consequences.

Two interrelated themes of the contradiction between hope and happening in schooling are entailed in the construction of evaluation at the level spoken about here.

1. There is the problem of selection: what knowledge is brought into schools through textbooks and national and local curricula? How can we understand the self discipline brought to the individual by the way curriculum is classified and framed? To what extent is current scholar-

ship about knowledge, language and social production of society incorporated in the selection of school content?

The public rhetoric of school knowledge focuses upon formal categories such as science and mathematics, or general educational purposes such as reflection, critical thought or problem-solving. But the construction of a subject matter gives these words a particular form and direction. What is that form and direction? How do formulations of the subject matter of science, art or literature create and respond to an epistemology about individuals and society?

2. We can also think of the everyday world of schooling as having differentiations that are produced through the social patterns of school life. The patterns of conversation and the practices of teaching are not common to all; they contain multiple layers of meaning and interpretation. In back of the rituals of a common institution are social differentiations: What knowledge is to be transmitted to whom? What are the different cultural and social messages transmitted in classroom interactions?

Although I have not exhausted any possible set of questions for considering issues of the enlightenment in schooling, I recognise that the paradoxes of knowledge and power relations also produce paradoxes for evaluation. The imposition of a curriculum assumes a transcendence of certain knowledge that has a potential for achieving a better society; yet to propose a single form of knowledge is to structure out other possibilities. This process is never neutral and never without social implications. Knowledge is always located in a social and material world. The contradictions of curriculum are those of our occupational roles. In focusing upon the issues of enlightenment as frames for evaluation, we return to the problem of irony, contradiction and dilemma that evaluations can illuminate.

As a final note, I would like to turn to a strategy for reform that has incorporated its pedagogical standards into evaluation. I pose it as an example of a comprehensive approach that approaches some of the issues of pedagogy but whose understanding is also related to its social field.

The National Council of Teachers of Mathematics (1989) adopted new standards for the teaching and evaluation of mathematics education in the United States of mathematical knowledge in schools, focusing upon the constructed quality of mathematical knowledge and recent trends in constructivist psychology in the United States. The curriculum standards are interrelated with problems of evaluation; the integrity of the curriculum is maintained through the construction of performance criteria. The production of the standards calls for a comprehensive approach for implementation: from acceptance of the standards by the fifty state governments to the production of new textbooks and evaluation schemes to monitor implementation and progress.

Multiple strategies for evaluation are proposed in the reform. These include a testing system. The standard developers recognise that test construction can assume a reality of its own in technologically driven societies.[6] (In a different context, the Israeli biological science matriculation examination was revised in the 1970s to give emphasis to problem-solving and laboratory work, the focus of their new curriculum. Israeli science educatoıs believe that combined with other strategies in teacher education and financial investments, the reforms were successful.) Testing in the form of evaluative approaches to the implementation of mathematics standards should provide evidence of the influence of national reforms by giving careful attention to the relation of the specific measurement schemes to the liberalising intent of the curriculum program. (Whether this will be successful within the context of school measurement in the United States is a different question).

The standards carry no legislative force, but their production occurs in a social field where there are multiple points of steering and monitoring. Though developed by a professional group of mathematics educators, the standards were financially supported by the US Department of Education, various philanthropic foundations and the departments in the National Academy of Sciences. The development of such standards requires an understanding of the various mediating institutions that exist in the decentralised state system of the US, including the role of professional associations, state and local educational agencies, teacher unions and philanthropic institutions. Further, any account of the production of standards needs to consider the tradeoffs and omissions that occurred during negotiations among the groups involved in drawing up the standards. Finally, it is important that the standards were given sponsorship by various agencies to produce a scientific and computer-related mathematics, consciously focusing on certain assumptions and directions while structuring out other relevancies.

The social field in which the standards were produced is not mentioned to limit the integrity of the proposal or the comprehensiveness of a strategy that combines the intellectual concerns of curriculum with evaluation. Rather it is to position the proposal and strategy within a debate and interests that occurred in the production of the text - a debate that will probably be submerged as the standards are implemented.

The problems of the standards and of the evaluation of pedagogy are intricately tied to the general tensions and transformation that I spoke of in the previous section. The structural transformations and fragmentations occurring in society compel educators to re-insert enlightenment issues in the study of schools as new forms for the development of social regulation and individual capabilities occur. We can read the international efforts for educational reform as a marker of social transformations and the need to reconsider the relations that occur within educational sectors.

Conclusions

We like to pretend that the world can be made rational, that progress is an obtainable goal, and that policy is the instrument of the modern version of salvation. I do not deny that we must keep on trying, but I also recognise that we know little about social and educational change. A focus upon ambiguity and uncertainty is my way to explore what Lundgren has called the tension between our hopes and happenings.

I have located some questions about the social transformations and pedagogical constructions of schooling as a central problematic of evaluation. I recognise that these problems are not easily measured or conceptualised. It is almost as if our role is like that of Sisyphus - never fully succeeding, but struggling to give attention to what is most important (even if what are collected as data seem imperfect and complex).

Finally, this chapter is written by an American who continually witnesses narrow criteria of competence, performance and outputs in the public discourse about education. The processes of evaluation are often implicated in these conversations. At the same time, there is a field of debate within educational arenas that tempers, modifies and makes less deterministic what occurs. I recognise as well that the social field in which these ideas and practices about evaluation develop seems less tenuous and problematic as the ideas and practices are exported to the worldwide educational economy. This essay has focused upon some of these issues through a cautionary tale and an horizon to a problematic of evaluation. Both themes recognise an historical importance in the shape and form that is given to schooling.

Footnotes

1. This is insightfully considered in Hans Weiler's contribution to this book.

2. See Bourdieu, 1989, for a discussion of problems in the social field of intellectuals.

3. I talk about this in Popkewitz (1984) and Popkewitz and Pitman (1986).

4. At one level, the current reforms can be seen as driving and being driven by such accounting procedures. The collection of achievement 'indicators', the construction of competency tests for teachers and the development of computer capacity to assimilate and analyse the data from all schools within the fifty states. The last federal budget increased the budget for educational statistics by 62 per cent; for educational research, less than 1 per cent.

5. Steiner Kvale, 'Evaluation and decentralisation of knowledge' (in this collection).

6. Gary Sykes' and Sigbrit Franke-Wikberg's discussions in this set of papers provide a general reference to these issues.

References

Billig, M. (1982), *Ideology and Social Psychology: Extremism, Moderation and Contradiction*, New York: St. Martin's Press.

Bourdieu, P. (1989), *Homo Academicus*. Stanford, Calif: Stanford University Press.

Foucault, M. (1988), 'The political technology of individuals'. In Martin, L. Gutman, H. & Huttan, P. (eds), *Technologies of the Self: A Seminar with Michel Foucault*, Amherst: University of Massachusetts Press.

Lundgren, U. (1983), *Between Hope and Happening: Text and Context in Curriculum*, Geelong, Australia.

National Council of Teachers of Mathematics. (1989), Curriculum and evaluation standards for school mathematics. Reston, VA: national Council of Teachers of Mathematics.

Popkewitz, T. (1984b), *Paradigm and Ideology in Educational Research: Social Functions of the Intellectual*. London: Falmer Press.

Popkewitz, T. & Pitman, A. (1986), 'The idea of progress and the legitimation of state agendas: American proposals for school reform', *Curriculum and Teaching*, 1(1-2), 11-24.

Popkewitz, T. & Lind, K. (1989), 'Teachers' incentives as reform implications for teachers' work and the changing control mechanism in education', *Teachers College Record*, 90(4), 575-94.

Chapter 8

Evaluation and decentralisation of knowledge

Steinar Kvale

Evaluation involves the power to define the value of something. The current decentralisation of the educational system in Norway shall be discussed here with respect to the consequences for the evaluation of knowledge. In the first part of this chapter educational evaluation will be analysed as an exertion of power. Two conceptions of what is evaluated will be contrasted - individual students vs. common knowledge. A conception of evaluation as knowledge constitution and censorship of meaning will be outlined. Educational evaluation involves here the power to define what is valid knowledge in the educational system.

In the second part of this chapter the role of evaluation by the decentralisation of power in the educational system is discussed. The question is raised whether the decentralisation of administrative power also involves a decentralisation of the power to define the quality, value and validity of the knowledge transmitted in the educational system. The relation of a national evaluation system and local evaluation here becomes tied to the emphasis upon a common cultural heritage vs. the value of local knowledge. The current move towards decentralisation is related to a modern crisis of legitimacy and the issue of objective vs. relative knowledge.

Evaluation, power and knowledge

To evaluate means to establish the value of something. An examination is an evaluation of a student's knowledge. This formulation of the topic of examination is, however, ambiguous:

(1) Is it the individual student who is being evaluated on the basis of his or her presentation of a discipline's knowledge?

(2) Or is it the common knowledge of the discipline that is evaluated through the student's presentation of his or her knowledge?

Evaluation as a test of individual students

The major part of evaluation research has, in line with common sense, investigated examinations as tests of individual students. Three main functions of examinations discussed have been selection, educational influence and power exertion (see Kvale, 1972, 1977).

Research has focused on examinations as a psychometric test concerning legitimate selection of students and efficient prediction of their careers. Studies have demonstrated a rather low intersubjective reliability for the grading of essays and orals, whereas the computerised multiple-choice test approached a perfect reliability. The predictive validity of grades for later achievements is relatively low within the educational system, and close to zero between final grades and later job success.

The educational influence of examinations in guiding and motivating learning has been little investigated. Some studies point to backlash effects as that the multiple choice tests may further superficial learning and that learning for grades may lead away from an intrinsically motivated learning to a less efficient, instrumental, motivation (e.g. Becker *et al.*, 1968; Kvale, 1980).

Examinations are an instrument of power, controlling access to educational privileges and influencing the learning process. I have interpreted earlier the manifest test and educational weaknesses of examinations by postulating more latent social power functions (Kvale, 1972, 1977). Examinations are a simple bureaucratic and legitimate selection for privileged educational and occupational positions. Although in fact involving a class bias, the sorting by exams grants an 'illusion of chance equality'. The importance of selection by grades lends a pressure to the social influence of examinations: a disciplining in school and a socialisation to the qualification requirements of the labour market. The learning for grades in school socialises the students to working for wages in occupational life.

Different as the selective, educational and power functions of examinations may appear, they have one common assumption - the focus on what the examinations do to the individual students.

Evaluation as a test of common knowledge

An alternative approach focuses on how examinations may contribute to the constitution of what is the valid knowledge of a discipline (Kvale, 1987). The individual students are then 'bracketed' as mere carriers of the knowledge to be evaluated. The emphasis is on the knowledge evaluated, tested, graded and certified by the examination as the legitimate knowledge of the discipline. The meaning of the same examination form is rather different with the two conceptions of what exams are about - testing individual students or testing common knowledge.

The two conceptions involve different answers concerning how to ascertain the validity of a given evaluation. The form of validation depends on what is investigated and why. In a test context, the what of evaluation is the individual student and why is legitimate selection and efficient prediction. The form of validation is the predictive validity of individual achievements, to be measured in correlation coefficients. For a knowledge concept of tests content validity pertains: that is how well the content of a test samples the subject matter about which conclusions are drawn.

Discussing the role of tests in a national evaluation, Lundgren (1990, pp. 37-8) outlines two paradigms of test construction that are close to the present distinction of evaluation of individual students vs. evaluation of common knowledge. The function of the first is selection, with test items discriminating between individuals, creating scales where individuals can be placed. In the second paradigm the test is assigned to measure a given body of knowledge, the test items are here to be discriminatory in relation to the structure of the content tested, creating maps on which individuals can be placed. In the second paradigm, the test constructors need not only master test theory but also need to master the knowledge structure and content that is measured.

Lundgren points out that the first type of tests are difficult to use by a national evaluation of the quality of the outcome of education, in that they only give information about the relative relations between the individual students, but not of how the content has been transmitted and the educational goals achieved. For the political governing of the educational system, for decisions on resource allocations, it is necessary with an evaluation of how well a knowledge structure is covered, of how the content has been transmitted and the goals achieved.

A conception of examinations as knowledge constitution goes further than appraising how well a given knowledge content is covered by a specific test by asking what the evaluation form does to the concept of the knowledge tested.

Constitution of knowledge

Knowledge is not merely something given, to be sampled and measured by a test; rather, the very operation of testing the knowledge of a discipline provides an operational definition of the knowledge of the discipline. Corresponding to the operational definition of intelligence as what is measured by intelligence tests, an operational definition of knowledge is for the students what is measured by the examinations. The examinations define the knowledge that is worthwhile to acquire and master.

The emphasis is here on how the very act of evaluation constitutes the values serving as the standards for evaluation. The focus is then changed from the content validity of a test to the constitution of valid knowledge through a test. A discipline's knowledge is not only transmitted in teaching and checked at examinations; the examination itself contributes to establish the valid knowledge of a discipline. In a literal sense, an examination is a test of knowledge, an examination of the value and validity of a discipline's knowledge. Examinations are an assessment of the knowledge of a discipline, a yearly testing and confirmation of the quality of the knowledge taught and acquired in a field.

The generally vague definitions of goals of learning and the lack of explicit criteria for evaluation leave large margins for interpretation by the examiners and censors; through their concrete evaluative decisions they operationally define the valid knowledge of a discipline. From the viewpoint of the sociology of knowledge, examinations are 'rites de passage', a confirmation ritual, contributing to the social construction of reality in the transmission and maintenance of a discipline's knowledge. The often harsh tests define what is the valid knowledge of the community, and to which the new recruits must pledge allegiance before they are acknowledged as full members of the community.

Examination committees and defence of dissertations

The examination committees in Scandinavia, which come close to the evaluation committees by dissertations, appointments and tenure, shall be discussed here as a case of the knowledge constituting and validating function of examinations. At the universities, the results of several years of study can be evaluated at one examination, often consisting of two days of essays and an ensuing oral examination. The examination committee consists of one or two faculty members and an external examiner from another institution, called 'censor'. The examiners read and evaluate the papers independently and then meet to make a joint evaluation. Only the final grade is public.

The attainment of a rational consensus among colleagues is a goal of an examination committee. It is essential that there is a genuine consensus about the final evaluation of a student's knowledge. The consensus is to be reached through a rational discourse about the quality of the knowledge presented, a mechanical computation of an arithmetic means testifies to a breakdown of a rational discourse of the value of the knowledge. The examiners are to be loyal colleagues, internal disagreements should not be made public, the examiners shall in union publicly represent the true common knowledge of their discipline.

This ideal description of the evaluation in a committee approaches the description of a discourse given by Habermas (cf. Bernstein, 1983; Løvlie, 1984) and represents an abstraction from the social power factors of real examinations, as discussed elsewhere (Kvale, 1987). A discourse is characterised by a rational argumentation.The participants are obliged to test statements about truth and falsity of propositions on the basis of argued points of view, and where the best argument wins. The discourse is a form of argumentation where no social exertion of power takes place, the only form of power is the force of the better argument. In the Socratic ideal of a dialogue, all motives beyond a cooperative search for truth is excluded.

The public defence of a dissertation is, taking account of the ritual form and the obvious power relations, probably the closest that an examination comes to a discourse, aiming at a convincing consensus about valid knowledge. There is an open dispute about the truth value of the candidate's thesis, the candidate argues and defends his or her knowledge claims in the public dispute; answering the critical claims of his official opponents and also of possible questions from the floor. The often tough public argumentation at the defence of a dissertation approaches the ideal of a discourse where the only force is that of the better argument.

Censorship of meaning

The establishment of what is valid knowledge in a field involves taking a position on what is true or false, right or wrong, and what knowledge is valuable enough to be furthered. A clear position taking on knowledge may, in a liberal society, be rejected as a censorship of meaning. An official religious and political censorship was common in earlier centuries, but has with the Enlightenment generally been abolished during peacetime in liberal states. The present issue concerns whether examinations today may function as a form of religious, political, and ideological censorship: Are modern examinations an official censor institution controlling what knowledge may obtain an official authorisation as legitimate knowledge in a field?

In the Germanic languages there is a linguistic link of examinations and censorship. In German the word 'Zensur' also means a grade, and 'zensieren' the activity of grading. In the Scandinavian languages one speaks of 'eksamenscensur', an external examiner is called a 'censor' and examining 'censur'. The topic of censorship has received little attention in examination research. And in the last few decades there has been a trend to replace the old, and somewhat negative terms of 'censoring', 'examination' and 'grading' by the modern concept 'evaluation'. As indicated by the word root, the issue of values remains. Reports of a censorship of knowledge tend today to be disclaimed as extreme, atypical, cases, and as a misuse of the examination institution.

In Scandinavian universities, there has in recent decades been controversies over whether psychoanalytic, critical and Marxist thought may be included in the social sciences. In given periods and departments, students who believed the work of Freud, Habermas and Marx were relevant for their topics, may have refrained from mentioning it in their examination papers, and some who did were failed when they tried to integrate these outside theories in their examination papers.

In such cases, there may be accusations of a censorship of meaning; between students and examiners, or between examiners, sometimes accompanied by strong emotional and personal conflicts. The basic issue experienced is less the particular grade assigned to a student than an attempt of invalidating what is the true knowledge standards of one's field. A few years later it may happen that the previously unaccepted theories become incorporated into the mainstream of the field. In Denmark, psychoanalysis, critical theory and Marxism were generally considered unscientific before 1968, but have since marched the long way through the examination system, to now to be generally accepted as legitimate ways of understanding in the social sciences.

Not every candidate who fails is politically persecuted or an unrecognised genius. The controversial censorship cases are statistical exceptions; from the present viewpoint, however, they are the deviant cases, the crisis in communication, which make visible the ordinarily overlooked knowledge constituting function of examinations, the marking of the boundaries of a discipline's territory. The censorship cases invoke a meta-evaluation, where the value frames for evaluation are at stake.

The description of an examination committee as negotiating what is true knowledge in a field may appear somewhat exaggerated. The routines of evaluation appear more commonplace as a checking of whether the basic concepts, methods and data of the discipline are presented convincingly in the examination paper. Fundamental epistemological disputes are not a common part of evaluation activities. It should, though, not be overlooked that the many routine evaluations also involve a meta-evaluation - here an implicit acceptance and certification of the knowledge passed at the examinations. Concurrently with the direct evaluation of the individual students, there takes place a meta-evaluation of the discipline's common knowledge.

Every evaluation of a student's paper also implicitly involves a confirmation of the value standards used for the evaluation. In normal stable periods of a discipline, the meta-evaluative aspect of an examination is hardly visible. In times of radical, paradigmatic changes in knowledge when the traditional values of a discipline are challenged, a meta-evaluative function of examinations may become visible, because of the necessity of defining the limits of a discipline, of re-establishing the core concepts, methods and data. During periods when a discipline simultaneously contains incommensurable frames of reference, a set of common standards have to be worked out anew in order to obtain unitary evaluations of the student's knowledge.

Implications of a knowledge-constituting conception of evaluation

The above outline of evaluation as contributing to the constitution of knowledge and values on a discipline is admittedly tentative. First, the analysis has departed from extreme cases of meaning censorship to understand the normal activity of evaluation. Second, the analysis has sought to understand the lower levels of evaluation from the higher levels; focusing on the advanced dissertations and university exams to understand also evaluation at more elementary levels of the educational system. Third, the relation between the two conceptions of examinations as respectively differentiation of individual students versus a constitution of common knowledge needs to be worked out.

Before applying the knowledge conception of evaluations to the issue of a centralised vs. decentralised evaluation, some general implications of a figure-ground reversal of evaluation - from certification of students to certification of knowledge - shall be pointed out. Thus, some of the disputes about form and procedures of examinations and grading, which appear bizarre from a psychometric point of view, may become understandable when examinations are seen as an institution of knowledge constitution.

The examination candidates as sacrificial lambs

Within a conception of examinations as knowledge-constituting and meaning-censoring, the individual student recedes into the background. The candidates are merely background figures, the supporting cast of the play, who bring forth knowledge for the yearly testing and confirmation of what is the valid knowledge of the discipline. In the continual task of maintaining and renewing the definition of the valid knowledge of the interpretative community, the individual candidates are sometimes offered in the internal faculty disputes about the true knowledge of the discipline. The candidates for the exams are the yearly lambs, some of whom have to be sacrificed at the examination table, in order to maintain the socially necessary common knowledge.

The artificiality of examinations

A common complaint about exams is that the test situation is artificial, the content and form of the examination tasks have little relevance for future work performance, the exams have little ecological validity. In a knowledge constitutive understanding of exams, this critique is beside the point. The similarity of the examination situation to later job situations is irrelevant if the function of the examination is the constitution of a consensually valid understanding of the discipline's knowledge.

Consensus - a starting point or a goal?

Evaluation research has documented an often low reliability of grading. Within a positivist conception, knowledge consists of objective facts. A low intersubjective reliability in grading is then due to subjectivity and error by the examiners. Within a hermeneutic understanding, knowledge is manifold and its meaning must be interpreted. The goal is, through a rational discourse, to arrive at a consensus about the meaning of a text. Initial differences among examiners about the value of an essay need then not be something subjective and negative. It is rather a positive accomplishment that examiners are able to, with the subtleties and ambiguities of knowledge, to arrive at a final consensus about the value of an essay. Within a hermeneutical approach, different initial evaluations of an essay are not something to be lamented, but a challenge to be overcome.

The return of the content

Studies of evaluation have focused on the formal side of evaluation, in particular by selection of individual students, stressing methods of evaluation, their reliability and predictive validity. Evaluation has mainly been relative to the achievements of other pupils, often to be distributed along a normal curve. Absolute evaluation in relation to given goals has been less frequent, Benjamin Bloom's (1971) mastery learning and goal taxonomies being exceptions.

There are some indications of a return of the content in educational evaluation, of the primacy of the knowledge to be evaluated. In the general public there is an increased concern with the quality of the educational content, as witnessed by the movements of 'back to basics' and of 'value clarification'. The public interest in Allan Bloom's (1987) massive critique of relativism in American education and advocation of a return to the great books testifies to a concern with true knowledge in education. It may also be mentioned that Lyotard's book, *The Postmodern Condition: A Report on Knowledge* (1984) was commissioned by the University Council of the Government of Quebec. An increased emphasis on the nature of the knowledge and values transmitted and evaluated in the educational system may again bring up the issue of meaning censorship involved in the older examination system.

With a change in emphasis, from form to content, from selection of students to selection of knowledge, the disciplines necessary for evaluation research change. Test theory, learning theory, occupational sociology and economics become less central for understanding evaluation; epistemology and ethics, sociology of knowledge and the history of education become relevant. Theory of knowledge and of value is basic to a theory of evaluation. The kinds of knowledge to be promoted become the criterion for judging specific evaluation procedures, of how they sample and further the knowledge goals of education. To the issues raised in a knowledge context are those of knowledge and power, of the ideal discourse versus social constraints, of logical argumentation versus rhetorics and demagogy. There is the issue of a quest for truth through discourse versus objectivist and relativist conceptions of knowledge. There is the issue of the constraints of a censorship of meaning versus the anarchism of an 'anything goes' relativism.

Decentralisation of power and knowledge

In the first part of this chapter evaluation was posited as constituting the knowledge of a discipline, as defining what is valid and legitimate knowledge in a field. The institutionalised educational evaluation involves the power to define the quality and the value of knowledge in the educational system.

The implications of this knowledge-constituting conception of evaluation shall now be discussed in relation to the current decentralisation of the educational system in Norway. This involves the questions raised by Lundgren: 'How can the expectations on national evaluation and its role in a decentralised educational system be realised? ... What kind of techniques and methods should be used within a national evaluation system? ... How can evaluations on a local level be used in a national evaluation system'? (1990, p. 39)

In the following discussion, the focus will not be upon individual evaluation as such, nor upon a system evaluation of educational programmes, but on the use of individual evaluation results as indexes of the quality of the educational system.

A main issue here concerns the implications of a decentralisation of administrative power for the evaluation of knowledge. Is it possible to decentralise on a legal and economical level and retain a central control of the knowledge transmitted in the educational system? Or will a decentralisation of administrative power also lead to a decentralisation of the power to define knowledge, to a move from a common national knowledge to a local knowledge? In other words, with power and knowledge intertwined, is it possible to confine decentralisation to management techniques and retain a central evaluative control of what is valid knowledge;in brief, can power be decentralised without also decentralising knowledge and truth?

Decentralisation of power exertion

Three forms of power exertion are usually discerned in educational systems - legal, economical and management by objectives. In the last decades, there has taken a transition place from a more rigid power exertion through strict rules and regulations to more flexible and less resistance-provoking financial instruments (Eide, 1968). And there is today a move towards management by objectives, to a result-oriented management through assessing attainment of educational goals (Lundgren, 1990). Hereto may be added examinations as a means of educational power exertion (Kvale, 1972, 1977). Lundgren includes evaluation as a fourth steering instrument, and posits that the looser and more diffuse the first three steering instruments become 'the more the evaluation will govern by giving interpretations in an operationalised way' (1990, p.14).

Today there is a move towards a decentralised power exertion in the educational system. Three common arguments outlined by Weiler (1990) are, with the wording slightly changed: (1) a democratic sharing of power, (2) increased efficiency of management, and (3) an educational interest in the local knowledge of the community.

In the Norwegian educational system, economic responsibility for the schools is today given to the local communities, with possibilities of adjusting the curriculum to the local cultural context. The examiners of the 1988 OECD review of educational politics in Norway remark that with the ambitious drive to decentralisation, it is essential that the local authorities and the ministry have qualitative knowledge of how schools work and of the state of knowledge throughout Norwegian schools. The OECD examiners recommend the build up of a central evaluation and information system on the progress of education, and 'On the basis of both quantitative and qualitative information there could be active evaluation and monitoring of what the schools do. Some of the monitoring might be in the form of tests' (Lundgren, 1990, p. 18).

The ensuing contradiction of decentralisation of educational administration and a national evaluation system is pointed out by Lundgren: 'What on one side turns out to be a change in steering systems directed towards a distribution of policy making from the center to the periphery, will on the other side be a strengthening of a central steering system' (p. 34). He discusses on a general level 'decentralisation and educational policy' and 'evaluation and monitoring' in the Norwegian educational system. Without more concrete description and analysis of the organisation of the evaluation systems and of the specific procedures and methods used it is, however, difficult to ascertain which of the alternatives he points out will be the strongest - a local participatory democracy with adjustment of the curriculum to the local cultural context, or a strengthening of the central political steering system.

If a central quality evaluation will be a main steering factor in the future educational system, the decentralisation of budget control and the incorporation of the local cultural context may well become a governing through an illusion of a local participation. There may occur a double communication - concurrent with an open move of legal and budget control from the central ministry to the local community, a central knowledge control through a less visible evaluation hand is built into a national evaluation system.

With a lack of detailed description of actual procedures and organisation of decentralisation and evaluation, the remaining comments attempt to outline a frame of reference for analysing the reforms taking place in the Norwegian educational system.

Decentralisation, evaluation and crisis of legitimation

Knowledge and values are in current society subject to a crisis of legitimacy. The validity and authority of traditional standards are dissolving. This concerns social knowledge and values at large, and in many university disciplines, the traditional body of knowledge, the basic concepts, methods and data are being disputed.

Rather than deploring the loss of universally valid knowledge and the collapse of the modern narratives of legitimation, postmodern writers as Lyotard (1984) recognise and welcome a primacy of the heterogeneous local language games. With the collapse of the global narratives of legitimation the local context becomes essential. With the dissolution of universal systems of modernity, the local knowledge comes into prominence. Heterogeneous and changing language games replace global horizon of meaning. In a postmodern condition, the local interaction, the communal network, is the point of departure. Rather than equating the universal laws with the objective and the individual with the subjective and relative, interpretations of meaning and truth are made in the local community by people who share decisions and the consequences of their decisions.

Within the context of postmodern knowledge, the decentralisation of educational management is not merely a new efficient management technique or an acknowledgement of local demands for a participatory democracy. It is also in line with a broader move from the modern centralised state to postmodern networks of communities and in accordance with a change from universal to local knowledge.

The emphasis on decentralisation and evaluation may be reactions to a crisis in legitimation of the authority of the modern state and of the validity of general knowledge; and, as pointed out by Weiler (1990), as compensatory forms of legitimation. With a loss of, or lack of consensus about, national goals of education, the aims of education may be left to the local communities. With a lack of universally, or nationally, valid knowledge, there may be a flight to a recluse in the local knowledge.

It is in the domain of knowledge that the issue of decentralisation of education becomes precarious. There is on the one side the argument that education should transfer a common cultural heritage, contribute to retaining a national unity and to assert national norms. On the other side there is the upsurge of cultural regionalisation, and interest in the local traditions and knowledge, and - particularly in Norway - the use of the local dialects. And there are educational movements linking school learning to the everyday life of the pupils in their local communities.

The strength of the current move to the local communities is rather open, it may be of mainly rhetorical and folkloristic interest, or it may be to leave basic decisions about worthwhile action and valid knowledge to the people of the community who share decisions and the consequences of their decisions.

Occasionally the move to the local communities may be accompanied by a grassroots romanticism, denouncing the central state as oppressive. Decentralisation may open for a genuine participatory democracy, and also for a local oppression by regional majorities and power groups, as in issues of religion and race. In some instances the central authorities may have the task of protecting local minorities against a local oppression.

Centralisation is often linked to a rationalistic model of the educational system. This model involves assumptions of an underlying order of the school organisation, predictability, students as passive objects and of objectively measurable competencies. The contrasting natural systems model of education points to absence of consensus on norms, values and objectives, emphases, arguments and bargaining, functional autonomy, de facto decentralisation and incomplete information (Darling-Hammond *et al.*, 1986).

In contrast to the implicit harmony assumption in the rationalistic model, Weiler (1990), maintains that conflicts are endemic in the modern state and its educational system. Pointing out that there are few areas in modern society that generate so much public controversy as education, and in particular educational reforms, he posits decentralisation as serving the political functions of conflict management and compensatory legitimation.

Decentralisation can be seen as a reaction to a loss of the authority of the modern central state, and evaluation as a reaction to a crisis in the legitimacy of a common knowledge. Evaluation has - in the form of examinations and grading - a long history in education; it is, however, first in the last decades that evaluation - of individuals and of systems - has become a main concern of the educational system. The current focus on evaluation may be interpreted as a reaction to an absence of clear, convincing and compelling educational goals and values. If something is convincingly valuable, appears as worthwhile in its own right, a demand for external evaluation of its value recedes. The quest for formal evaluation may also involve an element of distrust; there may be a suspicion about the general quality of education, a doubt about whether a special educational programme is worth the effort and investments, and a critical evaluation may be demanded to assess the value in doubt.

With a lack of consensus about what is educationally valuable, there is a proliferation of concepts and methods of evaluation. Textbook chapters on evaluation abound with conceptual distinctions of evaluation as formative - summative, absolute - relative, individual - system, etc. and with measurement techniques for evaluation. Weiler (1990) interprets the phenomenal rise of evaluation as in part due to its capacity of confirming scientific rationality and respectability upon the policy process, as a compensatory legitimation. The present argument goes further, stating that in face of confusion and loss of authoritative values and valid knowledge, the very focus on the concepts and techniques of evaluation may serve to uphold a belief in the existence of educational values and valid knowledge.

From the perspective of a legitimacy crisis in education, one may expect a move of emphasis in the exertion of power - from management by objectives to evaluational steering of the educational system. With a general lack of consensus about educational values and objectives, a result-oriented steering through explicit goals and taxonomies of content may invoke endless debates about the exact wording of the educational goals - between the diverse interest groups in the school boards, in the public and in some cases also in the Parliament. In the face of a lack of national consensus of the educational goals to be transmitted through the curriculum, a management through evaluation may be less controversial - the operational definition of values and knowledge is left to the secrecy of the examination committees and the anonymity of the test constructors. The evaluators are rarely required to defend publicly their operationally powerful definitions of what is valuable educational knowledge. From the perspective of a crisis of legitimation, the operational power of defining the educationally valid knowledge may today be moving from the curriculum constructors to the test constructors.

Standardised testing vs. humanistic-anarchistic exams

With a crisis in values and knowledge, and some disciplines being a mixture of relativism and local dogmatism, it becomes difficult to maintain a common rational discourse. A reciprocal argumentation about true and false knowledge is irrelevant in the milieu of both an objectivist clinging to a truth beyond questioning and a relativist indifference to the issue of truth and falsity.

To illustrate possible consequences of a centralised and a decentralised evaluation system two extremes shall be depicted - a technological standardising and a humanistic individualising.

The standardised multiple-choice test

With the technological reforms of examinations the validity of the knowledge tested appears unproblematic. The standardised tests imply knowledge as consisting of isolated facts and logical rules for combining the facts. This conception reflects a logical empiricist philosophy of knowledge and it is well suited to the current computerisation of knowledge. The question of valid exams has become a question of measuring techniques, of reliable and efficient techniques for measuring the existing objective body of knowledge.

The multiple-choice test is an important device. Some consequences of evaluating knowledge through answers to series of small questions shall be depicted. Knowledge tends to become decontextualised into atomistic data and formal rules of combination. The questions are to be answered as true or false, not allowing for the complexity and ambiguity of knowledge. The formulation of the questions and of the true and false answers is generally made by distant experts in test bureaux; they alone decide what is valid knowledge, with little possibility of questioning or discussion. The evaluation is computerised, leaving out any possibility of discourse.

The knowledge constituted by the standardised multiple-choice exams is objectivistic; knowledge is either true or false. Knowledge consists of answering the questions of others, not of questioning the knowledge itself.

The individualised humanistic evaluation

In the anarchistic 'humanised' open and often diffuse exams, a quest for valid knowledge is replaced by personal involvement. The diffuse exams are often legitimated by a humanistic and a therapeutic psychology, with the students' personal development and self-realisation in the centre. Teaching and evaluation is based on a therapeutically conceived dialogue, characterised by positive emotions and freedom of anxiety. Formal examinations are regarded as externally required bureaucratic formalities, with no intrinsic educational value.

The humanistic diffuse examinations have a variety of forms. The topic and the question for the exam may be chosen by the student himself, sometimes also the examiner. The essay may be written at home, both preparation of a paper and the orals may take place in groups, and the grading on a scale is replaced by a pass/fail decision. Evaluation of the knowledge product of a student's learning is de-emphasised to the advantage of an evaluation of the learning process, and with a change from teacher's evaluation to self-evaluation is an ideal. The importance of the formal examination situation is played down and replaced by informal counselling and supervision during the learning process. The requirements of formally appointed external examiners, censors, is often relaxed, whereby the likelihood of open disputes over the validity of knowledge is reduced.

The knowledge constituted by the humanistic diffuse exams is subjectivistic - the search for true knowledge is subordinated to the development of the person; knowledge is a means for the self-realisation of the individual student.

The question of valid knowledge has become irrelevant, knowledge is relativistic, the world consists of multiple realities with no necessity of finding out whether one reality is more true than another.

In conclusion, both the rationalistic standardised testing and the humanistic-anarchist exams appear as two opposite reactions to a general loss of authoritative knowledge. The definition of valid knowledge is either centralised to the anonymous test constructors or decentralised in extreme to the personal interaction of individual teachers and students. In contrast, the examination committees described earlier, with their potentials of conflict and censorship, allowed at least in principle, a rational discourse about the validity of the knowledge examined. And with the committees consisting of local examiners and centrally appointed censors, conflict and dialogue between local and central conceptions of valid knowledge is possible.

Knowledge evaluation and decentralisation

Some implications of a decentralisation of power and knowledge for evaluation practices shall now be raised concerning methods, backlash, validity and power.

Methods

The OECD examiners recommended in 1988 that on the basis of both quantitative and qualitative information there could be an active central evaluation and monitoring of what the schools do, and some of this monitoring could be in the form of tests (Lundgren, 1990, p. 18). The issue of quantitative vs. qualitative methods has been a discussion topic in educational research and evaluation during the last decades. Rather than discuss quantitative versus qualitative methods in abstraction, it appears more fruitful to ask what kinds of information for what purposes shall be provided by educational evaluation.

Today the most common use of educational tests is for the selection of pupils to higher levels of education. The evaluative information required by national selection of students is quantitative, precise, unambiguous and commensurable; the test scores and grade point averages are decontextualised, with the evaluation results in Oslo and Finnmark transparent and commensurable.

Tests may also be used as means of educational development (e.g. Bloom *et al.*, 1971). In addition to quantitative scores the educationally valuable evaluation may also be qualitative and contextual, tailored to the needs of the individual students and provide prescriptions for future learning.

And if tests are to be used for assessing the status of the knowledge of a field, they should not only yield information about the quantitative amount of knowledge, but also yield qualitative nuances and differences, including the complexities, ambiguities and controversies of knowledge. The emphasis upon one-dimensionality vs. qualitative differentiation will depend on whether the evaluative information is to serve in national or international comparisons on quality standards of education or to serve the development in the educational knowledge of the field.

The complexity and the intertwinedness of the different uses and consequences of evaluation procedures may be illustrated by the issue of the optimal number of steps on the grading scale. Given the often low reliability of grading, a final evaluation of an essay on a one-dimensional scale, even with decimals, may involve a pseudo-exactness. From a conception of evaluation as a constitution of knowledge, a finely differentiated grading scale may contribute to a preciseness of knowledge. If the task of an examination committee is merely to make a pass/fail decision, the conception of the knowledge at the basis of the evaluative decision need not be particularly precise. If the task is, however, to arrive at a consensus about the position of an essay on a finely differentiated scale of quality, this necessitates precise and intersubjective concepts of valid knowledge. A finely differentiated grading scale may then contribute to the development of precise and consensually valid knowledge in a discipline.

The legal profession in Norway has strict and finely differentiated evaluation procedures. This has earlier been interpreted from a socialisation perspective as indicating a necessity of establishing discipline, loyalty and rank order within the legal profession (see Kvale, 1972). From the present knowledge conception, the strict evaluative differentiation in the study of law also involves a coercion towards establishing precise and consensual interpretations of the legal texts.

Evaluation backlash

The OECD examiners mention that whereas elaborate systems of testing might give certainty about the quality standards reached, they may also have backlash effects on the quality of teaching, such as teachers teaching to the test (see Lundgren, 1990, p. 18). The backlash effects of evaluation upon learning and teaching are complex and little investigated. Some forms of evaluative backlash shall be briefly outlined here.

By the discussion of evaluation of individuals vs. knowledge earlier, three forms of relations between evaluation and knowledge went forth. A first, 'passive' relation of evaluation and knowledge involves evaluation as a mere final measure of the finished products of learning, the evaluation not influencing the knowledge measured more than a thermometer influences the temperature it measures. A second form of relation is more active, the evaluation procedures provide an operational definition of what is to be learned, with pupils learning, and the teachers teaching, to the test. And a third relation of evaluation and knowledge focuses on the activities of the examiners; on their definition, redefinition and negotiating the validity of the knowledge evaluated - horizontally between examiners, and, to a lesser extent, vertically between examiners and students. The 'active' relations of evaluation and knowledge may be further specified with respect to the forms and use of the evaluation, with simplification and erosion of knowledge as possible consequences.

Evaluative simplification of knowledge

A national evaluation system requires that the evaluations in different local communities are comparable. The demand for commensurability may be for reasons of accountability, with the pressures on objective evaluations forcing back a rather simplistic notion of evaluation (Lundgren, 1990; House, 1990). A stronger pressure towards commensurability and objectivity in evaluation today is due to the common use in many countries of test scores and grade point averages as the decisive selection criteria by restricted admission to university studies. To ensure legitimacy and avoid complaints, the evaluations have to be as standardised and appear as objective as possible.

Whether the demands for commensurable evaluations come from requirements of accountability to the state or from legitimation of student selection, there is a pressure towards standardised evaluation of objective knowledge. Such a conception of knowledge is also in line with a logical empirical philosophy of knowledge as consisting of isolated objective facts to be connected by logical rules; involving an assumption of knowledge as exactly measurable and commensurable across local contexts. Regardless of the reasons for the demand of the results of evaluation being objective and commensurable knowledge, the value of local knowledge is diminished by a national evaluation.

The form of evaluation best adapted to the demands of objective and commensurable evaluation results is the multiple choice-tests described above. These tests, with their standardisation of worthwhile knowledge, have a strong position in international education. The growing empirical evidence on the educational effects of these tests is usually overlooked - that the multiple-choice tests may lead to a simplification of the knowledge taught and acquired, emphasising memory of factual knowledge rather than more complex cognitive processes (Frederiksen, 1984).

Interpretations of knowledge evaluation as leading to a simplification or superficialisation of knowledge are not new. The Jesuits introduced evaluation by grades in their schools with the explicit purpose of promoting discipline, competition and diligence. Dürkheim (1977) has also postulated a desired cognitive effect of the Jesuits: to further a superficial learning of the Greek and Latin texts that the pupils were required to read as part of the general culture of the epoch. The Jesuits did not wish to further any deeper understanding of the content of the pagan texts of antiquity, and sought to focus the pupils attention upon the language, the grammar and the style of these dangerous texts. And a strong competition for grades was one of the pedagogical means of securing a superficial learning of the classical texts.

Evaluative erosion of knowledge

The form and extent of evaluative backlash does not only depend upon the measures applied, but is also related to the importance of measurement results, today in particular by the restricted admission to higher studies. Whereas selection pressure may provide a motivational incentive for learning, extreme degrees of selection pressure may lead to a simplification of, and even erosion of, learning, also by more open forms of evaluation as essays and orals.

A means-ends reversal may take place here, involving a 'goal trap' where the means of measuring the goals of learning themselves become the goals of learning. With the results of the evaluative measurements decisive for a student's future career an instrumentalisation of learning may occur. Knowledge obtains a commodity character, where the use value of knowledge recedes for its exchange value - what grades the acquired knowledge can be exchanged for, with grades as the basic currency of the educational system.

Instrumentalisation of learning through selection pressure, with possible simplification and erosion of knowledge, has received little attention in the psychology of learning and education. In observations of, and interviews with pupils and students in school, the effects of an instrumentalised learning appear more abundantly (e.g. Becker *et al.*, 1968; Kvale, 1980). Students may tell how they go to school with the explicit purpose of getting as good an examination as possible, with the least possible effort. They may deliberately focus on a simplistic learning, believing that it pays off at examinations: one does not experiment or take chances, but writes an orthodox essay, rather than one that would have been more exciting and worthwhile to write. Students may actually state the belief that if you really try to learn something, it will be a handicap with respect to grades. Several pupils note, somewhat astonished, how fast one forgets the knowledge learned after an examination. With an instrumental approach to learning, what has been called a 'memory clearance function of examinations' becomes reasonable - when learning only for a test, the knowledge has no value after the evaluation has been passed and may be forgotten or dumped.

The extent, strength and reasons of a grade perspective on learning is complex and little investigated. Its possible impact on learning and knowledge should though be taken in account in order to ensure that the quality control of education, rather than serving to develop education, may not involve a simplification and destruction of the educational goals.

Validity

The relation of a national evaluation to a local evaluation in education has implications for ascertaining the validity of the knowledge transmitted and evaluated. Within educational research and evaluation, validity has been treated as predictive validity and content validity, pertaining respectively to the prediction of student careers and the sampling of educational knowledge. Today there takes place a beginning expansion of the concept of validation in the social sciences - from mere observation of a correspondence between a measurement and the social reality, to also include communication with, and action in, the social reality investigated (Kvale, 1989). This move has been most clearly formulated for system evaluation, where there is an emphasis on communicative and pragmatic validity, whether the knowledge produced can be accepted and used by the participants in the system evaluated. House maintains in 'Evaluating with validity' (1980) that evaluation research does not concern mainly predicting events, but whether the intended audience of an evaluation report can see new relations and answer new but relevant questions. The utility aspect of validity has been further stressed by Patton (1980) who maintains that the ultimate test of the credibility of an evaluation report is the response of decision-makers and information-users to that report.

With the communicative and pragmatic extensions of validation of evaluative knowledge a decisive issue becomes who is the relevant audience, who are the information-users and decision-makers to validate an evaluation. In the present context it is conceivable that local and national information-users and decision-makers may pose different questions to, and make different use of an evaluation study.

These issues do not merely concern political aspects of validity and evaluation but are again related to controversies in current philosophy of knowledge as to the objectivity and relativity of knowledge, whether there exists universally valid knowledge, or only local language games. In the present context: Is the validity of knowledge to be ascertained on a national level, or can the local communities establish a local knowledge, valid for their decisions and actions?

Power

Students are taught in lectures that knowledge is power. At examinations they learn that power is knowledge. The examination committee defines for the students what is valid and legitimate knowledge in a field. The examinations provide an operational definition of valid understanding of the social reality, a definition that may be dangerous to contest for a student. He may be tempted to rephrase a Socratic question for the examination: Do the examiners represent a given conception of knowledge because it is true, or is the knowledge true because it is represented by the examiners?

The knowledge of a discipline is not constituted solely by examinations. The production and verification of knowledge takes place in scientific research, professional practice and public debates. The earth will not become flat, nor stand still, if an examination committee should decide so. It is, however, the examiners who decide the locally valid and legitimate knowledge, the understanding of science the students will pledge allegiance to before they are allowed, through the examination, to enter the profession. The power exertion through examinations thus goes beyond the social selection and disciplining of students to also encompass selection and certification of a discipline's knowledge.

With power and knowledge intertwined, decentralisation of power in the educational system may also involve a decentralisation of the power to decide what is the true, valid and legitimate knowledge to be taught in school and evaluated at examinations. The decisive question by the current reform of the Norwegian educational system is whether it is possible to decentralise only rule and budget control and retain a central knowledge control. A national evaluation system in a decentralised educational system involves a contradiction between local autonomy in the management techniques and the central state's authority to retain a common national culture by defining what is the legitimate knowledge to be transmitted and evaluated in education. The issue remains whether the local communities will remain content with the exertion of control over school budgets and rules, with the *de facto* control of the educational content exercised through national evaluation systems. Or will the move to more local responsibility in school management also lead to demand for local influence on the educational content, to participate in the decisions of what knowledge is valuable for their children to learn in school?

Conclusion

Decentralisation involves a transition of power from a national to a local level. Evaluation involves the power to define the quality and value of knowledge. With the current decentralisation of the educational system of Norway the question arises whether decentralisation can be confined to management techniques or will also involve a decentralisation of the power to control and define the value of the knowledge transmitted in the schools.

An answer to this question will require concrete case studies of the reforms taking place, also drawing in the concrete experiences from countries with an extensive local autonomy of the educational system, and a further theoretical clarification of the relation of power and knowledge in educational evaluation.

On the basis of the present analyses, emphasising the intertwinedness of power and knowledge, it is questionable whether educational management techniques can be decentralised and a central state control of knowledge retained. In this analysis educational decentralisation is not merely a formal modernisation of management techniques or a democratic distribution of power to the local community, but involves the political question of the value of a common national heritage vs the local culture and the philosophical issue of universal vs. local knowledge.

References

Becker, H., Geer, B. & Hughes, F. (1968), *Making the Grade*, New York: John Wiley.

Bernstein, R. J. (1983), *Beyond Objectivism and Relativism*, Philadelphia: University of Pennsylvania Press.

Bloom, A. (1987), *The Closing of American Mind*, New York: Simon & Schuster.

Bloom, B. S., Hastings, T. J. & Madaus, G. F. (1971), *Handbook on Formative and Summative Evaluation of Student Learning*, New York: McGraw-Hill.

Darling-Hammond, L., Wise, A. E. & Pease, S. R. (1986), 'Teacher evaluation in the organisational context'. In House, E. R. (ed.), *New Directions in Educational Evaluation*. London: Falmer Press, pp. 203-53.

Dürkheim, E. (1977), *The Evolution of Educational Thought*, London: Routledge & Kegan Paul.

Eide, K. (1968), 'Some financial instruments and efficiency incentives in educational policy'. In *Budgetting, Programme Analysis and Cost-Effectiveness in Educational Planning*, Paris: OECD.

Fredriksen, N. (1984), 'The real test bias: Influences on teaching and learning', *American Psychologist*, 39, 193-202.

House, E. R. (1980), *Evaluating with Validity*, Beverly Hills, Calif: Sage.

House, E. R. (1990), 'Decentralised evaluation for Norway', (in this volume). Kvale, S. (1972), *Prüfung und Herrschaft*, Weinheim: Beltz.

Kvale, S. (1977), 'Examinations: From ritual through bureaucracy to technology', *Social Praxis*, 3, 197-206.

Kvale, S. (1980), *Spillet om karakter i gymnasiet. Elevinterviews om bivirkninger af adgangsbegrænsning*, København: Munksgaard.

Kvale, S. (1987), 'Examinations - A psychometric test or a censorship of knowledge?', *Nordisk Pedagogikk*, 7, 221-235.

Kvale, S. (1989), 'To validate is to question'. In S. Kvale (ed.), *Issues of Validity in Qualitative Research*, Lund: Studentlitteratur, 73-92.

Lundgren, U. (1990), 'Educational policy making, decentralisation and evaluation', (in this volume).

Lyotard, J. F. (1984), *The Postmodern Condition: A Report on Knowledge*, Minneapolis.

Løvlie, L. (1984), *Det pedagogiske argument*, Oslo: Cappelen.

Patton, M. Q. (1980), *Qualitative Evaluation Methods*, Beverly Hills, Calif: Sage.

Chapter 9

National assessment of knowledge and proficiency: educational intentive or bureaucratic decision-making?

Ingemar Wedman

April 1989 was in its own way a unique month for the Swedish education system, when for the first time a completely Swedish national assessment of knowledge and proficiency was carried out, with the participation of nearly 400 classes from the second and fifth school year. Analysis of the results is already in progress, and will continue for a considerable period in the future.

The Swedish assessment programme provides the starting-point for the present article and contributes only indirectly to the debate over the corresponding Norwegian programme. My contribution thus differs from those of my co-authors. However, the divergence will perhaps be made acceptable by my dealing with some of the many concrete questions and problems connected with a national assessment programme. A further reason for basing my article on the Swedish programme is that there are actually many similarities between the Swedish and the Norwegian education systems. Experiences from the Swedish assessment programme can perhaps therefore be transferred and viewed seriously with greater ease than may be the case with other comparisons. A third reason for a Swedish perspective is naturally the close connection in time between the Swedish programme and a possibly corresponding Norwegian programme. The questions and problems may thus have greater topical interest.

Before continuing with a brief description of the Swedish programme and a discussion of some fundamental questions relating to it, it is essential - not least in view of the Swedish discussion, insofar as one exists - that I say something about what the concepts of national assessment implies. As far as Sweden is concerned it has as least two meanings. First, national assessment means the sum of all evaluation activities in progress plus any that may be expected to start within foreseeable future. Such a wide definition can include not only assessment of knowledge and proficiency - perhaps not even primarily this - but also evaluations concerning pupils' health, and follow-up studies within the framework of official statistics on school and/or education.

The second meaning, which in Sweden preceded the one mentioned above, is solely assessment of knowledge and proficiency. It is this second definition that underlies the present article, though in a somewhat wider perspective than the terms knowledge and proficiency usually imply - a modification that will be discussed later.

The Swedish assessment programme

The development of the Swedish national assessment programme for knowledge and proficiency has taken more than 10 years. It began with National Board of Education discussions that later resulted in a research programme, one aim of which was to investigate the possibilities for a Swedish national assessment programme. The research programme was concluded during the financial year 1986/87, since when the programme has been a regular part of the National Board's responsibility for assessment and follow-up studies. From the date mentioned, responsibility for developing the instruments to be used has been placed on a number of research institutions at Swedish universities - primarily departments of education.

There are many ingredients and many problems in the history of the Swedish national assessment programme, a number of which are specific to Sweden and need not be mentioned here. Others have more to do with general principles and may be of interest in a context such as this. I shall return to some of these problems later.

The creation of the Swedish assessment programme is also interesting *per se*, and in its sixties. As is well known, the first IEA measurements (IEA = International Association for the Evaluation of Education and Achievement) were made in during the 1960s, and a characteristic of this programme at the time was the strongly comparative element between the participant countries. In its early days, one of the principal ambitions of the IEA programme was to compare different school systems for knowledge and proficiency, and right from the start the idea aroused considerable criticism. Apart from the objections to the 'knowledge Olympics' idea that might be said to be latent in the programme, the criticism was also voiced that the special interests of the individual countries were far too often made to the second place to common international interests. Therefore, as many critics said, the results were of extremely limited value (even though the results also received a great deal of attention in the various national arenas).

One result of the criticism of the IEA measurements was that for the second series considerably more space were given to the countries' special interests in the area of knowledge and proficiency. However, international interests, or those common to several countries, were still important. For Sweden, the greatest response to the results was in the field of mathematics, though this was a central response only - on a local level the results were scarcely noticed except for the demands and instructions issued by the central school authorities.

In the light of these IEA measurements, and in view of the way they were criticised concerning the national application of the results obtained, and not the least the possibilities of national applications of the results, it can be of interest to note the development of the national assessment programme. Such a programme fits in very well with developments since the 1960s in the sphere of national assessment of knowledge and proficiency.

It is questionable, however, whether this 'neutral' explanation for the development of the Swedish national assessment programme is adequate.

As we shall see later, there do not seem to be merely educational purposes behind creation of the kind of national assessment programme that has recently been developed in Sweden. One can also discern what might be called a legitimising motive on the part of central and regional authorities. To put it in another way: From the point of view of central and regional school authorities, one important motive behind national assessment of knowledge and proficiency is that it will enable them to retain control on a local level at a time when quite far-reaching moves are being made towards decentralisation. Such a control function also provides the authorities with a high degree of self-legitimisation.

The construction of the Swedish programme is interesting for several of its aspects - three of which are worth our attention here. In the first place it is extremely comprehensive; in all, its completion takes 20 classroom periods, which in international terms is an enormously long time. In addition, the teachers involved carry out marking and estimation of the material used for an average of a similar number of hours. The extensiveness of the programme has of course certain advantages, among them that the breadth of the curriculum has been reflected in the various instruments. Here it should be noted particularly that the programme does not test only the so-called basic proficiencies, most often defined via knowledge and proficiency in Swedish (mother tongue), mathematics and English (foreign language). The programme also includes knowledge of the surrounding world, defined primarily via knowledge and proficiency in civics and science. In addition - and this is perhaps the most interesting element of the programme content - there are measurements of two so-called practical/artistic subjects, music and art education. There is thus a certain justification for claiming that the assessment gives a fair picture of the current curriculum. It is otherwise easy in evaluating knowledge and proficiency to concentrate one-sidedly on the subjects that above and elsewhere are called basic proficiencies.

Another interesting aspect of the Swedish programme is the design of the individual subject instruments. An express ambition in the development of the various instruments has been to pay special attention to so-called complex knowledge. The reproduction of simple, easy-to-measure knowledge has systematically been given less prominence than varying attempts to reflect complex knowledge. In the field of natural science, for example, is included the task of performing an experiment in small groups. Other instruments assess the ability to express attitudes and discuss incidents or a course of events in the outside world - problems to which there is no 'correct' answer in the traditional sense. In these and similar ways it is not only knowledge *per se* that the various instruments focus on, but also how the pupils deal with different kinds of knowledge.

A third interesting aspect of the programme is the background information that has been gathered in connection with the measurement of knowledge and proficiencies. Teachers, pupils, parents and county education departments have all been asked to give their opinion of school and teaching, and have thus provided a basis for better understanding of the results from the more specific measurements of knowledge and proficiency. Here the aim has been to provide a detailed basis for interpretation of the various results.

There are two further aspects of the Swedish programme that it would have been important to add to this list: how far the programme tends to contribute to educational incentive and regeneration, and how intensive the feedback of information is to the local levels, primarily teachers, pupils and parents.

However, the programme is not at all clear in respect of these last two points, and this gives grounds for interesting and fundamental consideration of national assessment of knowledge and proficiency. In the main, the rest of this article will directly or indirectly deal with these two questions.

Aims and ambitions relating to national assessment of knowledge and proficiency

It is not particularly difficult to find arguments for an assessment programme of the kind that has recently been carried out in Sweden, already exists in other places, and is now being discussed in Norway. One of the most important tasks for schools in Sweden, as in other countries, is to see that pupils acquire knowledge and, in the words of the first paragraph of the Education Act: '... and to practise (the pupils') proficiencies, while co-operating with the home to promote pupils' development into balanced human beings and responsible members of society'. If there is a law (or its equivalent), it is natural to ask oneself how far it is followed. One way of several is to assess pupils' knowledge and proficiency by means of a national assessment programme of the kind in question here. That side of the matter seems to be fairly problem-free.

It is, however, one thing to state that compliance with the law can be studied by means of a national assessment programme, and quite another to form an opinion about what such an assessment should be used for, i.e. which measures explicit as well as implicit, are associated with the programme. On this point there is immediately a central, fundamental question concerning a programme of this kind.

Put very simply, one may speak of different aims in a national assessment programme. On the one hand the programme may have a purely decision-oriented aim with the intention of directly converting the results into various kinds of decisions. With such an objective obviously weak results should be immediately convertible into concrete measures of various kinds, e.g. timetable alterations, arranging in-serving training for teachers and so on. The control function of a programme with such an aim in fairly explicit.

Quite a different aim may be to utilise the results for stimulating educational debate among the school system's consumers and other interested parties. In this case the aim of the programme is not to dictate conditions for change but rather to provide consumers and interested parties with a basis for better understanding of what happens in school, and to give them an opportunity to reflect over why things look the way they do. In the long run, part of such an aim is of course also that it should be possible to effect concrete measures. However, responsibility for initiating such changes will have shifted from national to local level.

In the light of both these aims the Swedish assessment programme is not without interest. In official terms at least, both aims are represented. On the other hand, as the programme has taken concrete shape it has become possible to observe that emphasis has been laid on a view inclining towards measures and decisions. It seems as if the previously described development from an international perspective loses momentum at the national level. Interestingly enough, the local level is not left by this means without a share; quite the reverse, in fact - it is allotted its own place in the Swedish assessment model. Here there is a distinction between central and local assessment processes.

Superficially, such a division of the process of assessment might appear far sighted and well-motivated. Decentralisation is not in fact complete as yet, and the national level is after all responsible for the school system as a whole, and in Sweden we do have a nationally applicable curriculum.

At the same time there is reason to ask in this connection why there is interest at the national level in national assessment. To put the question in another way: What use will be made of the enormous amount of information that has been gathered? The class that participates in the Swedish assessment programme will receive only extremely limited information on its own performance. From each of the instruments included in the programme each class will be informed about the results of some of the questions, isolated from one another and disconnected from the considerable amount of background information that exists. To express it somewhat differently, each class will only in a very restricted sense be informed about its own performance.

The aforementioned educational element will in other words be severely curtailed.

Thus the question remains of what use will be made of the results from the programme. While awaiting a reply to this question, I shall proceed to offer some thoughts concerning feedback of obtained results.

How should the results be utilised?

It seems to me that one important ingredient for achieving the above-mentioned educational aim is the feedback, i.e. the relaying of results to teachers, pupils, parents school authorities and politicians. During the period we have been working with the programme idea, it has become increasingly clear that the feedback is of vital importance for the efficiency of the programme. In this connection the experience of other countries is also unequivocal in its implications.

As things are at present it is the American programme (National Assessment of Educational Progress NAEP) that is most successful with feedback of results. Over the years the organisers have moved increasingly further from the neutral attitude they held in the early stages of the programme, namely, that the information was general and did not incline in any particular direction. Much remains to be done, however, if the programme is to reach and influence the various interested parties.

For the English programme (Assessment of Performance Unit, APU), which has not placed as much stress on feedback an NAEP, the following interesting results are reported in 'Monitoring Children' (Gipps and Goldstein, 1983). On asking local education authorities (LEA) what effect APU results have had on the authorities' own assessments and test programmes, the authors learned:

> The biggest group, however, almost a third (30 per cent), made no response to this question or gave an answer which was irrelevant. This together with the high proportion which said the APU had no effect suggests that perhaps half the LEAs in the sample had not really taken much note of the APU, as though it was going on somewhere else which did not affect them (p. 140).

On how far ASSP, an earlier Australian assessment programme, relayed its results to teachers, parents and other potential interested parties, Power and Wood (1984) made the following comment:

> Less than 2 per cent of schools made changes in lesson-time allocation, curriculum, remedial activities, teaching, or testing practice as a consequence of the testing programme. In most schools, staff did not even discuss the results. Half of the parent organisations contacted knew nothing of the project and only 11 per cent said they were clear about what was being tested and what interpretations were justified. Teachers' unions, professional organisations, and other groups with a potential interest were aware of the results from media reports, but only 12 per cent had discussed them, and even fewer took action (p. 375).

The weakness of most foreign programmes in the field is insufficient appreciation of the central importance of feedback so that results can be taken into consideration and utilised, and lead to improvements in teaching and education standards.

One might well say, without risk of exaggeration, that for a Swedish national assessment programme to succeed, we need both horizontal and vertical information flow and discussion. For the results to be utilised constructively, they must be known and discussed by the various groups with a potential interest in the programme: teachers, parents and children, school boards and education authorities. Politicians and the National Board of Education should conduct more comprehensive and long-term discussions. If the programme is to flourish there should also be an improvement in the exchange of information between the various interest groups and between the various levels in the education system.

In view of the way in which many teachers receive and react to information from central sources, we can be fairly certain that if we make use of the usual channels for reporting results the programme will be received in the same way as other pedagogic material. A few people will be actively interested in the results, whereas the majority will take a critical, negative attitude or remain unconcerned. Adding further to the complexity of the problem are some of the paradoxes, myths and notions that are often connected with large organisational systems (Stevrin, 1984). Of the phenomena reported by Stevrin, the following are of special interest to us in a design context:

1. *More of the same.* Solving problems by using the same solution as before, but to an increased extent. For instance, if it is felt that information is not reaching its target, the amount of information is increased without considering a change of content and perhaps of information channel.

Bearing in mind many teachers' attitude to pedagogic material, we must realise that we cannot simply use channels currently available but must find other ways and new methods of disseminating results.

2. *Negative problem-solving*. A method that predominantly focuses on rectifying errors and defects in the present situation, i.e. greater stress is laid on what is wrong now than on how things could be ideally. The consequence of this can be that the more things are improved, the more they continue to be the same as before.

From this we can learn that results should not only be presented as a description of the present situation and as basis for solving current problems, but also should focus equally on what we hope might be achieved in the future and thereby help interest groups to develop strategies for this.

3. *The utopia syndrome*. The aims of the operation are considered to be good, but the people who are to achieve them are seen as unsatisfactory because the aims are not achieved.

This is something often heard from teachers describing how they are frequently made the scapegoats for much of what is wrong with schools and the results they achieve (or otherwise). In an introductory phase a good deal of energy must therefore be used to inform people clearly that the programme is intended to be a support for teachers in their work and not a means of controlling or questioning their competence.

4. *Oversubscribing the future*. Unwillingness to make any sacrifices for the benefit of the future. Use of resources is restricted to the present, and they are insufficient to solve or deal with approaching problems.

Judging by the above-mentioned study of teachers, this phenomenon is significant for work in today's schools. The school day is so full of problems that all available time is taken up with finding solutions that can help people to function for the moment. As a result of this there is no room for pedagogic discussion or attempts to find working methods that might help the school of the future to avoid the problems of today.

5. *The information paradox*. This phenomenon has much in common with 'more of the same'. Briefly one could say that it means that excessive concentration on quantity of information will indeed increase knowledge of situation, but knowledge of action may very possibly decrease. One way of counteracting this might be to increase the quality of information.

This could mean concentrating on interpreting results instead of simply presenting statistical summaries - naturally bearing in mind the whole time the particular consumer/interest groups who are the targets. Another important principle is that interpretations and possible solutions should be presented according to the strategy of 'the unfinished'. An unfinished idea or solution has greater power than one which is completed. This strategy also caters for the human need for active participation to achieve a feeling of sharing in and contributing to a process of change.

6. *Reduced self-regulation.* A common tendency is that when external is increased there is a corresponding decrease in internal control, which in turn is seen as justification for a further increase in external control. If this vicious circle is to be avoided, efforts must be made to design the programme so that it is not seen as an organ of external control but rather as a means of helping those who work within the system. If successful, this can contribute to the creation of active discussion and a school climate where the work units themselves to a certain extent take responsibility for evaluation their own activities.

In addition to the above paradoxes, myths and notions, a further complication is that the people concerned are on different levels within the system and are also involved to varying degrees in direct school activity. Of these people, we see teachers, parents and children as particularly important interest groups.

It is probably accepted without question that teachers constitute an important interest group. That parents are also such a group is made clear by education law, have a vital role in cooperating with school to prepare children for adult life. Such cooperation requires, however, that the school is acquainted with the individual child and his/her family situation, and that the parents are acquainted with school, its aims and working methods. Results from our own study of parents (Karp, 1986) suggest, however, that this is not usually the case.

Instead it is clear that there is a gap between parents' view of school, its aim, its methods and work content and the view of the school itself. Helping to reduce this gap and to give parents a basis for knowing about and participating in discussion and cooperating with school on questions of teaching and education - all this should be seen as a self-evident task for a programme of the kind in question here. If the programme is successful on this point it will mean that other interest groups such as politicians, local education authorities and National School Board officials will have a more extensive part to play.

For the National School Board it may for instance be a question of utilising new information from the work in local schools and assisting LEA's might initiate local assessments by bearing in mind results and the activity that these can lead to out in the schools.

For the politicians involved, an effective programme should mean greater consideration paid to the views of the public they are elected to represent and thereby increased opportunity for acting in accordance with the democratic ideals we all support. More bluntly, one could say that if we are unable to stimulate and involve teachers, parents and pupils, the results of the programme will be of little interest to either politicians or state education officials.

Irrespective of which interest group the programme is intended for, there are some guiding principles to be borne in mind. It should be designed so that its results are seen as providing support or the means of dealing with a problem-filled existence. This means in turn that the programme will not be able to provide any definitive solutions, because the problems of school are a part of its daily life. Instead it should help those involved (heads, teachers, parents, pupils, politicians, education officials) to tackle situations as they are, on the basis of real conditions.

This means further that the results should not be presented solely as a description of the current situation and as a basis for dealing with existing problems, but should to an equal extent focus on possible future achievements and help the various interest groups to find strategies for this.

To put it in another way, the programme should not simply consist of instrument construction, information gathering and summaries of results; it must also contain an active component comprising interpretation of results and a well thought-out strategy for information design and its dissemination to the programme's interest groups.

Incorporating result reporting and information distribution right from the start is a prerequisite for achieving the pedagogic aim advocated here (see also Karp, Stage and Wedman, 1985, p. 44 and pp. 50-52).

Some concluding reflections

I have chosen in my article to discuss the question of national assessment of knowledge and proficiency on a very concrete basis, i.e. experience of the recently completed Swedish national assessment programme. There are undoubtedly risks in attempting to do this - not the least of which is that the theoretical perspective, of central importance, may take second place to concrete and practical questions.

I have also chosen to restrict the discussion to only a few parts of the national assessment programme. Other parts could easily have also been discussed.

It was not only laziness that led me to restrict myself to the questions I have dealt with. I find it interesting that even internationally there is still no analysis worth the name of the real aims of programmes like that discussed here, and even less any debate over the pedagogically interesting aspects of such programmes.

I find it also interesting to note (this too in the light of those experiences there always are in connection with programmes of this type) that the question of how to relay the results to those who provide the information and those who ultimately convert curricula into pedagogic practice is not considered very important.

Together these two complex questions lead to a situation where the educational value of national assessment programmes for knowledge and proficiency cannot be estimated and at worst might be negative. Perhaps in view of this one might even ask whether the central school authorities, and those who are ultimately responsible for the programmes, even have an educational end in mind. Perhaps programmes of this kind fulfil different, more important, functions for the central authorities?

References

Gipps, C. & Goldstein, H. (1983), *Monitoring Children. An Evaluation of the Assessment of Performance Unit*, London: Heinemann Educational Books.

Murray, Å. & Liljefors, R. (eds) (1983), Mathematics in Swedish schools (in Swedish: Matematik i svensk skola), Stockholm: Liber, Skolöverstyrelsen, Utbildningsforskning, FoU-rapport 46.

Power, C. & Wood, R. (1984), *National Assessment in Australia: An Evaluation of the Australian Studies in Student Performance Project*, EDRC Report, No. 35.

Stevrin, P. (1984), *Professional Problem Solving* (in Swedish: Professionell problemlösning), Lund: Studentlitteratur.

Part III

THE STATE OF THE ART: Creating evaluative systems

Chapter 10

The American research on educational evaluation and the national evaluation in Sweden

Sigbrit Franke-Wikberg

When EMIL, 'The Norwegian Project on National Evaluation and the Quality of Education', calls for papers (1989) the expressed aim is 'to attain an overview of international research and experiences on the "ecology" of decentralisation and evaluation' (p. 2). EMIL seems to approach its main issues in a promising way: critical learning through others' successes and failures.

As a Swedish evaluator who has recently spent a year in California[1] I will start to share my impressions of the American debate on education and evaluation. As you know, the pedagogical currents from the other side of the Atlantic sooner or later reach us, whereupon they often, without any reservations, are accepted and taken over. After having been filtered through 'Big Brother Sweden' Norway also, nonetheless unreflectingly, usually adopts them. Although the American influence seems to be ignored, as 'the spirit of European community' steadily grows, it will most certainly remain very strong. Many burning issues in the US can easily be spotted in the Swedish and Norwegian discussions and school reforms, whereas others will no doubt soon appear in one form or another. Even if some features are worth testing, others ought to be avoided or opposed.

After having drawn some parallels between the American and the Swedish 'ecology' of evaluation I will, in the second part of this chapter, give a brief outline of the main evaluation approaches, after which I will draw attention to the national evaluation programme that is being developed in Sweden.[2] The three main aspects according to my interpretation of the conference invitation, i.e. the demands on evaluation and the impact and the use of evaluation, are all touched upon, although very briefly and incompletely. Then again, a critical review of the Swedish attempts may offer some valuable experiences for the Norwegian project. My chapter ends with some normative comments on evaluation strategies in a decentralised system.

In relation to Chapter 3 by Ulf Lundgren, this chapter could be described as contributing a few more illustrations and confirmations of some of his analytical concepts and conclusions.

The American arena

What first struck me on the American education arena was the feeling of a serious crisis being whipped up. The focus has gradually climbed up the school levels during the 1980s and it has extended into the three R's. In the last few years high schools and now colleges and universities are highlighted. Even more than before teachers and schools of education have to act as public and sanctioned 'sputum cups'.

The national reports on education seem to play an important role as crisis-builders strongly supported by the mass media, whereas research work presenting a more balanced picture of the situation is passed over in silence. 'A nation at risk'[3] has a title symptomatic of the message delivered by these reports. An analysis of the three national reports on the critical state of higher education[4] reveals that their uninhibited conclusions are unfounded - they just refer to each other and these references are taken as the evidence of a prevailing crisis.[5] The miserable state of things is also fertilised by the bestsellers on education published in the last few years, all wallowing in terms of crisis. The public trust in education is undermined and this is, for example, expressed in the upswing of private schools and of voucher-suggestions as well as in the questioning of the relative autonomy of universities.[6] Reasons are given for a firmer federal and state involvement and control and certain conditions for centralisation are fulfilled,[7] all in accordance with what was said earlier (Chapter 3): 'What has to be reformed has consequently to be identified as being in a crisis and, furthermore, that the crisis must be identified as caused by what has to be the solution'.

In these flaming discussions proofs of satisfactory quality are, not surprisingly, demanded. The question about how the situation at school is to be evaluated is accentuated and formulated with renewed vigour in what Ernest House (1986) calls 'the new industrialization round', that education so clearly is subjected to. Concepts such as accountability, efficiency and rationality are, however, the prestige words and standardised tests are the passwords on the evaluation 'arena of realisation'.[8] Even if there are projects aiming at identifying indicators covering a broader spectrum of variables than specific knowledge and skills and even if evaluation problems are no longer only discussed as technical problems as was the case 15 or 20 years ago, it seems that in practice it is the students' results on several, but the same kind of tests, that are used as the quality measure of schools. In the cries for evaluation of higher education no attention is drawn to all that has been done so far to indicate the quality of undergraduate studies. The evaluation programmes being developed for universities and schools of education focus on direct measures of student performance. In practice test results are or will be the basis for rewarding or punishing institutions or the responsible persons while a seemingly more efficient education is being created.[9] When articles in the daily press presented the outcomes of the 5-year reform period in high schools[10] they did so in terms of comparisons of students' test results then and now and between schools in their own and in other states. Typically enough, references to specific contexts and conditions were seldom or never given.

I was also struck by the intense discussion about pedagogical content, used both to explain why this bottom quality of education was touched upon and to inform what has to be done if it is not to sink completely. When, for instance, Allan Bloom (1987) describes the degeneration of higher education in his bestseller *The Closing of the American Mind* he proposes his 'solution of good books' according to a classic ideal of education.[11] But Bloom, in his élite world, is not the only one arguing for the definition of a 'core curriculum' of education. However, related to compulsory school or high school 'cultural literacy' seems to be the key concept but with roughly the same meaning: to specify what knowledge all students must absolutely master after finishing school. In his book, *Cultural Literacy - What Every American Needs to Know*, E. D. Hirsch Jr. (1987) lays the blame on Dewey's and Piaget's dominating but empty pedagogically theories for the assumed miserable situation in school. Page after page he presents a list of names, concepts and years defining the core of knowledge that everybody should master. The same ideas are transferred to specific subjects by means of achievement tests in order to show how bad the situation is and to argue for the importance of that particular subject. The study by Ravitz and Finn Jr. (1987) on what 17-year-old students know about American history and literature is just one example of what is going on.

A lively discussion about content is healthy and important - of which, I think, there is too little in Sweden and probably also in Norway. At the same time the current American debate illustrates how ideologically marked the contributions to the debate are as soon as questions about what is taught or what to teach are asked. In the US neo-conservative demands for reforms obviously dominate the core curriculum discussions. The national touch is evident; there is much of 'Keep America American!' in the debate. It is, for example, feared that the already talented Asian students will become more numerous as well as cleverer.[12]

As in other Western capitalist countries there are growing problems of controlling education.[13] A natural solution in the decentralised American system seems to be the shift of policy-making towards the centre through different means one of which is evaluation.[14] The national reports and the programmes of evaluation in the form of standardised tests express these ambitions of centralisation as do the evaluation centres that are increasingly being built up in state capitals as well as in local communities. The public distrust makes this process easier. The steering problems and the solution strategy, the proposals to rise the standard and the quality of education as well as the national features of many reform attempts must, of course, be related to a keener international competition on the economic market, to a reduced national power and to the great importance attached to education in this context. The results of the IEA tests are taken into serious consideration. The requested proofs of quality must also be related to the harder struggle for resources between fragmentary sectors in which high costs for education have to be legitimised. All these matters push towards a thinking in terms of efficiency concealed in a philosophical spirit of business economics. Strong commercial interests held by the big testing companies also accelerate and influence the assessment of quality or efficiency of education. This partial and stunted evaluation has, of course, in its turn an impact on teaching and on learning. There is a risk that teachers may be tempted to teach in accordance with the tests in order to get as high results as possible. Five years after 'A nation at risk' a certain rise in the standard is reported on the basis of the test results of high school students, but it is also stated that the focus of teaching is on memorisation and recall.[15] The teachers claim that the students' 'gains come with low teacher morale, more bureaucratic red tape and political interference'.[16]

An already restricted teacher autonomy might, in other words, be still more cut down, which does not fit in well with ambitions of professionalisation in a deeper sense. Instead the professional teacher becomes the technician or the engineer of schools or of classrooms. The huge project on teachers and teacher training conducted by professor Lee Shulman (1988) at Stanford University aims, for instance, on one hand at determining the core curriculum or the knowledge basis for the profession and for teacher training, and, on the other, at constructing a programme of national evaluation. This programme will be the uniform test guaranteeing the standard and the quality of teachers and of teaching and it will make it possible 'to sift the wheat from the chaff' more effectively, to sort teachers into groups of 'the very good', 'the mediocre' and 'the bad'. The parallels to the system of a doctor's licence implies that the assessment might be used for decisions on giving or not giving the driving licence to teachers. Such a system aims, of course, at rising the current low status of the teacher profession but, as I have roughly outlined in the above, the cost will be high including a tough control, a limited freedom for teachers and a questionable philosophy of knowledge.

The Swedish arena

Some people may think that I have painted the American evaluation arena in too black colours, but I do not think that this is the case. Some may respond to it in the following way: 'Oh, how terrible it is over there! But it is not, and it will never become like that in Sweden - or in Norway'. Towards such a reaction I will draw attention to some current Swedish signs, which make it worthwhile reflecting more than once on where we stand and where we might be heading.

1. In the debate on the public sector, efficiency, productivity and responsibility have become the concepts of honour. The same philosophy characterises, implicitly or explicitly, the discussion and the documents related to schools. One recent and manifest example is the investigation of how time is used in high schools conducted by the National Board of Education and the County School Boards (1989). Another and implicit example is the exclusion of goals of equality in the Bill of the year, which is remarkable for such an important social democratic school text.

2. The interests in adjusting to the demands arising from the desired European cooperation are strong. In the Government Bill of 1989 high school reforms are justified by the discussions held in EC countries. The connection is made to industrial needs, to economic growth and to productivity. As such an initial position is not rejected, it is consequently accepted.

3. The renewed interests in evaluation express the rational paradigm now wide awake after more than 15 years of slumbering. Straight answers to questions of efficiency and productivity are required. Evaluation has at the same time become the main solution to the crisis of identity experienced by the two National Boards of Education in the last decades as the reform strategy of decentralisation is applied to solve the problems of steering the system of education. A national programme of evaluation has quietly been developed focusing on tests of 8 and 11 year- old students. In some years the turn will come to students in junior high and in high schools. At the university level the National Board of Universities and Colleges runs a project on 'performance indicators'.

4. In the discussion about the quality of the Swedish schools related to the OECD countries a positive and optimistic picture is given, the basis of which is the results of some standardised tests, i.e. the IEA tests and an achievement test in geography embracing nine countries. The need for easily comprehensible measures and seemingly fit for use in interna-

tional comparisons might push on these evaluation models now so dominant in the United States.

5. The arguments about school resources in terms of 'cash limit' is a good example of the current spirit. Proposals for individual salaries to teachers should be seen in the same light.

6. The concept of 'core curriculum' is already and without a Swedish translation being transferred to Swedish universities, where it tends to be adopted with few ideological reservations. Listening to the Swedish Minister of Education speak about cultural heritage may make you believe that the concept of 'cultural literacy' will soon and in its full meaning come into fashion.

Many more examples could be given,[17] showing that what is going on in the US is not too far away from the actual or the future situation in Sweden.[18] One important step of preparation for the development of national evaluation programmes is, in my opinion, to critically valuate trends and so-called modernities, to examine what they stand for and to take up a position for or against them in order not to be taken by surprise. The watchfulness has, hopefully, increased in one way or another concerning some of the aspects I have dealt with.

The main streams of educational evaluation

I would like to begin with an outline of the evaluation background I have in mind, and which, even if it is unnecessarily familiar and elementary to many, nevertheless is important for the understanding of my viewpoints of the national evaluation programme under development in Sweden.

The concept of evaluation has become more diffuse and woolly with its increasing use by more and more people. The general meaning, i.e. to express the value of or to make a qualitative judgement on something says something but not much of what it is all about. Nor does the fact that educational evaluation is basically a matter of analysing and commenting on how the goals and the outcomes of an educational programme are related to each other make the concept much clearer. The existing evaluation models nevertheless represent different solutions to the problem of how to describe and to interpret the relationship between the expected and the actual results. The model gives an answer to a solution, and it reflects a specific outlook on teaching and learning at the same time as it represents a certain paradigm of research. In order to be able to explain what evaluation is you must, to express it in other words, know why it is conducted, what is evaluated, to whom, by whom and how. Not until solutions and answers have been provided to such questions will it be possible to explain what an evaluation is actually about.

Evaluation as a phenomenon in the educational context has, from the 1960s onwards, become increasingly important. In the 1960s the so called 'technology of education' was flourishing and evaluation models manifesting ideas from the life of production were elaborated and used. The evaluation was often carried out in order to provide answers to questions of efficiency, effectiveness and productivity, the goals were described and broken down to measurable entities that were assessed through tests of specific knowledge and abilities. This enterprise was based on a firmly rooted belief in the possibilities to plan and steer the educational system in a rational way. The evaluation was often wanted by decision-makers on the central level. The evaluator was considered, by others as well as by himself, to be providing a neutral and an objective basis for the decisions. Descriptions and advanced statistical processings of test results from huge samples of students were characteristic features of this method. Sometimes these results were also compared with the results of other groups of students in order to establish how successful the educational programme was. It was a question of a summative evaluation, a summing-up control of goal fulfilment. In times of expansion and when the focus was on the issue of school organisation this type of evaluation, of which I have given such a simplistic picture in this chapter, was regarded as reasonably satisfactory by the decision-makers.[19]

During the 1970s, when the golden age was drawing towards its end and when optimism was replaced by pessimism as the expected outcomes in many cases did not appeal,[20] the confidence in reforms, in reform strategy as well as in the evaluation of these reforms was shaken. With more and more functions assigned to education in a changed and in a changing society the evaluation appeared to be too restricted and too narrow-minded. With a transition of the reform strategy from top-down to bottom-up and with the ambitions of decentralisation attached to it, the aim at exercising control was replaced by change and development as the main aims of evaluation. So called formative evaluations, contributing knowledge for the purpose of gradually improving education and which were primarily addressed to those directly involved in the educational process, were wanted. The focus on the issues of pedagogical content added to emphasising the inadequacy of the evaluations up to now. A number of models were developed in the 1970s aiming at capturing and portraying the reality of school in its full complexity.[21] No answers of methodology were given with these models, but various qualitative methods and techniques were applied to give as complete descriptions as possible. At the central level it became more precarious than before. Within this tradition the evaluator hardly could offer the neutral and objective basis for decision-making, which in the opinion of the administrators was necessary.

These main types of evaluation, briefly described, have existed since then and still exist side by side.[22] The two codes of evaluation have not, however, been equally alert at the same time. In the 1970s the evaluation oriented towards control and towards production took a nap while pink waves were roaring and starlings flew in the winds of 'the alternative pedagogics'.[23] Evidently, the rest has now come to its end and it is not surprising to find that the 'product-evaluation' has revived in the blue surgings overflowing this decade. If the dozing evaluation code of change will henceforth fall asleep or be brought back to a new life is somewhat uncertain at the moment.

'Theory-oriented evaluation' as the recommended approach

The kind of evaluation recommended by me, the so called 'theory-oriented evaluation', belongs to the second of the two approaches, of which the main aim is change. As with many other models of the 1970s, theory-oriented evaluation is to be regarded as a reaction to the simplified and misleading descriptions offered by 'product-evaluation', and to the whole outlook on education and evaluation that it represents. At the same time theory-oriented evaluation is also to be seen as a reaction to the more closely related models because of the two following reasons depending on each other: on one hand the ambition to give good descriptions but not seriously try to understand and to explain the picture presented by the evaluation and, on the other, the fact that the descriptions given with good reason could be accused of being too subjective and too specifically connected with the situation in question. To sum up, my main criticism could be described in terms of 'theory-lacking', something that would clarify the choice of name for the approach, i.e. theory-oriented evaluation.[24]

As time goes on I sometimes think that another designation would have been better, owing to the fact that theory is both very strange and pretentious to many people. What it is all about is, however, to formulate to yourself and to others a frame of reference related to the phenomenon to be evaluated, to indicate from what perspective the evaluation is conducted, to encircle the object of the evaluation and to clarify the meaning attributed to this object by providing it with a context. The frame of reference is simply the evaluator's formulated reflections about what is to be evaluated.

There are at least three reasons for working out such a frame of reference: it gives a steering-gear for the most important information to collect; it gives a screen for the interpretation of the information; and it gives a trade description that makes it possible for the interested parties to judge the standpoint and the value of the evaluation.

The theory-oriented evaluation approach offers a simple model of ideas including the three components: conditions (external and internal), process and results. These components must all be illuminated in every evaluation study if it is to inform why results are successful or unsuccessful and what could and what should be changed.[25] Theory-oriented evaluation lifts you above the simple level of description and gives you knowledge that goes beyond the specific situation. Knowledge is built up having a value of explanation and generalisation, knowledge giving you a basis for critical reflections on the education programme as well as a basis for change and improvement. Indeed, useful knowledge.[26]

It is important to emphasise that this evaluation approach is not at all reserved for researchers and/or experts. Theory-oriented evaluation is similarly useful to people responsible for evaluation on all school levels, e.g. to administrators on national, regional or local levels, to teachers at any specific school. It is true of all of us that nothing is as practical as a good theory. It is also true that thinking and acting according to theory-oriented evaluation is positive and constructive if the aim is to get a good basis for judgement of what to change, if anything.

The theory-oriented evaluation approach might be accused of still being too abstract and woolly in some respects. There are, however, several evaluation studies carried out that are to be seen as concrete examples of the approach.[27] Attempts at clarifying the approach and at showing non-researchers how to put it into practice have been made.[28] However, it cannot be denied that much remains to be done.

The Swedish national evaluation programme - in what furrow has it been planted?

My comments on the national evaluation programme being developed in Sweden are to be seen in relationship to the roughly outlined background given above. This evaluation programme represents essentially the same outlook and the same aim as 'product-evaluation'; it also reflects the current trends of evaluation in the United States, it seems to me. Even if more information is said to be added to the standardised tests of specific knowledge and skills, the main impression is that these tests form the core of the evaluation. They are assumed to describe the products of education and to be used by the National Board of Education to establish how efficient or how inefficient the school is. The National Board's interests in educational steering and control occupy, more or less implicitly, the seat of honour.

The national evaluation programme was first initiated just as a project of testing students and for years it was defined in accordance with that objective (cf. Wedman, 1987). Experts on test construction were very much in demand and became tied to the programme, whereas evaluation researchers working within a broader evaluation frame were looked upon as having little to do with the programme and nothing to contribute to it. The main effort in terms of time, strength and money was put on the part of the programme dealing with 'the tests of products'. Today, tests are ready-made and in the spring semester of 1989 they also began to come into use. The emphasis put on issues, such as testing representative groups of students and showing results of general applicability suggests furthermore that the evaluation programme belongs to the furrow of 'product-evaluation'. It seems to be very important to test a sufficient number of students dispersed all over the country to get information usable for comparing the efficiency of different schools.

My criticism of the Swedish national evaluation programme related to compulsory school is, of course, on the same line as the objections I raised to the dominating evaluation approaches in the 1960s and is thus in line also with my description of what floods the American educational and evaluational arenas and what slips into the Swedish ones in the 1980s. A rough summary of some of my comments on the evaluation programme under development commissioned by the National Board of Education is as follows:

1. It is remarkable how the National Board has presented or, more correctly, has avoided introducing this evaluation programme to the public. For years very few persons were informed about the extensive work on developing the tests. These standardised tests have taken form in a seemingly confidential silence. When the evaluation programme was presented at last, just some months before students in grade two and in grade five were to be tested, this was done as if being the overall and total evaluation of the Swedish school - which, of course, is not the case.

2. As was mentioned before, researchers representing broad and deep knowledge of educational evaluation (e.g. Urban Dahllöf, Erik Wallin, Ulf P. Lundgren) have not been involved at all in the development of the programme. Until recently only experts on test construction have been engaged by the National Board of Education in this huge and long-lived project.

3. The real aims and functions of the programme are, I suppose, to raise the central control, which has not been explicitly said, however, even in the appointed group of test experts. Different interpretations of aims and confusion about what answers to give to crucial evaluation questions have been manifested, i.e. by reducing the general feedback model of the programme to a small satellite project;[29] by choosing 'the wrong grades' (2 and 5) if considering that the curriculum is organised according to stages (1-3, 4-6) and not to grades.

4. As the very heart of the programme consists of these tests, the goals and quality of education is given a restricted and partial definition. It reflects an evaluation model within the rational paradigm at the same time as it represents a view on education, knowledge and on evaluation, which is too simplified. In other words: 'Education is conceived as occurring in an enclosed, formally administered world' (Popkewitz and Weklage, 1973).

5. The national evaluation programme does not fulfill demands of giving a basis for improving schools or teaching. It lacks knowledge of the external and internal conditions as well as of the process. Even if the strategy of adding up information is being desperately used now, no frame of reference seems to exist giving clues to what data to collect besides test information.

6. It is likely to expect a hectic activity of delivering information from classrooms up the school levels without anyone really knowing why and to whom this is done. Similarly, it is likely to expect the use of test results on central administrative level, not least for national and international comparisons of results, i.e. of educational quality.

7. A focusing on figures and diagrams showing students' test results can be predicted judging from the comments on the outcome of the IEA tests in the Swedish newspapers. Basic problems of a social political nature will be ignored both in the general school debate and in policy-making, I fear.[30]

8. Last, but not least, there is the risk that this evaluation programme will have a questionable impact on teachers, on teaching and on learning.

In other words: the Swedish National Board of Education has mistakenly developed a narrow evaluation programme for the compulsory school,[31] without having answered the basic evaluation questions in the first place and without having learnt much from others' experiences. As a consequence the Board can be caught in a trap of its own.

Some concluding remarks and some normative recommendations

It is high time to some way modulate the picture I have sketched above of the evaluation arenas and of the specific national evaluation programme. It seems important to me to explicitly stipulate, if overlooked by anyone, that I have deliberately polarised the main approaches of evaluation. These are described in their extreme forms as is also true of my description of the split elements of the national evaluation programme being developed in Sweden. As a consequence of that 'the product-evaluation' and the emphasis on tests on one hand and 'the theory-oriented evaluation' on the other are discussed as two unambiguous poles.

It is worth underlining that I have no objections to tests of knowledge and skills as such and I certainly believe that the actual tests may give interesting descriptions and important information about the results of the mediation of knowledge in school. The reservations made primarily apply to unfulfilled but legitimate demands on evaluation and to undesired use and impact of an evaluation with its focus on simple and specific products measured by tests.

I also fully understand that the activity in schools cannot be allowed to run wild and that some central control is needed. However, students' test results are not a sound and sufficient basis for such a steering, I think, a steering that involves more of ideological and political considerations than is explicitly pronounced.

Furthermore, I realise that it is not just difficult but impossible to design a national evaluation programme without objections. Anyhow, I will finish by very briefly presenting some totally unpretentious recommendations concerning evaluation that might be valuable to consider.

In a school system characterised by ambitions to decentralise decision-making there are some evaluation strategies that seem to be more in line with such ambitions than others. With the main aim being to get a good picture and a critical analysis of the real situation at schools, i.e. a well-founded basis of information to decide if and what to change, various evaluation activities are worth trying on different levels. On the local level internal self-evaluation in various forms is very useful and important, I assume. This evaluation should be closely connected with continuous developing work with teachers as main evaluators assisted by experts on evaluation, if needed. The models of 'peer evaluation', carried out for a long time at American universities and colleges as well as by CNAA in Great Britain, I have found can serve as rich sources of inspiration.

It is also high time to argue for 'bottom-up-evaluations' including not just students' evaluation of teaching and of teachers but also i.a. teachers' evaluations of the local, regional and national boards and how their function of steering and controlling the schools is really carried out.

On the central level one important task is thus to stimulate and to support evaluation activities on the floor. Another task is to obtain broad knowledge and statistics related to social and political goals of education, e.g. equal opportunities for children from different social classes and for girls and boys - besides information about what knowledge and skills specific groups of students have. A case-study approach is applicable when a lively overall and detailed picture of the school situation is wanted. As a result of studies like these, some aspects might crystallise as necessary to further investigate and illuminate through separate evaluation studies.

Administrators on the central level are also responsible for initiating and financing a thorough meta-evaluation,[32] which in any case is an important element in the build-up of an evaluation system that has been going on for years in Sweden and will now take place in Norway.

The role of educational researchers or evaluators is given in all of these respects mentioned above. And, as has been argued before, the thought-model expressed in theory-oriented evaluation is useful not just for these evaluators but also for administrators of all kinds as well as for teachers involved in evaluation activities - on condition that the main aim is improvement rather than control. Many issues of evaluation have been touched on in this chapter. Hopefully, EMIL will have something to learn from what I have discussed here, while considering some of the problems that have been pointed out.

Footnotes

1. As a Visiting Associate at the Center for Studies in Higher Education (CSHE), University of California, Berkeley.

2. This program is presented by the National Board of Education ('Skolöverstyrelsen' in Swedish) for instance in PM 1988-03-01(a) and in PM 1988-03-01(b).

3. The report was published by the National Commission on Excellence in Education (1983).

4. The three reports are *To Reclaim a Legacy. A Report on the Humanities in Higher Education* by W. Bennett, US Secretary of Education (1984); *Involvement in Learning: Realizing the Potential of American Higher Education* by the Study Group on the Conditions of Excellence in American Higher Education (1984); and *Integrity in the College Curriculum* by The Association of American Colleges (1985).

5. See Martin Trow's interesting analysis (1987).

6. In my paper *Evaluating Education Quality on the Institutional Level* (1989), the actual situation is characterised in more detail and with references given.

7. Among others: Goodlad (1987), Neave (1987).

8. See Franke-Wikberg (1989), *op. cit.*, footnote 1. The expression 'arena of realization' is from Lundgren (1989).

9. Cf. Ernest House's article in this book.

10. At the beginning of 1988 several articles were to be found, for instance in the *San Francisco Chronicle* (cf. Franke-Wikberg, 1989)

11. See also my review of Bloom's book in *Forskning om utbildung*, 1988.

12. See Franke-Wikberg (1989), *op. cit.*, if interested in a deeper analytical description.

13. See Lundgren's analysis of changed relationships between state and general education and between civil society and general education.

14. Evaluation could be characterised as the fourth steering system, where the other three are the legal, the economic and the ideological systems. (Lundgren, 1989, p. 33). For the centralisation process in the US see, for example, House, 1986; Popkewitz, 1988.

15. See *San Francisco Chronicle*, May 1988.

16. See *San Francisco Chronicle*, April 1988.

17. The idea of profiling schools, the talk about increased freedom of choice for students, proposals for permanent grouping of students in compulsory school according to ability, etc. etc.

18. When reading Lundgren's description of the situation in Norway (1989) you could add '... or in Norway'.

19. Some good examples of Swedish summative evaluations are the ones carried out by Härnquist (1958; 1960) as well as the curriculum studies by Dahllöf (1960) and Bromsjö (1965).

20. Härnquist's studies (1978a, b) were very important in this context. See also my analysis from 1981.

21. Swedish evaluators were most inspired by the so-called responsive and illuminative evaluation models (Stake, 1974; Parlett and Hamilton, 1973).

22. For interesting analyses of these main types of evaluations see House (1978) and Lindensjö and Lundgren (1983).

23. The metaphors are to be found in articles by Callewaert and Kallos (1976) and by Lundgren (1982).

24. For a description of the approach see e.g. Franke-Wikberg (1983) and Franke-Wikberg and Frykholm (1987).

25. The theory-oriented evaluation approach is strongly inspired by Urban Dahllöof's works (e.g. 1967; 1971) as well as by Ulf P. Lundgren's works (e.g. 1972; 1977). It was further developed by the author together with Martin Johansson at first (e.g. 1975; 1976) and together with Ulf P. Lundgren later on (e.g. 1980; 1981).

26. My definition of usefulness is broader than Lander's seems to be (Lander, 1987).

27. i.e. the evaluation studies conducted by members of the so-called Umeå-group and by researchers at the Stockholm Institute of Education.

28. e.g. Franke-Wikberg, 1983; Franke-Wikberg and Frykholm, 1987.

29. This main idea was continuously stressed by one of the experts, Ingemar Wedman.

30. Cf. also Popkewitz (1984).

31. The state of evaluation related to high school and to higher education is such that I found reasons for being more optimistic concerning these school levels. The strategy of evaluation related to high school is described by Johansson (1987).

32. A meta-evaluation was recently demanded in a government bill, see Prop. 1988/1989;4.

References

Association of American Colleges (1985), *Integrity in the Academic Curriculum: A Report to the Academic Community*, Washington DC: The Project on Redefining the Meaning and Purpose of Baccalaureate Degrees, February.

Bennett, W.J. (1984), *To Reclaim a Legacy: A Report on the Humanities in Higher Education*, Washington DC: The National Endowment for the Humanities, November.

Bloom, A. (1987), *The Closing of the American Mind: How Higher Education Has Failed Democracy and Impoverished the Souls of Today's Students*, New York: Simon and Schuster.

Bromsjö, B. (1965), *Samhällskunskap som skolämne*, Stockholm: Svenska Bokförlaget/Norstedts.

Callewaert, S. and Kallós, D. (1976), 'Den rosa vågen i svensk pedagogik', *Forskning om utbildning, 1976*, 3 (1), s 311-38.

Dahllöf, U. (1960), *Kursplaneundersökningar i matematik och modersmålet. Ak avh. 1957 års skolberedning III. SOU*, 15, Stockholm: Ecklesiastikdepartementet.

Dahllöf, U. (1967), *'Skoldifferentiering och undervisningsförlopp', Göteborg Studies in Educational Sciences*, 2, Stockholm: Almqvist and Wiksell.

Dahllöf, U. (1971), *Svensk utbildningsplanering under 25 år*, Lund: Studentlitteratur.

Dahllöf, U. (1989), *Tredje gången gillt: En ny start för svensk utvärdering! Manus*, Uppsala: Uppsala universitet.

Franke-Wikberg, S. (1981), *Arbete, familj och utbildning: Bakgrundsskisser för en analys av skolans studie- och yrkesorientering*, Stockholm: Liber Förlag.

Franke-Wikberg, S. (1983), 'Teoriinriktad utvärdering - ett fruktbart alternativ för en pedagogisk utvärderare?', *Forskning om utbildning*, 3, s 6-14.

Franke-Wikberg, S. (1988), 'Om krisen inom den amerikanska högre utbildningen eller Den bloomstertid nu kommer', *Forskning om utbildning*, nr 2, s 37-41.

Franke-Wikberg, S. (1989), *Evaluating Education Quality on the Institutional Level*, Department of Education, University of Umeå, May. (To be published as an OECD-report.)

Franke-Wikberg, S. and Frykholm, C.U. (1987), 'Utveckling och utvärdering - två sidor av samma mynt?' In Johansson, L. (ed.) *Vidare skola: Utvärdering - möte med verkligheten*, Stockholm: Utbildningsförlaget.

Franke-Wikberg, S. and Johansson, M. (1975), *Utvärdering av undervisning. En problemanalys och några empiriska studier på universitetsnivå. Akad avh*, Umeå universitet: Pedagogiska institutionen.

Franke-Wikberg, S. and Johansson, M. (1976), *Utvärdering av undervisning*, Lund: Studentlitteratur.

Franke-Wikberg, S. and Lundgren, U.P. (1980), *Att värdera utbildning*, Del I, Stockholm: Wahlström and Widstrand.

Franke-Wikberg, S. and Lundgren, U.P. (1981). *Att värdera utbildning*, Del II, Stockholm: Wahlström and Widstrand.

Goodlad, S. (1987). 'Editorial', *Studies in Higher Education*, 12, 3.

Hirsch, Jr. E.D. (1987), *Cultural Literacy: What Every American Needs to Know*, Boston: Houghton Mifflin Co.

House, E. (1978), 'Assumptions underlying evaluation models', *Educational Researcher*, 7 (3) 4-7.

House, E. (ed.) (1986), *New Directions in Educational Evaluation*, London: Falmer Press.

Härnqvist, K. (1958), *Beräkning av reserver för högre utbildning*, I SOU, 11, 7-92.

Härnqvist, K. (1960), *Individuella differenser och skoldifferentiering. 1957 års skolberedning*, II, SOU, 13, Stockholm: Ecklesiastikdepartementet.

Härnqvist, K. (1978a), 'Individers efterfrågan på utbildning'. In Franke-Wikberg, S. and Lundgren, U.P. (eds) *1980: Karriär och levnadsbana: En antologi om studie- och yrkesval*, Stockholm: Wahlström and Widstrand.

Härnquist, K. (1978b), *Det fria valet på grundskolans högstadium -motiv, tendenser och effekter*, Skolöverstyrelsen: Pedagogiska nämnden.

Johansson, L. (1987), 'Utvärdering i ett reformskede', In Johansson, L. (ed.) *Vidare skola: Utvärdering - möte med verkligheten*, Stockholm: Utbildningsförlaget.

Lander, R. (1987), 'Utvärderingsforskning - till vilken nytta? Pedagogiska röster och två exempel från forskningsfältet', *Göteborg Studies in Educational Sciences*, 64, Acta Universitatis Gothoburgensis.

Lindensjö, B. and Lundgren, U.P. (1983), 'Att utvärdera utvärdering', *Forskning om utbildning*, nr 2, s 6-20.

Lundgren, U.P. (1972), 'Frame factors and the teaching process: A contribution to curriculum theory and theory on teaching', *Göteborg Studies in Educational Sciences*, 8. Stockholm: Almqvist and Wiksell.

Lundgren, U.P. (1977), *Model Analysis of Pedagogical Processes*, Stockholm Institute of Education. Department of Educational Research, Lund: Liber Läromedel.

Lundgren, U.P. (1982), 'Between Schooling and Education: Notes on Curriculum Change within the Second Generation of School Reforms in Sweden', Invited address to the annual meeting of the American educational Research Association, New York, March, Washington: Educational Research Information Centre. Ed 218 193, 1982.

Lundgren, U.P. (1989), *Educational Policy Making, Decentralisation and Evaluation. An Invitation to Papers*, EMIL, The Norwegian Research Council for Applied Social Science. 1989-02-02.

National Commission on Excellence in Education (1983), *A Nation at Risk: The Imperative for Education Reform*, Washington DC: US Department of Education, April.

Neave, G. (1987), 'Crisis, What Crisis?', *Higher Education Quarterly*, 41, 2, Spring.

Parlett, M. and Hamilton, D. (1973), 'Evaluation as illumination: A new approach to the study of innovatory programmes'. In New trends in evaluation: Material for a conference on educational evaluation held at the Institute of Education, University of Göteborg, 22-23 October.

Popkewitz, T.S. (1984), *Paradigm and Idealogy in Educational Research: The Social Functions of the Intellectual*, New York: Falmer Press.

Popkewitz, T.S. (1988), *Teaching and Teacher Education Reforms: Reconstituting a State Bureaucratic Apparatus and Forming a Political Discourse*, University of Wisconsin, Madison, February.

Popkewitz, T.S. and Wehlage, G.G. (1973), 'Accountability: Critique and alternative perspective', *Interchange*, 4, 4.

Prop 1988/89:4. Skolans utveckling och styrning. Stockholm: Utbildningsdepartementet.

Ravitch, D. and Finn, Jr. C.E. (1987), *What Do Our 17-Year-Olds Know? A report on the National Assessment of History and Literature*, New York: Harper and Row.

Skolöverstyrelsen. Planeringssekretariatet, Lövgren, E: PM 1988-03-01 (a): Inriktning av nationell utvärdering.

Skolöverstyrelsen. Planeringssekretariatet, Lövgren, E: PM 1988-03-01 (b): Policyfrågor som kan belysas genom nationell utvärdering.

Stake, R. E. (1974), *Program Evaluation, Particularly Responsive Evaluation*, reports from the institute of education, University of Göteborg, no 35.

Study Group on the Conditions of Excellence in American Higher Education (1984), *Involvement in Learning: Realizing the Potential of American Higher Education*, Washington DC: National Institute of Education/ U.S. Department of Education, October.

Trow, M. (1987), 'The national reports on higher education: A sceptical view', *Educational Policy*, 1, 4.

Wedman, I. (1987), 'Vad kan dom? Eleverna alltså! Ett nationellt programme för att mäta kunskaper och färdigheter'. In Johansson, L. (ed.), *Vidare skola. Utvärdering - möte med verkligheten*, Stockholm: Utbildningsförlaget.

Chapter 11

Some notes on a Norwegian evaluation programme

Erik Wallin

It might seem somewhat presumptuous to use Norwegian in the title of this chapter. My contribution is not exclusively focused on the Norwegian scene but more oriented to general problems of a programme of evaluation. My point of observation is a Swedish one reflecting experiences from the development of the Swedish school that in basic respects has been parallel to what has happened in Norway since the 1950s.

The state and control of education

In both countries, and especially during the last decades, the state has had a firm grip of the school development. As is said in the background paper this is due to the need to control the implementation of the reforms. To this should be added that this need was so much more strongly felt as educational reforms were consciously part of reforms in other areas of politics of a welfare state in being. The Swedish educational reforms cannot be understood as to intents and resistance if not related to social policy.

In both countries, thus, there has been a need for control by the state. Centralisation has become a hallmark and particularly so in Sweden. As is also said in Chapter 3 there has always been more local autonomy in Norway than in Sweden and this difference is primarily due to the topographical and infrastructural conditions of Norway. It might seem trivial for this audience to point to the interest of the state to control education (and schooling). Irrespective of whether we stress the integrating function of the state or give accent to dominating values the state has primary interests in education and its control. This seems too often to be forgotten when discussing educational reforms, and their implementation as well as decentralisation and evaluation of educational systems.

Sweden offers a nice illustration of the need for control when during the end of the 1870s (1) the state decided to pay most of the teachers' salaries; (2) we got the first national curriculum; and (3) the state inspectorates of schools were established. In other terms, from these days the interest of the state to steer (govern) education has become obvious and evident. This interest of the state that implicitly carries the seed to vertical organisation and bureaucracy encounters the plural interests of the modern differentiated society. In this encounter is created the conflict (or dilemma!) of centralism and decentralism. There is also created the basic problem of evaluation.

The problem of control as part of a decentralisation strategy in a pluralistic society has to be complemented by adding the problem of the legitimacy of the school. This is discussed in a generative way in Chapter 3. Nonetheless it is of such importance that it should be given attention even here.

It is a well-known fact that the educational system of the western countries has suffered from a legitimacy crisis during the last decade or so. For different reasons education has met with decreasing confidence from its audiences. Whether this reflects success of education or its opposite might be discussed, but it is a fact. Related to a national programme for evaluation the decreased confidence in education/schooling, however, has consequences. The responsible state authorities need to encounter attacks on the system by proving its advantages and success. On the Swedish scene there is an obvious - and legitimate - endeavour to prove that the school has been 'successful'. Again, this endeavour may lead to great problems.

The problem in focus

The background paper to the conference sets the stage for discussion of the problem in a generative and concentrated way. There is a quotation in the OECD review of 1988 that further pinpoints the main problem:

> This leads us, therefore to think about the ways in which the Ministry can secure better knowledge of the working of the system. First, it needs a far more secure quantitative data base enabling it to know how the resources it distributes are used. It needs, too, to have more secure knowledge about the part played by educational institutions in the flow of students and their access to institutions of different levels.
>
> Secondly, and more difficult, it seems essential that both the local authorities and the Ministry have qualitative knowledge of how schools work. As we have indicated earlier, a move from a centralized system cannot mean that the central ministries simply abandon the national stage. In order to perform these functions adequately, and to take a central role in continuing development of the system within the frameworks agreed in Parliament, they will certainly have to adopt an evaluative and monitoring function. Equally, local authorities have a political responsibility for the maintenance of their school. As far as the schools are concerned we would hope that they will develop a strong practice of self-critique and self-evaluation. In brief, we are concerned

> not with the reintroduction of national controls but with considering in which ways good norms of educational practice can be established and disseminated better in Norway. Good practice need to be identified and disseminated. The process of education as well as its outcomes need to be considered (pp. 17-19).

A basic observation in the quotation is that evaluation is a matter of securing good knowledge of the working of the system being evaluated. This means taking stand against a naively rationalistic conception of evaluation as a quantitative relation between a standard (objective) and an outcome.

In the quotation is also pointed to the need of collecting quantitative data. This seems to imply data on allocation and use of resources and, more generally, data on an organisational level. It does not imply data on educational outcomes as measured by tests and related to process variables. The former kind of quantitative data will not be further discussed.

It is further said that evaluation should be a responsibility of different levels of the system and that good practice should be identified and disseminated.

It is stated also in the quotation that qualitative data about the system is needed. This is a crucial point for an evaluation programme that emphasises 'knowledge more than plain figures'.

The issue of criteria

Before continuing I will summarise the previous sections as far as concerns control and evaluation. A national programme of evaluation has three main functions:

1. of control, which can be split up in two:
    - as part of decentralisation and
    - as part of goal steering ('managing by objectives')
2. of legitimation; and
3. of implementation, which might also include a subordinated function of encouraging school personnel.

As related to a reform, i.e. being an instance of planned change, the evaluation programme highlights the issue of goals or rather the issue of interpretation as giving meaning to stated goals. This becomes the issue of criteria. This issue can be illustrated by taking goal steering ('management by objectives') as an example.

The major idea of goal steering as system management is that rules and more or less detailed plans are substituted by clear goals (objectives) and methods for evaluation of the achievement of the goals (objectives). To be effective goal steering has to be executed from the centre as well as from the periphery, from top as well as from bottom. In the terms of Lindensjo and Lundgren the goals are formulated on the 'formulation arena', i.e. here on the state level. On the local level different parts of the (educational) system transform the goals into their own objectives and decide upon their means of reaching the objectives/goals. This defines 'the arena of realisation'.

Between the two arenas, i.e. levels of the system, there is a problem of balance. There is no guarantee that the activities on the local level do move in the direction set down in the goals.

In order to overcome the risk of imbalance there is a need for a common base for action through the whole (educational) system. The term (and concept) used is often 'enterprise culture'. There follows a need for establishing a common culture by development and training measures. It is said (cf. Ramstrom, 1988) that a common culture has to be formed or created. This may be a problem, but the very essence of the problem is that in the (educational) system there already exists, by training and learning, a culture of the school and of schools. Forming or creating a new culture, therefore, is to replace an already existing culture by another.

This example shows implicitly how goal steering as management by objectives has its roots in the world of enterprises and business administration. Profit maximisation, divisionalisation and accountability are catch words and transferring these into education may prove disastrous. Now however, the matter is how the example illustrates the problem of interpretation of goals.

The problem illustrated is not only a problem of goal steering but, also in its general sense, inherent in all aspects of goal setting and goal interpretation in the educational system. To a national programme of evaluation it means that an evaluation never can be absolute and made against fixed criteria. Not only has the school its culture or state authorities as their base for action but it is due also to 'the general public': politicians, parents, pupils, etc. Anyone concerned with construction of observation schemes or achievement tests has his/her own 'culture', i.e. system of norms and values concerning education and schooling.

As stated, evaluation can never (but in trivial aspects of schooling) be absolute. It is relative in relation to the 'culture', to the conception of schooling, to the system of norms of those who are responsible for the evaluation in terms of instruments for collecting information of the system being evaluated.

A holistic approach to evaluation

The perspective discussed in the previous section on the relative character of evaluation is - important as it is in itself - part of a more general holistic approach to evaluation. In order for evaluation data, quantitative or qualitative, to give knowledge about the system being evaluated, they have to be related to 'what has lead to what'. This is due, of course, when the aim of evaluation is to guide implementation by giving 'good norms of educational practice' but it has a general implication related to all instances of evaluation.

In 1967 Dahllöf presented his frame factor theory of educational processes. In this the general model looks like this:

$$\text{Frames} \rightarrow \text{process} \rightarrow \text{results}$$

When applied to evaluation it pinpoints the need for taking into consideration as well the process as the condition for the process leading to a given result.

As a transactional model for evaluation the Dahllöf model has a more general scope in theoretical terms than that of Stake (1967). As intended more explicitly for evaluation Stake gives strong emphases to what he calls the rational. This can be the rational of the system being evaluated, but more important in this context the rational of the evaluator. Wallin has used the term 'base of interpretation' for rational and included both intentions of the system and of the evaluation in the concept. In the terms of Franke-Wikberg and Lundgren 'theory-based' evaluation stands close to all the mentioned authors. Common to them is a holistic approach to evaluation.

Conclusion I

In practical terms the implication of a holistic approach is that the evaluation intended should be motivated and justified as to aims and as to aims of the system to be evaluated. Instruments used for observation and/or measuring results should be rationalised (and, therefore, also interpretable) in terms of, e.g. background in the educational system, in conception of knowledge and conception of content. The results measured, in their turn, should be relatable and interpretable - i.e. given a meaning - in relation to the process and its conditions.

Only in this way can an evaluation be meaningful. If we again look at the three functions of evaluation stated above it can be said:

1. of control (in relation to both decentralisation and goal steering): those controlling will be able to respond to the system being evaluated in a way making change of action possible and to give grounded arguments for change. In the case of a national programme of evaluation the audiences of reporting/responding will also include the general public and educational politicians and planners;

2. of legitimation: again the most important consequence seems to be the possibility to give grounded arguments and, on stated premises, rational reasons for curricula, schooling and teaching;

3. of implementation: those responsible for implementation are in a position to give not only technical directives but also guides for action, i.e. 'good norms for educational practice'. (The very essence of this point is that a holistic approach recognises teaching as actions and not as applying techniques.)

Conclusion II

Who should do the evaluation? The question has to be related to the setting up of a national programme for evaluation. Anyway, it seems as if the answer should be that the evaluation might be carried out on different levels:

- on ministry level and county level
- on local (municipal) level
- on school level

The demands of the holistic approach are due on all and each level and of course even to the total programme. It might be supposed that the level that could give the most illuminating and in all senses meaningful knowledge of the system would be the school level - provided the school is able to analytically and descriptively handle all ingredients of the approach. If this is not the case - and it is doubtful if it is - evaluation on the school level would not be meaningless but evaluative data cannot be used for integration on a higher level. Data would lack meaning to the receiver.

Anti-conclusion

What will happen if a national programme of evaluation is not planned and run according to a holistic model? Concerning the aim of giving 'good norms for educational practice' it will not succeed but only give technical directives without a rationale. Teaching or other activities in school will not be influenced.

In terms of control and legitimation the consequences will generally be identical. Any evaluation report presented to the state authorities or to the general public will primarily lead to a discussion of how data should be interpreted. If data are presented without a context anyone interpreting will, more often than not, implicitly use his or her own criteria for interpretation. The discussion will be reactive instead of focused on arguments for and against ends and means of education. In its extreme this will mean setting the carriage in front of the horse: there will be a discussion of the data instead of a discussion about ends, form and content of education.

An example of a reactive discussion of evaluation data is one where an aim of the evaluation programme, because of lack of rationalisation, is to give a base for judging whether the results of education are 'satisfactory', 'adequate', 'show improvement' and similar. A discussion in these terms will be a discussion on usually implicit premises where different interest groups express their meaning without any clear point of reference. The risk is great that a discussion of this kind will dominate when evaluation is used for legitimation purposes. It is then near to focusing on whether the school has been 'successful' or not - and the problem is to define success. The discussion is again reactive on the premises of different participants of the discussion and will reflect what they 'think' of the system. The discussion will be a wrong discussion in the sense that it is not related to the aims of the educational system. In the same sense it will also run the risk of being an instrumental discussion in a technical way without instruments/means being related to ends.

The 'anti-conclusions' in terms of risks for an evaluation programme leading to wrong discussions can be expressed in words that are still more general.

If an evaluation programme is set up and run without reflected theory and value premises it will take form and content on the premises of the educational system itself. This will mean a restriction of perspectives and might lead to a discussion without rational arguments. If so the evaluation programme will contribute to a restriction of the public discourse and, in the end, to a restriction of democracy.

References

Dahllöf, U. (1967), *Skoldifferentiering och undervisningsforlopp* (Ability Grouping and the Teaching Process), Goteborg Studies in Educational Sciences 2, Stockholm: Almqvist & Wiksell.

Lindensj, B. & Lundgren U.P. (1986), 'Politisk styrning och skolreformer', *Skol overstyrelsen*, I Brannpunkten B 86:3, Helsingborg: Lieber Utbildingsforlaget.

Ramstrom, D. (1988), 'Målstyrning i utbildningen - skåpmat eller en reell fornyelses-kraft', *Forskning om utbildningò*, Nr. 2/1988, p. 14.

Stake, R.E. (1967), 'The countenance of educational evaluation', *Teachers College Record*, 68 (7), p 523-40.

Chapter 12

Evaluation in the context of national policy and local organisation

Gary Sykes

Introduction

This chapter is an account of a set of observations concerning the role of information in the regulation of education, with the term 'regulate' meant to include both its hard version of 'control' or 'govern' and its softer version of 'steer' or 'influence'. By 'information' I mean to indicate nothing very precise, but rather the collection of all kinds of data that might be useful in helping to describe, interpret, understand and perhaps even influence educational policy and practice within a society.

The United States will serve as the case for an unsystematic review of experience with the collection and use of information at two levels of the policy system - the nation and the school. However, an eye will be kept throughout on the case of Norway and emerging policy developments there, notably the trend toward decentralisation. This choice of levels needs justification for each country's policy system has five levels. In the US, policy may be established at the federal, state, school district, school or classroom level. In Norway the levels that roughly correspond are the national, the county, the municipal, the school, and the classroom. The similarity of course is inexact on many dimensions, not least of which is scale: 50 states, 15,000 school districts, roughly 80,000 schools and several million classrooms serving a population of 240 million compared with 19 counties, 454 municipalities, some thousands of schools, tens of thousands of classrooms and a national population of 4.2 million.

In both systems decision-makers at each of the five levels require information for policy-making. As authority flows among the levels over time, so will demands for information. In the US, for example, the recent explosion of state-level policy-making has escalated demands for information there, whereas in Norway, county and municipal officials face important new decisions about budget allocations and implementation of national educational goals that may be informed by the collection of data.

Given limitations of space and competence, I will concentrate on the two levels mentioned, thus failing to supply a more systematic treatment level by level (but see Kogan,1989). I select the national level because the international arena is an increasingly important context for national policies. Most nations today operate in global economic markets where competition requires a dynamic and well-qualified workforce. Such competition places direct pressure on the education system. Developments afoot also indicate the dawn of a new international age that is likely to pose challenges, puzzles and opportunities to most nations. I refer here to the approach of the European Economic Community, a potential East-West détente following on the heels of Glasnost and Perestroika within the eastern bloc and the potential opening of China (recent events there notwithstanding) and the emergence of a powerful economic challenge on the Pacific rim. Those nations with the greatest understanding of their own circumstances stand a better chance of reaping the benefits and minimising the costs of the new order, and so national policy is likely to assume increased salience in the coming years.

On educational grounds I emphasise the school as the critical unit of educational production and improvement. Here I reflect the emphasis of the last decade's scholarship in the US that concentrates on school factors and processes as the point of leverage for change. In the US evidence and experience over the past decade has converged to form a conventional wisdom that the school is the unit of change. The literature on school effects (see, for example, Barr and Dreeben, 1983; Chubb, 1988; Chubb and Moe, 1988; Purkey and Smith, 1983; Rosenholtz, 1987; Rutter *et al.*, 1979) and its ideological counterpart in the effective schools prescriptions (e.g. Brookover and Lezotte, 1979; Edmonds, 1981; Edmonds and Frederickson, 1979); the emphasis on individual school cultures as a central phenomenon (e.g. Sarason, 1982) with parallel attention to the concept of culture in business organisations (e.g. Deal and Kennedy, 1982; Peters and Waterman, 1982); the testimony and strategies of school improvement advocates (e.g. Goodlad, 1984; Lieberman, 1988); and the emergence of school-based policy initiatives (most notably the California School Improvement Program) all reflect and support the belief that the school is the most effective level at which to target improvement efforts.

Some emerging work in the US has begun to concentrate on the importance of other levels, including the state (Odden and Marsh, 1988), the district (Little, Long and Guilkey-Amado, 1986; Rosenholtz, 1989) and the department as an intermediate unit within the high school (e.g. a research focus for the federally funded Center for Research on the Context of Secondary School Teaching). However, the weight of opinion today still rests on the school as a focal point, and so I shall adopt the orthodox perspective.

Three parts, then, to the analysis: a review of US experience with data collection and use at the national level; a perspective on evaluation as an organisational process within the school; and a set of concluding remarks.

Evaluation and national policy

In the US a steady restlessness over the distribution of authority and responsibility among the levels of governance has characterised our educational history. Recent developments include the relative decline of the federal government, the increasing activism of state governments and of district-level policy-making, and the continuing residual control exercised by street level bureaucrats in schools (i.e. administrators, teachers) over the actual provision of education. In contrast, the 1987 Mønsterplan in Norway sets the stage for decentralisation, with the national role underspecified, and questions about the relative influence of county and municipal units.

In the US it is commonplace to observe that the 'bottom' of the system has considerable power over the top. Local educators have wide latitude in interpreting, distorting, and ignoring central mandates, and policy most often appears a weak and blunt instrument for affecting change (see Green, 1983). In many European nations with a strong ministry of education and a national curriculum and assessment system, the top may wield relatively more influence, although traditions of local control are undoubtedly strong in Norway where cultural tensions among regions (e.g. cosmopolitan, urbanised South vs. rural, conservative North) further complicate the possibilities of national control. The first point to note, however, is the instability that characterises patterns of authority within educational systems.

Evaluation as an emergent concern in system building

Within the shifting configurations of authority in most nations, the function of evaluation typically assumes increasing importance with the maturity of the system. Initially, nations must concern themselves with the creation of an educational system and its steady expansion. Table 12.1, drawn from Thomas Green's analysis (1980, p. 10), sets forth the modes of system growth.

Most nations have expended considerable policy effort in these modes of growth, for system development is the most potent strategy available to influence education through policy. Once the basic system is in place, marginal development likely will continue indefinitely. So the US turns attention to pre-school and child-care in public institutions, and in Norway policy goals include the extension of kindergarten to a larger proportion of the population.

Table 12.1 - The modes of educational system growth

1. The system may expand in response to increases in the school-age population either by increasing the number of units in the system, or by increasing the number of students in units of the system, or both.
2. The system may expand by increasing rates of attendance and survival. Growth in attainment.
3. The system may expand by adding levels either at the top or at the bottom. Vertical expansion.
4. The system may expand by assuming responsibility for educational and social functions that are either new, that have been ignored, or that have been carried out by other institutions. Horizontal expansion.
5. The system may expand either by differentiation of programs or institutions or both. Differentiation.
6. The system may expand by intensification, that is, by attempting to do more in the same time or the same in less time. Growth in efficiency.
7. The system may expand by extending the school year or the school day.
8. The system may expand by increasing the number of persons needed to staff it independently of the number of students and number of its units, the magnitude of the school-age population, rates of attendance, survival.

System growth demands planning, resources and coordination between sectors and within the educational sector, but poses relatively minor challenges for evaluation. When, however, government seeks to learn what children are learning, and what effects that learning has on such large matters as economic productivity, the civic virtues, national defence and the standard of living, then the need for information increases dramatically, and the challenges are joined in earnest. Policy preoccupations shift from the question, 'Is the system in place and functioning reasonably well?' to 'Is the system achieving its goals, serving its fundamental purposes for the individual, for the community, and for the nation?'

The distribution of authority over education as inherently unstable

Two constants render unstable any distribution of authority over education. There will be a steady-state of dissatisfaction over education subject to some waxing and waning in intensity and public awareness; and there will be an inability to know what is going on. These constants, of course, are not unique to educational policy-making and are related to one another. A plausible case always can be made that education is in a sorry way because it is difficult to tell, because means-ends connections are indeterminate, and because goals are multiple, conflicting, and tradeoff in complex, ill-understood ways.

This assertion overstates the case, but contains enough truth to suggest a point about centralisation-decentralisation. At every level of the system interests concentrate that exercise influence and are therefore capable of abuse. One predictable policy response to perceptions of failure or decline in education is to re-allocate authority over the enterprise. However, dissatisfaction will be constant and the results of any such reallocation will be uncertain, so every pattern of authority distribution eventually will be challenged and modified.

The dynamics of this process is the subject of institutional choice theory, the selection of a decision-maker based on judgments about agreement over substantive goals and about capacity to achieve those goals (Clune, 1987). The logic, or method, of choosing institutions is sometimes called 'comparative institutional advantage' and begins with 'institutional distrust' or criticism. As distrust of institutions emerges (e.g. that universities cannot train teachers, or that schools fail to educate children) pressures form to re-allocate authority: increase external controls over schools and universities, or delegate core tasks to other institutions. However, distrust alone is inadequate in determining the comparative competence of one institution over another. Distrust proves nothing by itself in the absence of a superior alternative, and every alternative involves a mix of advantages and disadvantages. 'The real world offers a "least worst" choice of imperfect institutions (e.g. not an ideal education but the best education possible from some configuration of real governments, schools, teachers, and students)' (ibid., p. 118). Information, of course, is critical in making and justifying these comparative choices.

In Norway, decentralisation appears to be the general direction of institutional choice, but the precise configuration of authority remains open. Should central policy strengthen the hand of the county at the expense of the local municipality? Should universities be encouraged to play a larger role in the delivery of in-service education and the dissemination of innovation? Should local school councils composed of parents, teachers and community representatives be given a larger role in school improvement? These are questions of institutional choice, and the collection and aggregation of information in the system will reflect and be reflected in the unfolding of institutional choice.

Information at the national level: a cautionary look

In the US considerable interest has emerged lately around the notion of an educational indicator system. The analogy is often made to economic indicators - the unemployment rate, for example, and other signs of economic health. One report defines an educational indicator as, 'a statistic about the educational system that reveals something about its performance or health' (Oakes, 1987), and provides three key elements: (1) an indicator should provide a referent point. The referent point may be a previous value, the value of a comparison group, or some socially determined standard; (2) an indicator should provide at least one of the following: information about the education system's performance, features known to be linked with desired outcomes, central features of the system, potential or existing problem areas or information that is policy relevant; and (3) an indicator should measure ubiquitous features of schooling that are enduring, easily understood, feasibly measured and generally accepted as valid and reliable statistics.

This appears straightforward. National policy-makers would simply organise a set of common indicators under the conventional rubrics of inputs and resources, processes and outputs, establish a set of reference points, then track the performance of the system. For example, inputs might include student enrolment counts and trends, flows in the components of teacher supply and demand, fiscal measures such as per pupil expenditures, expenditure 'effort' corrected for wealth, budgetary breakdowns by major spending categories, and so on. Processes might include courses offered, time allocations to particular subjects, student course-taking patterns, deployment of instructional methods, teacher and student absenteeism, and other indicators of educational process. And outputs might include rates of dropping out, of educational attainment, and of educational achievement as measured by a variety of tests.

National policy-makers require such information because . . . information is power, and that power is of two basic kinds: indicators and monitoring. In its indicator mode, information is powerful as a tool of social problem solving. For example, the trends in student achievement and attainment can be compared with trends in academic coursetaking to assess the impact of that development. In its monitoring mode, information is powerful as a method of control. As a policy instrument, information is a centralising influence almost by definition (because it collates dispersed data, whether at the state, district, school, classroom, or student level); and the comparative advantage of central authorities in looking at information is either perspective or leverage (Clune, 1987, p. 124).

The indicator function appears rational and illuminating, but there is an inevitable tendency to utilise indicators for monitoring purposes, so that in the political hurly burly the functional distinctions tend to blur.

Norway may well wish to invest in some form of national data collection system, but a look at the US experience will suggest some cautions and some guidelines.

Problems of interpretation, conflicts over control

The interpretation of many indicators will be problematic. For example, the US has now had over 50 years of experience with the estimation of unemployment, but the interpretation of trends continues to be the source of controversy and complexity, although much progress has been made in identifying the causes of fluctuations in unemployment (see Murnane, 1987). Similarly, when US policy-makers noticed a long-term, steady decline in SAT scores, that trend set off a search for causes that produced multiple, competing explanations rather than a single, definitive account.

As I write, the US Department of Education has just issued its annual 'wall chart', a compilation of state-by-state comparisons on a set of educational statistics, and every newspaper in the country has picked up this event with typically misleading stories. For example, a highly salient statistic is the school dropout rate, and comparisons are made over time and between such jurisdictions as states or districts within states. However, the definition of 'dropout' varies from locale to locale, making comparisons suspect, and tracking students who move around the country is difficult, so no one is sure about the exact rate (see Williams, 1987).

There are three technical problems here. First, we cannot adequately model relationships among elements within the educational system for purposes of attributing and partialling causes. This means that the selection of input, process and output factors will be a judgment call insofar as the relationships among these factors are not understood and may be indeterminate and unstable. Second, the definition, measurement, and validation of key indicators will create significant challenges and require years of technical work to pin down. Dropouts are a case in point in the US. Third, there are difficulties in collecting the necessary data in a cost-effective, non- burdensome manner. Consider, for example, the challenge faced by the US Census Bureau in entering ghetto neighbourhoods to collect regular statistics on households from suspicious minority residents who may have a stake in concealing, not revealing information. Put simply, the value of indicators to central authorities is not matched by the value of cooperation to local authorities (or respondents) who must collect (or provide) the data. Weak and fallible information may be better than none at all, and technical quality and capacity may be steadily improved upon, but danger lurks in connecting indicator information to policy decisions in a facile manner.

Some 20 years ago, the US developed a system of 'shallow sample' performance testing known as the National Assessment of Educational Progress (NAEP). This system tests a random sample of 9-, 13-, and 17-year-old students in reading, mathematics and science. The data are aggregated to the national level, but disaggregated by such factors as region, gender and race (but not class) to allow trend analysis overall and within sub-populations. The regular reports issuing from NAEP have provided extremely important and valuable information on academic achievement in selected subjects in the US, and recent additions to NAEP include writing samples and assessment of critical reasoning skills as well as basic achievement.

For political reasons the decision was made originally not to disaggregate data to the state level. States were understandably nervous about comparisons. However, in 1985, the organisation of state education chiefs voted to support state-by-state comparison of test scores. Whether this turns out to be a courageous or foolhardy move remains to be seen because the use of indicators for comparative purposes is a double-edged sword: 'Without question, publishing comparative information about educational quality can bring to bear on institutions tremendous political pressure to improve. But this pressure also produces some measurable pressure on schools to make results look better than they actually are - or even to pervert the reporting system' (Smith, 1988, p. 490).

The reactive effects of measurement is an old story in fields as disparate as physics, psychology and politics, and the wisest course appears to avoid politically divisive comparisons, at least in the initial phase of assessment. Note too that the cost implications of such disaggregation are substantial: to produce state-level NAEP data likely will increase costs from $4 million to $13.5 million by one estimate, due to the necessity of larger, more precise samples.

Indicator trends should trigger search, not policy. Typically, the meaning of any trend or pattern of trends is unclear. NAEP serves as a thermometer, alerting policy-makers to the possibility of educational fever in the body politic, but not indicating the cause of the malady. There should be parallel systems to explore possible interpretations of national trends in education indicators, getting beneath the numbers to find out what's going on. Investigative journalism, not science, is the right metaphor. Such inquiry might be institutionalised in the form of an inspectorate or of school accreditation standards and processes and/or pursued on an ad hoc basis as the need arises. For example, in response to alarming evidence of gross inequities in school finance or dramatic declines in achievement or attainment, or serious shortages of qualified teachers, or any number of other problems signalled through indicator trends, the national government might form a commission of inquiry authorised to explore the problem in depth and make recommendations.

Such reliance on indicator trends, however, will mislead in failing to distinguish problems from conditions. The baseline against which to measure fluctuations may not represent a normative standard. For example, it is probably accurate to claim that since the inception of the Common School, there has never been an adequate supply of well-qualified math and science teachers in the US. Elementary teachers typically know very little maths or science and so ignore these subjects or teach them badly. Secondary schools cannot compete with business and industry for scientific talent: whereas history or English teachers must forego $1500 or so of annual income to teach, graduates with math/science backgrounds must forego $8,000-9,000 in choosing teaching over work in industry

(Levin, 1985). Consequently, the supply of maths-science teachers is in a chronic state, structurally determined by the level of public investment in education and the market for scientific talent that produces large public-private salary differentials. The moral is that indicators alone, no matter how cunningly constructed, cannot supply a normative basis for policy-making.

The US has become a test-mad society and this suggests another caution. The suspicion is beginning to form in the minds of many policy-makers that we have organised assessment around the wrong set of outcomes that are now driving teaching and learning in unfortunate directions. Most standardised tests in the US target minimum competencies and basic skills achievement, but vanguard opinion is focusing more strongly these days on the necessity of teaching for conceptual understanding of subject matter, for critical thinking and problem-solving, for active and self-directed learning and so on. The instructional strategies that have evolved to produce increases in basic skills as measured by the all-powerful tests increasingly appear to be anti-thetical to the new agenda for the schools. Beware that you may get what you test for.

The psychometricians have come to dominate conceptions of assessment in US education to the general impoverishment of the enterprise. Standardised, multiple-choice tests that meet the criteria of psychometric reliability and validity, low cost and feasibility/efficiency of administration have driven out most other forms of assessment at policy-making levels above the classroom. Ironically, the evidence indicates that teachers do not pay much attention to test scores and are quite capable of evaluating student learning informally but accurately.

In the US, interest grows in the exploration, development, and use of innovative forms of assessment for learning. Some educators are beginning to look to the experience of other countries, as the following quote indicates:

> In this country we have been so enamoured of efficient testing that we have overlooked feasible in-class alternatives to such impersonal testing, which are already in use around the world. The German *abitur* (containing essay and oral questions) is designed and scored by classroom teachers, who submit two possible tests to a state board for approval. The APU in Great Britain has for more than a decade developed tests that are designed for classroom use and that involve interaction between assessor and student. What is so striking about many of the APU test protocols is that the assessor is meant to probe, prompt, and even teach, if necessary, to be sure of the student's actual ability and to enable the learner to learn from the assessment (Wiggins, 1989, p. 709)

It will be difficult to turn around the US system of assessment because standardised tests have become the barometer for our educational weather. With shallow sample testing, however, forms of assessment are feasible that require complex, open-ended responses and that utilise human judges in scoring. Mindful of this experience, Norway might well invest in multiple forms of assessment that seek to capture a range of outcomes, building the samples, the procedures and the outcomes gradually over time as budget, technical capacity and political consensus permit. Multiple outcome indicators that supply time series profiles rather than single lines of evidence appear to be a promising approach.

Information, equity and rights

So practical a review of experience with indicators, performance measures in particular, may send chills down the reader's spine, conjuring images on the one hand of Orwellian depersonalisation and spying as the government relentlessly stalks local educators; and on the other hand of a set of cost, technical and logistic problems likely to defy successful resolution. However, before rendering a categorical judgment, it is worth examining the US experience with regulatory monitoring for compliance. Consider first the values that justify national government intervention in local education. In the US, the value placed on individual rights, equity and social justice has most often justified intervention. In the US, injustice and inequity are woven deeply into the fabric of society. Schools, for better or worse, are widely viewed as frontline agencies in the struggle to create a more equitable, just and democratic society. Consequently, judicial and legislative actions frequently bring the coercive power of the state to bear on local education.

This perspective provides a counter-image to Big Brother, for what frequently drives authority upward is the aim of protecting the weak, the disenfranchised and those in the minority. The central collection and use of information will influence the balance of local interests because knowledge is power. Information allows government to monitor compliance with authoritative policy, to detect injustice, inequity and the systematic abrogation of rights, and to pinpoint sources of responsibility and accountability.

Consider the following cases:

- Without legal and legislative intervention from the national level, the US might still be operating a racially segregated, two-class school system that served to perpetuate the legacy of racism while providing a demonstrably inferior education to poor minority students.
- Until Title IX of the Educational Amendments of 1972, most US schools and communities provided highly unequal resources

to the education of boys vs. girls together with gender-biased educational practices that maintained opportunity-limiting gender stereotypes for boys and girls alike. In the last 15 years, the US Office of Civil Rights has enforced implementation of sex equity guidelines that have improved the resources and opportunities provided to girls, particularly in the area of athletics.

The US Supreme Court decision in the case of Lau vs. Nichols and the ensuing regulatory remedies spurred development of instructional strategies and targeted resources for non-English speaking students in US schools, many of whom were systematically denied access to education because local educators failed to supply appropriate instruction. Bilingual education continues to be a contentious area of social policy in the US, but I believe it is unarguable that without judicial and legislative intervention, local communities would continue to underserve linguistic minorities, failing to supply access to cultural knowledge.

- Public Law 94-142 required that handicapped children be mainstreamed into regular classrooms, thus ending decades of neglect, segregated schooling, inadequate funding and social stigma for millions of exceptional children. Implementation of this federal policy mandate has been halting, difficult and conflict-laden, but there will be no turning back.
- Again under the spur of courts and legislatures, states have had to reform school finance systems to redress gross inter-district disparities in spending. In the US school funding has long been tied to local property taxes, but finance reform tends to shift the burden from local to state levels. Some states have made substantial progress in reducing spending disparities between rich schools and poor schools, whereas others have not, and the struggle continues to equalise school finance.

The government gathers a wide range of information in conjunction with these social mandates, and the aim is to serve the weak in our society - immigrants, black and Hispanic citizens, the gender-oppressed, the handicapped, the poor. Such use of information must appear noble, but the record of results is sadly mixed, for government policy has also produced a set of adverse consequences. Government auditing and reporting requirements have resulted in disruptive patterns of 'pull-out' instruction in schools; increases in paperwork, bureaucracy, proceduralism and rigidity; a profusion of testing requirements that dominate instruction in some schools; and an emphasis on student rights, due process and litigation that has undermined the moral authority of the school. Furthermore, federal mandates are typically underfunded and ignore the lack of local capacity to provide appropriate instruction to the many special categories of student. So the implementation of social policy has produced a fair measure of chaos, disruption, demoralisation, community conflict and even violence in US schools.

It is not possible, then, to render a simple, global judgment about these matters. If federal and state governments do not monitor the educational system, this constitutes a tacit policy of acceptance, a triumph for the status quo, a belief that there are no injustices and no inequities, or an admission that they are socially, politically and morally tolerable. But the US case suggests that pursuit of social change through central policy is fraught with hardships, pain and dislocation. The stakes, then, are high in either case, for the dispossessed have a claim in all humane and decent societies.

Evaluation and local organisation

The large matters just reviewed will have effects on schools, but schools have lives and cultures shaped by more than policy. A second context within which to view evaluation is the local organisation of school. Evaluation can be and often is a pro forma ritual within schools that has little impact on either individual or organisational effectiveness. However, it can also serve as a powerful mechanism for control, direction and learning within organisations, particularly as it is coordinated with other organisational processes such as personnel recruitment and socialisation, goal setting and school planning, in-service education, formation of work norms and task conceptions, and creation of shared expectations.

Within the US today, two broad, contending strategies have emerged that bracket the possibilities for evaluation as an organisational process.[1] My colleague Brian Rowan (1989) has labelled these 'commitment' and 'control' and each is worth brief characterisation.

Evaluation, organisational control, and the reduction of uncertainty

The control strategy seeks to design educational organisations around a standardised technology of teaching and learning that dramatically reduces the 'loose coupling' identified by organisational theorists in the 1970s as a prominent feature of schooling (see Meyer and Rowan, 1977; Weick, 1976). The emerging metaphor within this conception is 'alignment', or the nature of the coupling between input, behavioural, and output controls established within a hierarchical system of management. Input controls consist of standard texts and materials, curriculum objectives and guidelines, pacing guides, remediation routines and so on. Output controls include norm- and criterion-referenced tests and course requirements and standards for promotion and graduation. Behavioural controls involve centrally directed in-service education explicitly linked to both inputs and outputs. The control strategy as evidenced in full-scale instructional management systems operated from the state or district levels bends evaluation to the cause of organisational control. Evaluation becomes a management tool to be used in alignment with other policy tools to routinise the core technology of schooling.

Evaluation and the creation of school culture and commitment

The alternative strategy posits the formation of school-based professional commitment as the key to improvement rather than the design of an instructional management system. In this view, organic forms of management are necessary to foster professional cultures that emphasise normative controls achieved through collaborative goal-setting, increased collegial interaction and involvement in decision-making, job redesign that introduces new staffing patterns and leadership configurations and so on (see Lieberman, 1988; Weick and McDaniel, 1989). 'Network structures replace hierarchical structures, and technical work is guided by rich information and advice received from colleagues rather than by centralised statistical reports or standardised task instructions' (Rowan, 1989, p. 10).

This approach regards teaching and learning as requiring complex, non-routine technologies wherein workers must engage in frequent searches for solutions to difficult problems. Continuous learning and problem-solving become the hallmarks of organisational effectiveness in this view, and the collection of evaluative information should serve these functions.

The strategies compared

I have little doubt where Norwegian sympathies lie, and the first model may appear as a peculiar Anglo-Saxon perversity (allowing for emerging developments in England); but suspend judgment for a moment to note the alternative definitions of the problem. With the first strategy, the problem is defined as uncertainty, a debilitating uncertainty at both organisational and individual levels. When the ends of an enterprise cannot be fixed, and when means-ends relations are weak and unclear, then the resulting wide latitude for practice will produce a correspondingly wide range of outcomes. This range may be related to the sensitive adaptation of practice to clients and circumstances, or to simple incompetence - inept practice that is disciplined neither by common aims nor by shared professional norms, nor by standard technologies.

Much research on teaching and schooling in the US has detected patterns of accommodation that result in inadequate education, and a few examples will suffice:

- Studies of elementary teachers suggest that expectation processes operate to shape teacher behaviour in interaction with students. Many teachers hold low expectations for students and fail to challenge them academically while communicating their poor opinions of student ability (Cooper and Good, 1984).

- Other work suggests that elementary teachers' grasp of mathematics, science, and other subjects is weak, so they tend to underplay these subjects in the curriculum (see, for example, Goodlad [1984]).
- Studies of secondary schools suggest that the curriculum has become fragmented and highly stratified as a means of managing conflicts of purpose in secondary education (Oakes, 1986).
- Ethnographic work at the secondary level suggests that many teachers negotiate 'bargains' with students that exchange behavioural compliance for lowered demands and watering down of academic content (McNeil, 1986; Powell *et al.*, 1986). The overwhelming emphasis on the need to control student behaviour enlists knowledge as one more teacher resource to be used in the struggle over control.

These and other examples suggest precisely that teachers operate in a system so loosely structured that they will manage and interpret their work over time in ways that minimise stress and difficulty while failing to produce quality education. According to this view, then, the gravest danger to educational improvement lies in the lack of systematic direction that structures competent role performance. Control strategies are necessary to reduce the endemic uncertainties of teaching and learning.

Turning next to the commitment strategy, the conception of the problem changes dramatically. Here, the argument is that organisational control systems that rely on impersonal rules and procedures to achieve integration and coordination have important effects on worker commitment, defined as motivation and engagement in tasks, sense of efficacy, and feelings of cohesiveness within the work setting. The problem here is not uncertainty and the absence of external control but lack of commitment and engagement on the part of teachers and students alike. In this view, the imposition of routine technologies through bureaucratic procedures serves to exacerbate the problems of alienation and disengagement. Professionalism becomes the alternative of choice, for this strategy relies on the creation of school-based learning communities formed around shared norms, goals, and instructional arrangements that foster commitment to learning among teachers and students alike (Sykes, in press).

The two strategies described here are not mutually exclusive, but are difficult to blend into a single system. At the school level, the aim is to create structures, processes and norms that favour learning, consensus-building around shared goals and engagement in school tasks. School improvement relies on problem-finding - critical scrutiny of existing practices in a regular, ongoing, institutionalised manner. But commitment to such scrutiny is difficult to foster and requires a supportive climate of trust, mutual respect and dedication to mission. External control of school processes and outcomes tends to foster problem-hiding within schools, and can foster a climate of suspicion, distrust and defensiveness. So there is a tension between the imperative to gather information for purposes of monitoring and oversight, and the imperative to support critical inquiry within individual school cultures. If the state does not monitor education, then it cannot detect pockets of incompetence, ignorance, backwardness and inequity. However, external monitoring can become heavy handed and intrusive, disrupting the fragile culture of teaching and learning that must arise within individual schools if they are to be successful.

Conclusion

Constructing a multi-level system of evaluation in pursuit of learning and of control is a complex and conflict-laden process. Conflicts of authority are inevitable among levels and between purposes, for information requirements in service to the goal of control cut against requirements in service to the goal of learning. This chapter's organisation might suggest that higher levels of governance collect information for control, whereas at the operating level (i.e. the school), information serves the purpose of learning, but this conjunction is mistaken. Government, too, must function as a learning system for society, particularly in areas where policy and practice are unstable and non-routine. As Donald Schon (1971) writes:

> For government to become a learning system both the social system of agencies and the theory of policy implementation must change. Government cannot play the role of 'experimenter for the nation', seeking first to identify the correct solution, then to train society at large in its adaptation. The opportunity for learning is primarily in discovered systems at the periphery, not in the nexus of official policies at the center. Central's role is to detect significant shifts at the periphery, to pay explicit attention to the emergence of ideas in good currency, and to derive themes of policy by induction (p. 177).

This may appear a singularly American conception of policy in light of most nations' centralised education systems, but the pursuit of learning is a necessary goal at all levels of the policy system. Regulation and control are similarly necessary functions at the local level, so the task is to construct checks and balances in the evaluation system. 'Simultaneous loose-tight coupling' is one formulation for this elusive mix, a management slogan meant to indicate tight control exercised through creation of shared norms and values with maximum local autonomy for innovation, flexibility and responsiveness to local circumstances. The US case suggests that the national government has a legitimate role in monitoring the educational system for purposes of both compliance (or control) and assistance (or learning) (see Elmore and McLaughlin, 1982). As Norway's central government decentralises certain aspects of their education system, there may be corresponding need to exert more control over other aspects to maintain a dynamic balance in national-local interests. The collection and use of information is one such function. This chapter has explored some of the issues and dangers in the systematic collection of information on education, but on balance it is difficult to imagine steady improvement in education without a rich and varied body of reliable information, so the risks appear worthwhile. Ignorance, after all, poses its own risks.

Footnote

1. This depiction of approaches to reform is not inclusive and there are other alternatives that I do not review. For example, many policymakers are interested in introducing greater consumer choice into US schooling, to create market mechanisms that send evaluative signals to schools. So there are open enrollment plans, discussion of tuition tax credit and voucher schemes, and experiments underway with choice arrangements on both the supply- and demand-side.

References

Barr, Rebecca and Dreeben, R. (1983), *How schools work*, Chicago: University of Chicago Press.

Brookover, Wilbur, and Lezotte, L. (1979), *Changes in School Characteristics Coincident with Changes in Student Achievement*, East Lansing, MI: Institute for Research on Teaching, Michigan State University. (ERIC Document Reproduction Service No. ED 181 005.)

Chubb, John (1988), 'Why the current wave of school reform will fail', *The Public Interest*, 90, 28-49.

Chubb, John and Moe, T. (1988), 'Politics, markets, and the organisation of schools', *American Political Science Review*, 82(4), 1065-87.

Clune, William (1987), 'Institutional choice as a theoretical framework for research on educational policy', *Educational Evaluation and Policy Analysis*, 9(2), 117-132.

Cooper, Harris and Good, T. (1984), *Pygmalion Grows Up: Studies in the Expectation Communication Process*, New York: Longman.

Deal, Terrence and Kennedy, A. (1982), *Corporate Cultures: The Rites and Rituals of Corporate Life*. Reading, Mass.: Addison - Wesley.

Edmonds, Ron (1981), 'Making public schools effective', *Social Policy*, 12, 56-60.

Edmonds, Ron, and Frederickson, J. R. (1979), *Search for Effective Schools: The Identification and Analysis of City Schools that are Instructionally Effective for Poor Children*, (ERIC Document Reproduction Service No. ED 170 396.)

Elmore, Richard and McLaughlin, M. (1982), 'Strategic choice in federal education policy: The compliance-assistance trade-off'. In Lieberman, A. and McLaughlin, M. (eds), *Policymaking in Education: 81st Yearbook of the National Society for the Study of Education*, Part I, University of Chicago Press, pp. 159-94.

Goodlad, John (1984), *A Place Called School: Prospects for the Future*, New York: McGraw-Hill.

Green, Thomas (1980), *Predicting the Behavior of the Educational system*, Syracuse University Press.

Green, Thomas (1983), 'Excellence, equity, and equality'. In Shulman, L. and Sykes, G. (eds), *Handbook of Teaching and Policy*. New York: Longman.

Hawley, Willis and Rosenholtz, S. (1984), 'Good schools: What research says about improving student achievement', *Peabody Journal of Education*, 61(4), 1-135.

Kogan, Maurice (1989), *Fitting Evaluation Within the Governing Levels*, Oslo, Paper prepared for the Norwegian Research Council for Applied Social Science, May.

Levin, Henry (1985), *Solving the Shortage of Mathematics and Science Teachers*, Stanford, Calif.: Institute for Research on Educational Finance and Governance, Stanford University, January.

Lieberman, Ann (ed.) (1988), *Building a Professional Culture in Schools*, New York: Teachers College Press.

Little, Judith W., Long, C. and Guilkey-Amado, J. (1986), *Expanding Professional Collaboration in Schools: Can Districts Organize Leadership by Teachers?*, San Francisco: Far West Laboratory for Educational Research and Development.

McNeil, Linda (1986), *Contradictions of Control: School Structure and School Knowledge*, New York: Routledge and Kegan Paul.

Meyer, John and Rowan, B. (1977), 'Institutionalized organisations: Formal structure as myth and ceremony', *American Journal of Sociology*, 83, 340-63.

Murnane, Richard (1987), 'Improving education indicators and economic indicators: The same problems?', *Educational Evaluation and Policy Analysis*, 9(2), 101-16.

Oakes, Jeannie (1985), *Keeping track: How Schools Structure Inequality*, New Haven, Conn.: Yale University Press.

Oakes, Jeannie (1987), *Educational Indicators: A Guide for Policymakers*, New Brunswick, NJ: Centre for Policy Research in Education, Rutgers University, November.

Odden, Allan and Marsh, D. (1987), *How State Education Reform Can Improve Secondary Schools*, Berkeley, Calif.: Policy Alternatives for California Education.

Peters, Tom and Waterman, R. (1982), *In Search of Excellence: Lessons from America's Best-run Companies*, New York: Harper and Row.

Powell, Arthur, Farrar, E. and Cohen, D. (1985), *The Shopping Mall High School: Winners and Losers in the Academic Marketplace*, Boston: Houghton Mifflin.

Purkey, Stewart and Smith, M. (1983), 'Effective schools: A review', *Elementary School Journal*, 83, 427-52.

Rosenholtz, Susan (1987), 'Effective schools: Interpreting the evidence', *American Journal of Education*, 95, 534-62.

Rosenholtz, Susan (1989), *Teacher's Workplace: The Social Organisation of Schools*, New York: Longman.

Rowan, Brian (1989), *Commitment and Control: Alternative Strategies for the Organisational Design of Schools*, unpublished paper, Michigan State University.

Rutter, Michael, Maughan, B., Mortimore, P., Outsen, J. and Smith, A. (1979), *Fifteen Thousand Hours: Secondary Schools and Their Effects on Children*, Cambridge, Mass: Harvard University Press.

Sarason, Seymour (1982), *The Culture of the School and the Problem of Change*, 2nd edition, Boston: Allyn and Bacon.

Schon, Donald (1971), *Beyond the Stable State*, New York: W. W. Norton.

Smith, Marshall (1988), 'Educational indicators', *Phi Delta Kappan*, 69(7), 487-91.

Sykes, Gary (in the press), 'Teachers and schools: The profession as locus for improvement', In Elmore, Richard (ed.), *New Roles in Public Schools*, San Francisco: Jossey Bass.

Weick, Karl (1976), 'Educational organisations as loosely coupled systems', *Administrative Science Quarterly*, 21, 1-19.

Weick, Karl and McDaniel, R. (1989), 'How professional organisations work: Implications for school organisation and management'. In Sergiovanni, T. J. and Moore, J. H. (eds), *Schooling for Tomorrow: Directing Reform at Issues that Count*, Boston: Allyn and Bacon.

Wiggins, Grant (1989), 'A true test: Toward more authentic and equitable assessment', *Phi Delta Kappan*, 70(9), 703-13.

Williams, Patricia (1987), *Toward a Definition of School Dropout*, Madison, WI: Centre for Policy Research in Education, Wisconsin Centre for Education Research, University of Wisconsin.

Chapter 13

Evaluation and political governing in a decentralised educational system

Lise Vislie

This chapter will focus on the evaluation-decentralisation issue by orienting the discussion specifically to the Norwegian scene, and by highlighting at the same time a specific set of policy demands also made on the Norwegian education system, (see the reference to 'integration of the handicapped in education' as a national policy concern in the title of this chapter).

'Decentralisation' and 'integration' are strongly intertwined ideas in Norwegian policies. The combined effect is a system that makes evaluation not only difficult but also rather 'resistant' to evaluation. By examining the issue of evaluation from a combined policy perspective one should be able to explore and reflect more deeply into the meaning of 'decentralisation' in the Norwegian context, and probably also get a better grip of evaluation as a 'problem' in a concrete setting.

There are other reasons as well for going beyond the general policy of decentralisation and to include more specific educational policy goals in discussing the evaluation issue.

First, whether national evaluation efforts are discussed in terms of forms of organisation or in terms of concrete programmes, they should be based on, oriented towards and serve national policy objectives. Evaluation is not a goal, but a means towards steering and control. It may seem a trivial point but for political, economic as well as professional and practical reasons, evaluation must be controlled in the first place - by policy objectives. Second, it should be remembered that 'policies' are of different kinds, and that some are more easily evaluated than others. Take, for example, Norwegian pre-school policies, which have been mainly concerned with expanding the number of places available on a national scale and not with whether the expansion takes place in full-time or part-time provisions, - and compare with policies for equality in education. Policies for equality in education is a 'mixed bag' of complex challenges for implementation.

Finally, it is also worth noticing that 'policies' that appear on the agenda in most countries under the same heading, for example the 'equal opportunity policy' or the 'comprehensive school policy' etc., have different status, and highly different meanings and implications in different countries. The British or German versions of the 'comprehensive school policy' are fundamentally different from the 'school for all policy' as found in the Nordic countries (cf. the gap between the idea of a 'school for all' and for 'almost all'). Again the point is illustrative of the rather trivial fact that evaluation of 'similar' educational policies will require different schemes across the mentioned settings.

The point is of course highly relevant also for 'integration' as a policy concern in education. The policy emerged as a dominant policy issue relating to the organisation of schooling for handicapped young persons in most of the Western countries in the late 1960s and early 1970s (OECD, 1981). In 1978 OECD/CERI initiated a project on the education of the handicapped adolescent, which focused (particularly in its first phase) on integration policies and practices in member countries. Norway was actively involved in this project, as the following examples illustrate.

In 1982 Norwegian authorities invited the project to participate in an examination of Norwegian policies in the field. As part of these activities a background report *Integration of Handicapped Pupils in Compulsory Education in Norway* was published on the initiative of the Ministry (Dahl *et al.*, 1982). A group of OECD Examiners visited Norway in autumn 1982, and their report (OECD, 1983b) was presented and discussed at an international Conference arranged by Norwegian authorities in Oslo in February 1983.

At a high level conference arranged by the OECD Project in Paris in 1986 and attended by Ministers and senior representatives from 21 OECD Member Countries (OECD, 1987), the Norwegian Minister of Education made a strong statement in favour of integration policies. She emphasised the high priority such policies have had in Norway during the last two decades and would continue to have in the immediate future.

The Examiners' Report of 1983 is mentioned in the OECD *Review of Educational Policy in Norway* of 1988 (p. 4), but this specific policy area is not particularly focused on. From an outside perspective and for the purpose of an overall review of the system, this policy area may easily go unnoticed, because it has to do with 'the few' and thus may seem relatively unimportant. In fact it has to do with the 'integration of all' in the common school, and hence the importance. Apart from being the most ambitious dimension of Norwegian educational and social policy, it also gets to the core of the most vital concerns of educational policy in Norway throughout this century.

As it is this important the policy area in question should at least be within the scope of the discussions at the conference. The policy area is therefore presented below, as a separate idea and as related to major trends in Norwegian educational policies and practice in general. Integration and decentralisation are analysed and discussed in relation to evaluation. In the final part of the article I present a few (preliminary) conclusions regarding the question of a national system for evaluation of education in Norway.

Integration policies in Norway

This section should be seen in relation to the introductory chapter. It is not meant as a correction to his account, but as a supplement particularly aimed at an international audience.

'Integration' as a policy concept

The examiners who participated in the OECD review of Norwegian educational policies undertaken in 1974 noted particularly that integration was a vital issue in education policies in this country. The term 'integration' was, however, not easy for an outside observer to understand 'since it does not convey any specific meaning outside Norway, and also in Norway itself no concerted effort has been undertaken to specify its meaning. Nevertheless, it crops up again and again in discussions of Norwegian policy' (OECD, 1976, p. 31).

To come to grips with the meaning of 'integration' for Norwegian education the examiners had tried to trace the areas in which policies for integration had been implemented. They found many such policy areas, of which some were recognised by the examiners as actually being policies initiated for achieving equality of educational opportunity or policies to increase participation. As relevant examples mentioned under these rubrics were: 'integration' of rural and urban schools to make them more comparable and to provide equal educational services and; 'integration' of primary and lower secondary schools to create the 9 year comprehensive school; 'integration' of school and community through policies for participation; even the grading policies can be understood in terms of their contribution to integration of class levels, streams and institutions within the sector of compulsory education' (*loc. cit.*).

To this list we may as well add policies for the integration of handicapped pupils in education, because when the rights of the handicapped in society came to the forefront in Norwegian policies by the mid-1960s, the fundamental problems were seen as largely the same: that of diversities and divisions and the resulting injustice and conflicts about power.

The Norwegian 'enhetsskole' - a revisit

The history of 'the school for all' (folkeskolen) - in its modern version - started in Norway by the passing of the 1889 Education Act. Step by step this school has been improved and ensured by new legislation throughout the 20th century, i.e. in 1936, 1969 and 1975.

A fundamental aim of the educational policy pursued in Norway during this century has been to raise the general educational level of the population as a whole, and to provide equal educational opportunities for all. Historically the Norwegian approach to this objective has been closely linked up with the comprehensive, common school model ('enhetsskolen'). Such a school was established in Norway in 1920 for the whole period of compulsory education, lasting 7 years, characterised by a common, mostly neighbourhood organised local school, a common curriculum, no streaming of pupils according to ability and stressing the principle of automatic movement of pupils from lower to higher grades. After the end of the Second World War began the expansion of compulsory schooling to cover nine years, a reform that was fully implemented in accordance with the mentioned principles by the passing of the 1969 Education Act.

This is one part of the history of the Norwegian 'enhetsskole' and of the gradual implementation of policies for integration over almost a century. There is, however, another side to this story that is worth noticing as well. When the legal rights of all children to compulsory education was first stated in the 1989 Education Act, handicapped children were not included. At the time when the fundamental comprehensive school principle was first formulated and gradually gained support in Norwegian education, it was required simultaneously that specific categories of handicapped children would have to be excluded from a school that intended to 'comprise all children'. A section on exclusion was therefore incorporated in the Education Act. In spite of the rhetoric - from the point of view of the handicapped this important Act represented a first formal decision of segregation (Dahl *et al.*, 1982, p. 16).

In the following decades, when the comprehensive (local) school principle was further consolidated in Norwegian education, several reforms concerning the care, treatment and/or educational provisions for the handicapped were introduced, the provisions always being formally placed under the responsibility of the state. The genuine importance of some of these reforms to the persons concerned have been questioned. They were probably more important to the comprehensive local school, which by the introduction of special legislation under the governance of the state could even further disclaim its responsibility for the so called handicapped populations. The segregating effects of the early reforms related to the care and education of the handicapped children were also further intensified by the fact that the provisions introduced were not taken seriously by the central authorities. Consequently it may be said that during this important period of educational and social reforms in Norway the handicapped children became segregated from the local school and mainly neglected by the central authorities (ibid., p. 17).

This was the situation up to the end of the Second World War, when the planning of reforms and expansions of compulsory education immediately appeared on the political agenda. Educational provisions for the handicapped were also to be expanded. The first plans presented indicated that the principle of segregated provisions was firmly settled by that time. The idea was to establish a system of special schools spread out over the whole country under the governance of the Ministry. In accordance with this model a joint Special School Act was passed in 1951.

In the mid 1960s plans for the concrete localisation and the building up of a network of state special schools in Norway were presented to Parliament. Instead of approbation the whole plan was set aside, and a new policy programme based on 'integration' was launched. In accordance with the new policy programme, steps were immediately taken to prepare for a full merger of the Special School Act 1951 and the Education Act, and this 'legislative integration' was achieved when a set of supplementary regulations to the Education Act 1969 was passed in 1975.

The new legislation took effect on 1 January 1976. The Special School Act was then abolished. A series of other education acts that were either revised or first established in the early 1970s, i.e. the Upper Secondary Education Act 1974, The Kindergarten Act 1975, and the Adult Education Act 1976, were both based on the same integration principle. More specifically this means that all these laws regulate provisions for all at the levels in question, they include regulations concerning 'ordinary' as well as 'special' education, and no distinctions are made between the two in terms of overall responsibility and governance.

Integration, normalisation and education policy

The sudden change in educational policy orientation that took place in the late 1960s does not make sense in itself, neither do the policy implications of the change, unless presented in a broader political perspective.

First of all it should be mentioned that matters concerning handicap and disability became an area of particular policy concern in Norway in the mid-1960s. As a consequence of intensive discussions a White Paper to Parliament of 1966/67 stated normalisation as the overall principle for policies and further public intervention in the field. The main message of the policy document was that instead of charity disabled people should have rights. More specifically this meant the same rights as other members of the society to all services and social 'goods'. The extended increase in public responsibility in the field should, however, not lead to a corresponding increase in segregated services and provisions. The aim of the reform was therefore twofold:

- to improve the living conditions of the handicapped by increasing their command over such resources that are regarded to be of central importance to people's welfare in general (i.e. medical care, employment, education, recreation and leisure activities); and
- to do so within the frames of the public services that are responsible for serving the population in general.

These basic policy points have been emphasised and repeated in later policy documents to Parliament, and all political parties have so far unanimously consented to the policy.

The new overall policy orientation related to handicap and disability had - as was described above - an immediate effect on educational policies in Norway, of which the following key points are to be mentioned here:

(a) The overall purpose of the compulsory school had previously been formulated as broad and covering the interests of all children. In 1975 the purpose was broadened so as to formally include also the interests of the handicapped. As a result the right to education was reformulated: According to present Norwegian policy and legislation all children and young persons have the right to an education in accordance with their own needs, interests and capabilities. Since 1974/75 this principle refers to compulsory and upper secondary education.

(b) According to the Education Act 1975 the right to education - in the revised form - is unlimited, not reserved for handicapped pupils, but something to which every student is entitled. In fact the act does not refer to handicap or any categories of handicap at all. Neither education, nor special education, was any longer linked to categories of handicap.

(c) The right to education will, under particular circumstances, include the right to individual or what might be considered as rather special programmes. A kind of 'basic change' in the overall educational philosophy with wide implications for the organisation of the school and teaching in particular is here implied and deserves a particular comment.

Whereas the policy of the Norwegian 'enhetsskole' up to the end of the Second World War can be characterised as mostly regulated by the idea that 'all are equal, and shall be treated equally, no one favoured', it had been realised that the problems of inequality are complex and intricate and cannot successfully be dealt with as easily as that. The theory of non-intervention was therefore given up and substituted by a principle of positive discrimination. The basic insight behind this change was that a school for all has to accept inequality, and must therefore assist all children and young persons who, because of social background or environment, sex, ethnicity, mental or physical handicap, have a special difficulty in becoming integrated in school and society and sharing on equal terms its opportunities.

Consequently, providing adequately for all - not similarly for all - became the core of the new concept of education and teaching. The right to an adjusted education implied in principle that the school and the educational programmes have to be adjusted to the needs of the students (not the students to the school). Extra stimulation, extra support, or, if necessary special education is a general right, which according to the law, must be provided whenever necessary.

(d) This emphasises the need for content variation and differentiated programmes in every local school and classroom (cf. the curriculum principles laid down and being developed in the Mønsterplan of 1974 and 1987). In relation to this principle it should particularly be noticed that (advocated by the Ministry and supported by Parliament) it has been stated that most students should receive their education in regular classes (special classes or schools shall not be used unless there is a need for a total change in the social as well as the educational environment of the student).

Special classes had slowly started to grow up locally (before the Second World War actually). They first appeared in some of the bigger towns, probably because this was the only way the local schools and communities could either get rid of - or control - a number of 'difficult' or 'disturbing' pupils, who were either too 'good' for the special schools or for whom there were no places left in centrally organised facilities. The early local provisions were mostly organised as special classes and located at the ordinary schools, but some local special schools were also established.

In 1955 local authorities were legally instructed to provide special education for pupils 'who could not otherwise profit from teaching in ordinary schools'. As a consequence a differentiated system of special classes and other, more flexible arrangements for the provision of special education grew up on a local basis. As a result of the highly varied nature of the support given, the actual number of pupils receiving such support was not systematically registered. According to some estimates made in the beginning of the 1970s more than 60,000 pupils (10-11% of the total pupil population) were offered special support of an 'integrated' kind. It would, however, be misleading to refer to all these pupils as handicapped, but actually many of them would 'normally' have been regarded as special school clients.

From 1955 the responsibility for providing special education was placed either with the State or with the local authorities (the lack of clarity as to who had principal authority in this field was a problem in itself, which we will not go into here). There is no doubt that special education expanded under the local system and - in spite of existing official plans - stagnated under the state system in this period. Many also became aware of the fact that it was not educational reasons but a variety of other circumstances, mostly unrelated to educational considerations, that decided under which of the two special education systems a particular handicapped child would obtain its educational training. To the child and its family the question of 'system' was highly relevant, particularly because a provision in the state special schools normally required that the child left its home, the family and the neighbourhood for most of the year - for years. A strong demand for local provisions was the basis for one of the more specific principles for the organisation of special education laid down by Parliament in 1967, which stated that 'the child should to a great extent be allowed to live in its natural environment' and not be required to move out 'unless it is considered absolutely necessary'.

On these terms a fully decentralised system of special education was established in Norway, i.e. the local authorities became responsible for catering for all pupils living within their local territories. For this purpose the local education budgets were strengthened by a system of new earmarked economic transfers from the state. In general the local authorities were expected to be capable of offering provisions for all within the ordinary, local schools. However, if they could not offer a proper provision for a particular child, they might apply for a place in any of the special schools (still) run by the State or apply for a place in a local special school outside the commune in question. The point is that the local authorities would have to find a suitable provision and pay for it.

Another significant point also worth noticing here is the fact that since 1980 the final decision concerning the possible placement of a child in a special school has been left to the parents (according to another supplementary regulation). Thus the local school cannot transfer a handicapped pupil to a special school against the will of the parents.

Integration, decentralisation and evaluation

In the preceding sections an account of 'integration' policies as a significant and vital constituent of Norwegian educational policies in general has been given. I have tried to go beyond mere abstract ideas by linking the policy to more concrete, but still central goals and to particular events. Norwegian educational policy may appear over-ambitious when systematically outlined from the integration policy perspective, but it is not 'just rhetoric' and therefore deserves to be seriously taken into consideration when a national system of evaluation is to be discussed.

Furthermore, the policy dimension here outlined may illustrate, probably better than most other examples one might choose for the purpose of such discussions, how deep into the educational system and school practice decentralisation have actually been extended in Norway, and - consequently - how difficult the evaluation issue has in fact become. The nature and extent of the difficulties for evaluation will be further examined in this section.

First, it should be observed that few countries, if any, have gone further in eliminating 'unnecessary' distinctions between children with special educational needs and others. Consider for example, the fact that all special legislation in the field of education has been abolished, the total lack of registration by labels (categories) for administrative purposes throughout the educational system, the large extent to which ordinary and special education are overlapping provisions within the system, and the mixed roles of special and ordinary teachers in the local schools. One of the few important distinctions in this field that existed in the first decade after the introduction of the reform, was financial (earmarked budget transfers for special education or 'integration' purposes), but this distinction also disappeared with the introduction of the new income system for the communes (and the counties) in 1986.

Whereas the development of local decision-making are common tendencies in most countries, it is particularly characteristic of the Norwegian situation that there are relatively few matters left that require formal decisions. At the same time as standards concerning learning and knowledge acquisition have become individually based, examinations and other assessment procedures have been reduced to a minimum for all pupils. Another characteristic particularly related to special education and the integration of handicapped pupils is that decentralisation of responsibility is to a very little extent balanced by 'national safeguards' in the Norwegian system.

A combined effect of the integration/decentralisation policy is therefore that most of the distinctions, points of registration and quality measures that are traditionally used as 'indicators' for evaluation purposes, are not immediately 'at hand' and easily available in the Norwegian system.

The difficulties discussed so far are mostly practical barriers to evaluation. Other difficulties are of a more tensional kind, indicating the conflicts implied and the fact that the system in its present shape represents a delicate balance between central and local power that may be disturbed by the introduction of a centrally based, national system for educational evaluation. As far as the more conflicting set of difficulties are concerned, the following experiences may serve as examples.

From the point of view of the handicap organisations, individual persons and their parents, decentralisation was closely linked with the demand for 'administrative normalisation' (cf. section II. 3 above). It was a question of equity, but also a question of getting a better, more flexible provision. Decentralisation of services and provisions was also regarded as a crucial step towards social and (finally) societal integration for handicapped people.

All agreed to the principle, but many without necessarily being willing to limit the range of options accordingly, i.e. they wanted to take advantage of a decentralised provision as well as having the option or the safeguard of a national programme in addition (cf. OECD, 1987). Similarly, as far as local provisions were concerned, they wanted to take advantage of a fully integrated programme in the local school as well as having the possibility to choose a provision in a local special school or special class. Briefly, they wanted two systems of provision among which they could move as freely as possible and according to individual interests and needs - from time to time.

From a central political-administrative point of view operating two separate systems of provisions in this field is obviously connected with great difficulties. Under the current political-social conditions a 'cheap' special school system could no longer be defended, and if both systems should be of good standard, the economic consequences would be remarkable, particularly in a country where the size of the population is too small to run one system on an economically 'sound' basis.

Furthermore, a special school system will by necessity have to be established and operated on the basis of some kind of conceptualisation concerning 'special populations'. From an administrative point of view the experience is, however, that it is generally very difficult to distinguish logically and coherently the 'special' populations from the so called 'normal populations' on the basis of any such distinctions (OECD, 1983a). In a modern society where the pressure on the ordinary school system is considerable, demands for special provisions and for the elimination of 'difficult' children for a variety of reasons are correspondingly strong, the consequences of operating a 'special' system, parallel to the ordinary one, may be insurmountable. Not only will the special system tend to expand beyond economically acceptable limits, but also the high number of the population in special provisions will threaten the ideological basis for the school in modern societies.

In a wider perspective the 'services for all' approach can therefore be regarded as a measure for the purpose of stabilising society in its (post)modern form. The role of the school is of course fundamental in this respect, which may explain why education is normally the first public sector where the principle has been fully adopted.

For reasons already mentioned, 'services for all' approaches cannot be economically effectively operated from the centre. Thus decentralisation becomes necessary for using limited resources more effectively, in accordance with wide and flexible purposes, but also by practising the necessary controls. Decentralisation may also be useful for raising resources not available, or impossible to generate or mobilise for certain purposes from the centre (Weiler, 1988).

The last point is not the least important in relation to the wide 'resource concept' one must have in mind when the issue is the integration of handicapped young people. However, to obtain such effects, decentralisation will actually have to go beyond the local authority administrative level and down to the 'street-level-bureaucracy' (Lipsky, 1980).

All these arguments point to the local administrative level as generally more capable of making decisions and finding solutions in this policy field than the central authorities. Other arguments point, however, to the central political level as being in fact unwilling to make unpopular decisions (such as limiting demands for expansion and extra resources) and therefore more or less avoiding to take responsibilities in policy areas where ideological resistance is likely to turn up (Eckhoff, 1983). According to this argument decentralisation is not so much the question of the state being deprived of its power, but as an example of the state having actually resigned from using it. Weiler describes this as 'the fundamental ambivalence of the state' in relation to decentralisation.

In finishing this section it is emphasised that the central authorities have in fact played a rather passive role in the implementation of the integration policy, and that the more active part has been played by various actors at the local levels. This may explain why Norway is a mixture of 'integrating' communes (or local schools), 'segregating' communes, and 'in-between' communes (Dahl *et al.*, 1982; Lindbekk, 1987).

A national system for evaluation of education in Norway

Considering the outline of educational policy and the Norwegian situation given in the sections above, what conclusions could possibly be drawn in response to the proposal for a national system of evaluation in Norway?

The list of 'points' presented below should neither be regarded as a set of exhaustive nor conclusive responses to the question, but as an attempt to clarify some implications of the preceding discussions.

1. From a professional point of view there is no doubt that evaluation is a useful instrument in education. Education without evaluation is in fact an unthinkable possibility! Thus the question is not whether we shall have evaluation, but the framework for it and how to do it.

My first concern is that if a national evaluation system is to be established in Norway, the policy area that has been outlined above should be included in the programme. This is vital for at least two reasons:

(a) The policy area in question needs to be stimulated. Evaluation - according to carefully designed schemes - may have a stimulating effect on policies, cf. that what is evaluated is important, and that non-attendance may indicate neglect and that the policy intentions with related practice may gradually vanish.

(b) A possible (unintended) effect of a sharpened focus on evaluation as a governing system in education is a narrowing down of policy goals. Compare (a) above and the well-documented fact that data easily 'at hand', what can be registered by standardised techniques, measured by size, weight or numbers and analysed accordingly may obtain priority, particularly when the intention is to cover larger systems (national programmes). It is therefore necessary to ensure that evaluation efforts are confronted with the complexities of educational policies and that what count as 'policies' and not just fragmented elements of such ideas, are guiding and controlling the evaluation programmes.

2. A second main concern, which follows directly upon the previous point, is to ensure that approaches to evaluation, including the development and selection of indicators for assessing the qualities of Norwegian education, are regarded as a challenge for a political-professional oriented and broadly skilled expertise (rather than a task for a neutral-technical expertise, cf. OECD, 1989, p. 32).

Given the character of Norwegian education policy priorities a variety of assessment strategies and techniques are definitely required. Traditional methods must be improved to serve as proper instruments, but the development of new indicators and assessment methods is even more important. Particularly to be mentioned here is the need for a system of assessment that could go beyond formal indicators and also bring out, for example, qualitative insights from significant participants/actors at various levels within the system (Neave, 1987).

3. As previously mentioned the Ministry has played a rather passive role in the implementation of the integration policy. The idea of a national programme for evaluation of education seems to imply a politically stronger and more active centre than we have so far seen in this field in Norway. One implication of a national evaluation programme is that it requires policy purposes to be interpreted into practice (according to evaluation technology we should rather say 'operationalised'), which the Norwegian political centre, as far as we have just seen, for various reasons has mostly resigned from doing. A logical conclusion on this point is therefore that a (strong) national programme of evaluation is not likely to be established in Norway - at least not under the present political circumstances and management conditions.

The Ministry is of course interested in evaluation (and control), and it is also under a certain political pressure for providing evaluation programmes. However, it is also aware of the difficulties and the contradictory elements involved (compare the complicating factors mentioned in section III - above). By initiating the EMIL project, under which auspices this Conference is taking place, the Ministry signals its interest in evaluation, as well as wins time, - for considering the situation and for searching out models or schemes of evaluation on which it can - if necessary - safely land.

Less ambitious models are definitely needed, i.e. particularly models that can give the centre a less demanding role in relation to evaluation activities and that can balance the power and control and other related interests between the centre and the periphery at the point where it can be politically accepted. For the sake of illustration a few examples of possible 'less ambitious evaluation schemes' are briefly sketched out below:

(a) A first response to the demands for evaluation might be to launch a programme for improving the educational statistics in Norway. Also the national system for school documentation needs to be extended and improved. Such efforts may not be evaluation in the real sense, but it is actually the kind of information many have wanted, and so the demands have been put under the evaluation umbrella.

(b) Instead of a systematic programme of evaluation, single projects may be taken up when required, and may then be dealt with on an ad hoc basis - preferably by dispersing contracts between different research groups and types of institutions (universities, district and other regional colleges). This is more or less the scheme presently operated by the Ministry. It places the Ministry in a (relatively hidden) position of governing and control whereas at the same time representing a 'democratic' and 'decentralised' approach.

(c) One problem with scheme (b) is that if evaluation activities should increase, the Ministry would not be able to deal with the workload (neither politically nor administratively). It would need an 'extension', e.g. an external body which could operate as a national centre in close cooperation with the Ministry and by applying more or less the same strategies of negotiations and contracting as described under (b).

The Advisory Councils (for Basic Education, Upper Secondary Education, Adult Education, etc.) are established outside the Ministry, but they are too sectorised to take on overall responsibilities in this field, and probably neither 'close' enough (to the Ministry) nor independent enough (from practice) to become the seat of such a strategic and evaluative body as here outlined. The newly established 'Programme for educational research' (established in 1988 upon a joint initiative between the Ministry of Education, the Ministry of Cultural and Scientific Affairs and the Norwegian Research Council for Science and the Humanities) would probably be a better alternative for such purposes.

References

Dahl, Marit, Tangerud, H. and Vislie, Lise (1982), *Integration of Handicapped Pupils in Compulsory Education in Norway*, Oslo: Universitetsforlaget.

Eckhoff, T. (1983), *Statens styringssmuligheter*, Oslo: Tanum-Nordli.

Lindbekk, T. (1987), 'Autonomy and local policies in Norwegian educational authorities', *Scandinavian Journal of Educational Research, vol.31, pp. 181-90.*

Lipsky, M. (1980), *Street-level Bureaucracy: Dilemmas of the Individual in Public Services*, New York: Russel Sage.

Lundgren, U. (1989), *Educational Policy Making, Decentralisation and Evaluation: An Invitation to Papers*, EMIL Conference document, Oslo: NORAS.

Neave, G. (1987), 'An overview', paper prepared for CERI international conference on 'The Role of the Central Inspectorate in Defining, Assessing, and Reporting on Quality in Education', Oxford.

OECD (1976), *Reviews of National Policies for Education: Norway*, Paris: OECD, Education Committee.

OECD (1981), *The Education of the Handicapped Adolescent*, Paris: OECD.

OECD (1983a), *The Education of Minority Groups: An Enquiry into Problems and Practices of Fifteen Countries*, Paris: OECD.

OECD (1983b), *Integration of Handicapped Pupils in Compulsory Education in Norway: An Appraisal of Current Policies and Practices*, Paris: CERI HA/84.01.

OECD (1987), *Active Life for Young People with Disabilities*, Paris: OECD.

OECD (1988), *Review of Educational Policy in Norway: Examiners' Report and Questions*, Paris: OECD, Education Committee.

OECD (1989), *Decentralisation and School Improvement: New Perspectives and Conditions for Change*, Paris: CERI/CD (89) 4.

Weiler, H. N. (1988), *Education and Power: The Politics of Educational Decentralization in Comparative Perspective*, Stanford University.

Chapter 14

Decentralised evaluation for Norway

Ernest R. House

In his excellent analysis of the evaluation issues posed in a decentralisation context (see Chapter 3), Ulf Lundgren has presented four models for the governing of education, arrayed along the central-local and political-professional dimensions:

	Political	*Professional*
Central	A	B
Local	D	C

In this chapter I would like to suggest what idealised evaluation procedures might consist of at each of these levels in a decentralised national educational system.

These constructions are necessarily idealised rather than real because implementation of actual evaluation procedures depends on the particularities of the real world, on the workings, organisation, and politics of Norwegian education.

Two general considerations guide this presentation. The first is that the primary causal factors of classroom learning are under direct control of local teachers, who essentially determine classroom learning processes regardless of restrictions and mandates imposed by political authorities. Consequently, significant improvements classroom instruction must necessarily engage local classroom teachers intensively. This consideration is counter to policies currently being implemented in the educational systems of the US and UK, which increasingly impose mandates from above, and with quite unproductive results. Professionals actually control classrooms and must have considerable authority and latitude in their professional work if classroom learning is to improve.

The second consideration is that other groups, including parents, local and national government authorities, and the public at large, must have better knowledge of the schools. That is, there are legitimate demands for accountability to which professional educators must respond. Different groups have needs for different kinds of information about the schools.

Parents want to know about local school operations, whereas national leaders want to know how the schools fit into national goals, such as national economic development.

Local government leaders have yet other needs for information, such as budgets and community impact. Hence, the schools must provide evaluation information of different types to various audiences. Conflict arises from the fact that educators must be accountable to external groups while simultaneously maintaining enough autonomy to improve.

So beginning with the local level I present a pure form of decentralised local professional evaluation, then proceed to accountability to local political groups, then to the central political level, and finally to the central professional level. I conclude by discussing briefly the limits imposed by the international economic order.

Local professional evaluation

What would a model of decentralised local professional evaluation look like, without regard to pressures from the other levels? Imagine a small school or a department within a large school in which the teachers of the unit come together to evaluate their own performances. The master teacher has tape recorded one of her classes, and she plays the tape recording for the other teachers, stopping it often to make comments and criticise her own performance, taking care to explicate the reasons for her actions at different points in time. The other teachers make cautious comments about her teacher performance and ask questions. Why did she call upon that student at that time? How was she able to keep young Henrik under control, considering that he is so difficult to handle? How will she test for the material she is teaching? Is a copy of her test available? Through commentary, explication, and questions by herself and her fellow teachers, the master teacher proceeds with a critique of her own lessons, using herself and her own teaching as an exemplar of classroom critique.

After a while the other teachers begin contributing comments and mild criticisms about how the lessons might have been handled better. The younger, novice teachers listen intently, learning why the master teacher does the things that she does, hearing her reasons for her actions. They discover that she has doubts about her own teaching, worries about how she has handled particular students. It is apparent that she cannot solve all the problems that arise in her classroom. They learn the professional wisdom of the master teacher's experience accumulated over the years, and also that she has fallibilities. In later sessions that year the next best teacher exposes her lessons to similar critique by the group, and so on, until by the end of the year, the novice teachers feel confident enough to expose their own classrooms to analysis and to admit the serious difficulties they are having in their teaching.

Teacher talk during these sessions is always about specific incidents, specific lessons, rather than about the broad and distant generalities of research. The teachers talk about particular students they share, and there is a check upon what they say since they have considerable knowledge of each other's teaching and classroom performance. None of this information or discussion travels outside the group. No school administrator or outsider is privy to the internal criticisms of this group of colleagues, so that the teachers' discussion is privy to the internal criticisms of this group of colleagues, so that the teachers' discussion is phrased in the specifics of the classroom, the advice is highly relevant to action that can be taken immediately, centring on the controllable specifics of the teachers' everyday lives.

From this sort of self-critical process, over a long period of time, one might expect gradually improved teacher performance, more camaraderie and better morale. One might expect not only that individual teacher performance would be improved but that also the collective performance of the school as a whole would be improved as the school faculty developed a collective wisdom that was passed on to new generations of teachers. That is, the school faculty would be generating particular knowledge of their field of endeavour, much as university faculties generate knowledge of special research phenomena. It is critical that no administrators be intimately involved in this process, because such exposure would be too threatening and intimidate the teachers into silence and confusion, and hence into no improvement. Rather, administrators should serve as facilitators for this professional self-critical development.

This model, of course, is one of pure decentralised collegial evaluation, not unlike that of a university faculty when it is working well. It is one version of what Lundgren calls the 'local professional' model. It offers promise of slow but steady improvement in classroom practice, improvement in terms of the factors that are under direct teacher control. It provides teachers the opportunity to control aspects of their teaching environment and stands in contrast to models of imposed teacher performance in which it is assumed that some external authority can determine what teachers should do in particular circumstances, an assumption that is almost always incorrect.

Local political accountability

Of course, such a system of pure decentralised professional evaluation is incomplete. Its limits are that it ignores factors that lie outside teacher control - these are many in modern educational systems - and that it offers no accountability, or indeed no account to parents, the public or other government authorities. Peer evaluation does not address the concerns of parents and public officials who have other responsibilities, although such procedures do hold great promise for improving classroom instruction and student learning.

In his incisive analysis of educational accountability, Kogan puts the problem succinctly: 'The policy problem is that whilst education is financed and sponsored as a public activity, it is offered in institutions which are largely closed to public scrutiny and difficult to supervise from the outside' (Kogan, 1986, p. 17). Our model of pure professional peer evaluation deliberately and necessarily excludes others and does not provide any means of understanding schools or influencing them from the outside. Typically, local political accountability is provided by a lay council or governing board that oversees the local school. However, this form of local political accountability is not entirely satisfactory. Lay boards seem to be dominated by professional educational administration who carefully control the information fed to them.

Other local accountability procedures include reports of test scores and supervisory visits by the local inspectorate. Recent innovations include a 'report card' on each school, similar to that issued for pupils, which reports local test scores and a wide array of information about the school, and vouchers for parents to place their children in schools of their choice, a resort to market mechanisms. These trends correspond to Kogan's three main models of accountability: public or state control (usually manifested in managerialism), professional control and consumerist control. Kogan argues persuasively for the maintenance of at least some state control, and I concur that state control is extremely important.

Test scores, statistical report cards and vouchers do not provide an accurate picture of what is happening in the schools themselves. An additional idea would be to have members of the public team with trained professionals to produce case studies of particular schools and programmes, these cases then being presented to the general public for review and discussion. Such an approach would provide an intimate portrait of local school operations, with all the good and bad such familiarity would entail. The case study might include interviews with teachers and students, classroom observations, examples of the students work and even video and audio tapes of the classes themselves, all with the teachers' permission, of course. This combined public-professional team approach would mitigate against professionals providing a whitewash of the schools. Producing such case studies would be costly in time and effort, however, and require special training for team members. Simons (1987) has presented a rationale for such school self-evaluation.

Central political accountability

At the national level such case studies by social scientists or joint projects by professionals and public would be useful but insufficient. For example, in an evaluation of the Promotional Gates programme in New York City, the central Board of Education found case studies of classrooms to be quite informative because the Board members were so far removed from the city's millions of students and thousands of teachers. However, large-scale units also need other information. Education is of such importance in the modern nation state that there are legitimate concerns at the central level of government that extend beyond the schools themselves. Who is being educated to what level? What are they learning? How much is it costing? What effect is education having on the larger society? What social groups are benefiting at the expense of what other groups? One would surmise from reading an historic sketch of Norway that there is strong concern for social equality and for the preservation of Norwegian culture. It would be useful to have indicators of both economic equality and the cultural content learned by students.

A system of national educational data collection seems reasonable, even in a highly decentralised educational system - provided the data are handled in the proper way. The major problem with national data collection schemes is that they are used to attempt to control educational results rather than to seek information. For example, most American states have implemented vast testing programmes in attempts to mandate educational outcomes. The intent is not to secure information but rather to establish numerical indicators and standards for which teachers and schools can be held directly responsible. For example, in 1981 New York City stipulated that no child could be passed on to the next grade level unless he or she had attained a particular score on the district wide achievement test. The idea behind this scheme was that teachers and students were not working hard enough, and that the attachment of student promotion to test scores would induce both students and teachers to work harder. After three years this scheme was abandoned because the students were scoring no higher on the tests than before.

Using mandated achievement tests to coerce is a common mentality among legislators, governors and central administrators. This thinking derives in part from frustrated attempts to control educational events. Empirical studies indicate that these coercive testing schemes fail eventually. Where strong pressure is applied, teachers comply by teaching the tests. For example, when a judge ordered the San Diego school district to raise the test scores of minority students, the school district did so by teaching the students the actual test items. Although one might argue that such behaviour deserves the deception that it engenders, these machinations introduce vast amounts of distrust into the educational system and absorb efforts that could be directed to improving education. The public at large is led to believe that education is improving when in fact it is not. Appearance in the form of test scores substitutes for reality.

There is good reason why such uses of tests do not result in improved education: the causal factors that can improve education are simply not attached to indicators such as test scores. The problem is akin to changing barometric pressure by manipulating a barometer. The true causal factors lie elsewhere. Yet this detachment of the factors that can actually cause educational improvement from the indicators themselves continues to elude many central authorities. Test scores cannot be used successfully as instrument to coerce educational improvement. National governments have good reason to collect test data to inform policy decisions, but this is quite a different use.

Test scores are a desirable part of national information about schools so that one can discern what students are learning. However, tests lend themselves to far less decisive policy interpretation than one might think. Different tests measure quite different things, even when they are supposed to be tests of the same content. Testing requires specifying particular content to be tested for, which dictates that other important knowledge will be neglected. So tests do not provide a universal picture of student learning as the public generally believes. The content of tests must be examined carefully because tests can reflect only a small fraction of what is learned. Still, such partial information can be useful at the national level provided the results are not misinterpreted.

One would think from the history of Norway that certain cultural knowledge might be deemed valuable, in addition to the traditional content of mathematics, science, language, and social studies. Other useful information at the national level might be school costs, attendance, level of attainment, numbers of students and teachers and so on. Of special concern for a democratic country so dedicated to equality would be tracking the inequality in the schools and the society at large. To guard against improper pressures on the test scores themselves, thin sampling schemes might be employed. Of course, test scores and other educational indicators provide only a partial picture of schooling itself. More vivid assessments of the schools and students could be provided by qualitative case studies sponsored by the central government.

Central-professional

So far we have presented a picture of an idealised evaluation system in which the local professionals are busy critiquing their own work, in which the local community and political authorities are being provided with case studies, reports and accounts of schooling that they help produce, and in which the central government is collecting a range of statistics on equality and student achievement and sponsoring studies of the internal workings of the schools by social scientists and professional evaluators in order to address national problems and to provide a portrait of the national educational system. What might be done at the central level for professionals?

Teachers operating within the local community are necessarily focused internally and parochially. Professional support at the central level might entail introducing teachers to new ideas from outside, such as from research and the universities. It would also be good to have professionals conducts studies of their own professional development. The central government might sponsor teacher research of teacher activities or even teacher research on aspects of the total educational system with a view to national reform. Ideally, the teachers organisations would be involved in evaluation in something more than a cursory role. The central authorities might also promote research skills among the teachers, especially as it relates to developing the critical skills necessary to critiquing their own practice. Research concepts and methods supportive of such evaluation practices have yet to be developed and will be eventually require an investment of sophisticated research talent.

The international economic order

As Lundgren notes in his analysis, national governments are no longer totally in control of many aspects of their national lives, particularly their national economies. All countries are now tied into global international trading markets, and economic decisions affecting national life are made in places far away and for reasons other than national benefit. Market economies bring all facets of society into their orbit and have a destabilizing effect on society because they dissolve traditional structures and social relations (Gilpin, 1988).

This internationalisation is reflected in calls for education to produce certain types of students and knowledge so that nations can compete successfully in international markets. In many countries these pressures have resulted in increasingly centralised educational systems, and with standards being mandated from above in the form of standardised tests and national curricula. The United States and the UK stand as examples of this trend. However, it is by no means certain that centralised national educational systems and narrowing their focus will indeed produce the benefits that advocates contend, i.e. a more efficient national economic system that will compete successfully with the Japanese. In fact, the evidence of recent educational reforms in the United States, which have been carried out by political authorities without consultation with professional educators, is that the educational systems are becoming increasingly inefficient and unproductive - which in turn calls for more centralised reform. In other words, the effects of the reforms are the opposite of what the reformers expected (Elmore and McLaughlin, 1988; McNeil, 1986).

Norway exhibits a provocative departure from the current international pattern. In spite of much talk about decentralisation as a potential development strategy in education, true decentralisation has rarely been tried anywhere. The Norwegian decentralisation provides a fascinating contrast to the apparently ineffective and counterproductive reforms now underway elsewhere in the world. Norwegian decentralisation must also be set within the context of an international economic order that is rapidly falling apart. That is, the United States has lost its ability to enforce the liberal trade order has dominated the world since the Second World War. What will follow the disintegration of this international economics order is unknown, but the emergence of more nationalistic trading blocs seems highly likely (Gilpin, 1987).

Economic nationalism asserts the primacy of politics over economics, that the market should be subordinate to the interests of the state, as opposed to liberal theory, which asserts the market should be free of political influences and that economics and politics exist in separate spheres. For liberals social classes, ethnic loyalties, and national boundaries are assumed not to exist. For nationalists the self-sufficiency of the nation is valued over economic interdependence (Gilpin, 1987).

The point is that Norway may be unique in its decentralisation reforms, but the strong economically induced external pressures on national educational systems may be abating, or at the very least changing in character over the next several years as the international political economy undergoes a major metamorphosis. Norway in its decentralisation may be as well prepared to contend with these sweeping changes as any other country.

References

Elmore, R. F. and McLaughlin, M.W. (1988), *Steady Work: Policy, Practice, and the Reform of American Education*, Santa Monica, Calif.: The Rand Corporation, February.

Gilpin, R. (1987), *The Political Economy of International Relations*, Princeton University Press.

Kogan, M. (1986), *Education Accountability: An Analytic Overview*, London: Hutchinson.

Lundgren, U. P. (1989), *Educational Policy Making, Decentralisation and Evaluation*.

McNeil, L. M. (1986), *Contradictions of Control: School Structure and School Knowledge*, London: Routledge and Kegan Paul.

Royal Ministry of Cultural and Scientific Affairs and Royal Ministry of Church and Education (1987), *Reviews of National Policies for Education: Norway*, report to OECD, Oslo.

Simons, H. (1987), *Getting to Know Schools in a Democracy*, London: Falmer Press.

Chapter 15

Evaluation in a decentralised school system: where do we stand? Where are we heading?

Tom Tiller

School evaluation - an instrument for what purpose?

The Norwegian school system is celebrating its 250th birthday this year. Not exactly a senior, but old enough to enjoy adult status and to make its decisions more independently. The ideal of innovation has picked up speed during recent decades. Norway has apparently believed in 'the good development project', as well as 'the successful solution'. Even if this belief has become somewhat frayed, new projects in the 9 year compulsory school and the upper secondary school are continuously being launched. Does the school benefit from all this innovation? To a certain degree it probably does, but doubt obviously prevails. Could we have done things differently? Should we have considered matters more carefully?

School evaluation is a new project with the aim of creating a better system. School evaluation and decentralisation must be regarded as related issues. We possess one of the most decentralised school systems in the world, and maybe one of the least externally controlled. This fact is both the school's strength and its weakness. The individual school has been given a far more extended mandate for development through decentralisation. This is evidence of its adult status, or more precisely: the school as an institution has become a grown-up servant.

It did not take many years after decentralisation, however, before reservations appeared: Are we going in the wrong direction? Are the authorities losing control? A lurking centralism can be identified. Symptoms indicate that the authorities are confused. The reins have already been somewhat tightened. On the drawing board, the stricter lines become visible: A state consultative body has proposed replacing the expert councils with a smaller and more efficient educational directorate organised to regain control and efficiency.

Systematic evaluation is to re-establish the control that was lost through the intense decentralisation measures. So there we are, in the same boat as a number of other countries, and with our share of the same antagonisms and conflicts. School evaluation is probably regarded a tool for obtaining different goals. Should the new project serve to control or to develop? This could turn into a difficult conflict in the years to come, especially if we fail to discuss such subjects from the beginning.

School-decentralisation can be compared with general tendencies in the political and economic systems on several points. Nelson Polsby characterises the question of centralisation-decentralisation as one of the great topics of modern politics. (Polsby, 1979). Current events in education are deeply rooted in society. Hans Weiler illustrates this clearly in a paper debating education and power. Behind the surface advantages of decentralisation greater efficiency, apportionment of goods and increased learning, can discern deeper purposes: decentralisation as a tool for the handling conflicts concerning educational questions, which will always be present in a modern society and decentralisation as a compensatory legitimation (compare Chapter 3).

The strong and partially concealed political background for decentralisation in the school system is perhaps first of all noticeable in the conflict between the advantages of the new profile, and the loss of control and direction that are associated with the old methods. All genuine decentralisation will necessarily involve distribution of power and control to a certain degree. Strong tensions usually arise when one tries to maintain as much central control as possible, and at the same time argues heartily in favour of decentralisation (Polsby, 1979).

In this chapter, I consider seriously the decentralising of our education system. I do not speculate in hidden arguments about school evaluation. I therefore mainly underline how this may be reinforced on the local level, in the individual school. The reasoning so far is quite simple: the schools have received a substantially larger development mandate through decentralisation. This mandate also calls for enlarged, self-imposed quality control and evaluation. What are the basic conditions for the schools being able to manage these new tasks in a satisfactory manner? What advice can we give the teachers and the school authorities?

Our modern society demands quick decisions and fast action. The school authorities feel pressed in the question of decentralisation and school evaluation. The danger of the development processes being forced too strongly truly exists. Think thoroughly, and systematise the best of the available knowledge in this field is thus a good advice. Talk to the leading researchers and thinkers, listen to these persons' advice, but consider the usefulness and advantages in relation to the distinct character and goals of the Norwegian school.

The need for good orienteering maps

Map and compass are essential in this situation. The terrain is very difficult to follow with a number of steep and dangerous cliffs. The fog still rests quite heavily on the landscape. I think it would be an idea first of all to work out a survey of the terms and concepts that are now being used. The concepts provide information about the activities, but do not present the whole background. Thus, it is necessary to study the school's everyday life, as well as the actors' understanding of it on the scene. For example what do most teachers understand by the new term 'school evaluation'? Not long ago, I gave a lecture on the relationship between school development and school evaluation. My preparatory work consisted of talking to teachers about their perception of the term 'school evaluation'. They were all very insecure. One statement, however, was given all-round support: 'In a way it sounds frightening. We perform lots of daily evaluations of pupils, each other, parents and the school management, but this is a more flexible evaluation, which is adequate for our competence and working situation. I suppose that this new thing has to do with the school being evaluated according to the top-down perspective, but I of course hope that teachers will play an active part in this process'.

The teacher focus on a key issue with this statement. Part of the school evaluation project will obviously be 'top-down', whereas we may hope for, and should work for, a better backing of the school's self-evaluation programme. I see the internal, school-based evaluation as the most exciting and challenging part of the project, as well as the incentive that may really bring the development onto a new and prosperous track. It is a national aim to come up with measures that can strengthen and renew the school system. The country should therefore be interested in stimulating more conscious and systematic work on the part of the individual schools in their evaluations, and safeguarding high quality.

Strong decentralisation has created a need for distance and space. What happens in this field in other countries? What activities and concepts are reflected in the general evaluation context, and especially in the area of school self-evaluation? I have chosen to begin with experiences and conclusions from a European Council conference on evaluation, held in Scotland in December 1988.

It was quickly realized that the representatives from the thirteen participating countries had very different understandings of the contents of this term. Everybody seemingly agreed that evaluation was important and had a future, but how the new tool was to be applied created much heat discussion. Different opinions of and attitudes towards evaluation reflected different basic values, attitudes towards authorities and accountability, and consideration of how both development and control could be marshalled. Professor John Nisbet summed up the conference by drawing

Figure 15.1 Evaluation - a cognitive map

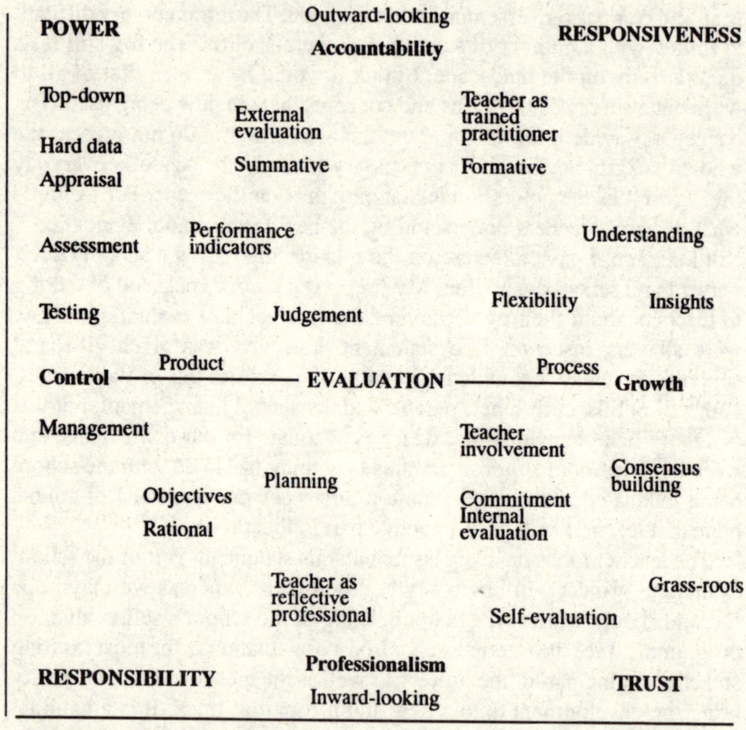

a cognitive map (see Figure 15.1), based on terms that had been used during the discussions in groups and plenary. This map enabled a rough sorting of underlying values, principles, activities, opinions and interests. Moreover, the intention of the cognitive map was to provide a basis for considering action in the field of evaluation.

The cognitive map in Figure 15.1 expresses tension both between north-south and east-west. There is a visible tension between evaluation as an instrument for direction and control, and evaluation as a tool for increased professionalism and school development. We further see the conflict between external and internal accountability. Nisbet divides the field into four main sections, which may facilitate the identification of our own stand: power, responsiveness, trust and responsibility. Even though these are roughly divided sections, and hardly a model giving clear guidelines for action, Nisbet's framework may help to throw new light on where Norwegians stand, as well as our main direction in the continuing evaluation debate.

Where do we stand and in what direction are we going? What opinions are predominating in society, and what impact will they have on school self-evaluation and external evaluation? In what direction should we move? What answers can be found in the curricula for the 9-year compulsory school and the upper secondary school? There is an abundance of questions and answers! Questions and information are plentiful.

The most recent school language tells something about where we stand and where we probably will go, if we do not pay greater attention to a more thorough debate and analysis. We have seen a strong growth in the fields of organisation and management in the later years. Terms like rational planning, strategic planning, management, and so on, in a relatively short period of time have permeated our thinking and action. As far as I can see, technological and bureaucratic rationality has increased considerably through these new measures. Digging a little deeper into the causes will probably reveal some clear tracks of a system-theory. The question asked, among others, is whether this is a modern concealed example of the means-ends thinking. (Løvlie, 1984; Tiller, 1986). From the view of such observations and considerations, it is not surprising that the demands for more conscious and systematic evaluation contains strong arguments for more efficient control and direction. Words like testing and measuring appear at regular intervals. The idea of a Norwegian inspectorate body has been carefully aired. Signals calling for greater competition between schools, about stronger rights to in-service training, and more alternatives for the parents are evident, especially on the right wing of Norwegian politics. This no doubt goes in the direction of accountability and control on Nisbet's cognitive map (Figure 15.1). The foundation is clear enough: power.

However, we also see other ideas, arguments and signals going in the direction of growth and professionalism. Speeches concerning school policy contain many full marks concerning the need for school development and reinforcement of the teachers' competence. A white paper on Norwegian teacher training was recently published in which the keynote is the desire for an increased competence that may lead to school development being based on the ultimate objective in the national curriculum. (NOU, 1988: 32, *For et lærerrikt samfunn*).

The teacher organisations/unions argue that the school's main goal is to take care of the pupil as a whole person. Researchers have warned against taking the school for a profit-based organisation. The school's basic concept is learning, and the schools' primary work consists in providing meaningful and positive learning conditions. Teaching is an instrument for learning. The teacher's task is to coordinate the meeting between the pupil and the school (Tiller, 1989).

These type of arguments, which are also stressed by some politicians and bureaucrats, indicate what Nisbet calls 'inward-looking professionalism' and growth in the sense of actual development of the school as an organisation and institution. The basic values may here be defined as 'trust'. A comprehensive school-evaluation project of the kind that RVO (National Council for Upper Secondary Education) has implemented emphasises trust, self-evaluation, the actor's perspective, experiential learning, ownership and so on (Bjørndal, 1989). This project relates the national level to the regional and local levels, but particularly underlines the need to increase the individual school's ability to develop these desired qualities through self-evaluation.

In addition to these relatively clear points of view concerning value, we find a row of mixed relations. Many will claim that there is no difference between increased professionalism on one hand and control on the other. Furthermore, one can easily imagine that increased accountability required of school managers and teachers would be an excellent instrument for school development.

With reference to these considerations, we recognise that clarifying the Norwegian debates and activities concerning evaluation is not easy. Neither is it an easy task to express anything definite about the direction the development will take. What we can say for sure is that at present, we are able to identify clear differences in values, as well as the seeds for a number of conflicts in this field in the years to come.

At a time of an unstable economy, academia has shown the will and capacity for innovation. History proves that this is often so; ideas, creativity and drive increases in times of crisis. It is now up to us to promote this receptiveness for learning and development, and interconnect creativity and pedagogical enterprises in a fruitful manner. School evaluation could prove valuable in promoting the process, but regretfully, it may also put a spanner in the works.

Teachers and school managers have greatly emphasised the importance of making decentralisation function in practice. Pragmatism has been predominate. Analysing, reflection and basic thinking have not really prospered; some negative consequences of this are already appearing. Schools have been looking for other alternatives, and have opened their doors to oncoming new ideas and suggestions. The gurus have entered the scene, and the schools jump from one guru to the other. This kangaroo school is now turning into a problem. Present symptoms indicate that the actors are suffering from an increasing weariness, and are getting discouraged from repeatedly trying new ideas and proposals, which do not create the results hoped for.

In these opportunistic times, certain ideas 'sell' better than others. In a high-pressure every-day life, it is often a matter of finding solutions that can make tomorrow a little easier than today. Highly prioritised items on the list of wants will therefore be techniques and methods. The technological way of thinking and acting prospers in fertile soil in such situations.

Arrangements in favour of the 'responsibility' field on Nisbet's cognitive map (Figure 15.1) are the way forward for the next few years. The crucial question is what direction should the development take? Will it turn towards responsiveness, power or trust?

However, what is of great interest to us, is not where the development goes, but where it should go. Furthermore, it will be important to develop thoughts, ideas and practical alternatives, for action that are able to stimulate and guide the development process onto the right track. The educationalist should have a critical-constructive role. The educationalists must descend from the terrace and enter the field of play. To a greater degree than before, they must enter the schools and, in cooperation with the teachers, construct reasonable models and alternative actions. They of course must be careful not to lose the distance necessary in order to present sound analyses and clear perspectives, but Norwegian educationalists still have a lot in reserve.

Public attention is often attracted when evaluation and evaluation arrangements are on the agenda. We are talking about one of the most sensitive nerves of the school system and the society. There will always be a great deal of public rhetoric attached to such sensitive areas, and there will always be lots of disguised schemes as well as hidden knowledge and silent perspectives.

This tangle of values, tensions and open and latent messages, I believe calls for a number of simple and basic questions. The approach to the problems must be direct and without delay, or else this will lead to an arbitrary exploitation of the evaluation system. A situation like that is not desirable, and probably would soon result in a demoralising and subversive effect.

My simple question must thus read: Should the values and goals in our national curriculum still be taken seriously? Are these goals to be the primary guidelines for school evaluation? If the answer is yes, we also know something about where we would like to find ourselves in a few years, when we again take a look at Nisbet's cognitive map.

Locally based school self-evaluation: the new challenge

The self evaluation, of individual schools will present a new challenge. Some may ask 'what is new?'. Haven't the schools always carried out evaluations? Isn't school evaluation an established tradition? The teachers perform continuous evaluations of the pupils. A great amount of time is consumed for evaluation, preparing tests, giving tests, and correcting them. Individual pupils are discussed both in breaks and at the many staff meetings.

The complete perspective and a more conscious and systematic approach are new concepts of self-evaluation for which criteria for evaluation have been made clearer.

Complete perspective means that the evaluation is to consist of more than just an evaluation of the pupils, their skills and social qualifications. The other groups of actors, teachers, school managers, other employees and parents, are now the aim of systematic evaluation, and will have to participate more actively than has previously been the case. Equally, the school's relationship to society is an interesting field for evaluation. The entire school society has come into focus. The question will be how the school as an organisation manages to realise its goals. This work demands active participation in evaluation from all parties in the school society, including the pupils.

According to this, a tentative definition of school self-evaluation would be: 'School self-evaluation is a systematic and long-term analysis of the school society, where the aim is to evaluate the results of the pedagogical and subject-related work, the social environment, the organisational and administrative relations, as well as the relationship between school and society.' (RVO, 1988).

This work needs to be systematically planned. The evaluation must take place over time, as this is a matter of processes in a complex social system, a system with long and tough roots into the society that the school is serving. We are talking about institutionalising new arrangements in an organisation that has fixed its traditions throughout 250 years. In the past evaluations have tends to be unsystematic accidental, and undigested. The new approach to evaluation concerns institutionalisation of a new practice that involves radical new forms of activity. A serious school evaluation must also take the pupils seriously. The pupils' perspective must also be incorporated in a school self-evaluation. Quite a number of persons will feel this as threatening. Things take time, and things in this field should definitely be given the required time.

What qualifications are lacking, and what resources must be called on in order to enable the individual school to fulfil these requirements? We must move from descriptive to analytical competence; from the teacher as a consumer to the teacher as a producer. Lawrence Stenhouse's terms state the objective as 'the teacher as researcher' (Stenhouse, 1975). We need the researching teacher and a thinking school. This cannot be achieved overnight. We must thus ponder thoroughly, debate the new ideas for quite some time, and carefully proceed with the action. I do not believe much in quick and easy solutions. What is needed is a carefully considered and stage by stage development scheme. We must find out whether our authorities will consider such a development, and whether they dare go in for it on a long-term basis. In any case, I believe that researchers and the school staff must outline the stages of long-term schemes in a clear and convincing manner. The school itself must be able to create environments where cooperation, trust and reflection are central themes of every day life. They must find the strength to do something about the three 'isms': conservatism, individualism and presentationism. Schools must reveal and replace basic rules like privacy, territory and hierarchy through critical responsibility, openness and autonomy. Helen Simons among other things states: 'Unless schools are prepared to face the fundamental reversal of institutional traditions, and commit themselves to a new concept of what John Elliot calls intraprofessional accountability, it is unlikely that school self-evaluation can lead to constructive institutional development' (Simons, 1987, pp. 244-5).

In these development efforts, we must therefore be aware of the fact that something old must be thrown out and new rules and alternative actions must be implemented. This is a time-consuming and toilsome work. If we are to succeed in exposing the teachers' individual work in the public arena, where critical construction of the good alternative is the aim, we need both access to adequate arena and a reasonable adoption period in order to develop responsible and constructive conduct.

However, is it possible to bring this kind of message to the schools? Would they resist such development perspectives? Would it be safer to be evaluated externally, e.g. by state-appointed inspectors? We undoubtedly face many obstacles, but suppressing the challenges and requirements that school self-evaluation presents is poor strategy. It requires review and insight into possibilities, consequences and obstructions. John Elliot is one of those who underline that 'the full consciousness' is deficient when new school-evaluation arrangements are initiated (Elliot, 1979).

The school as a conflict organisation - consequences for the evaluation work

It is crucial that teachers and school managers acknowledge and understand what values pervade prevailing social structures and organisational arrangements. An important starting point for school evaluation is to recognise the school as a conflict organisation. (Pupils of the 9-year-compulsory school for example do not attend voluntarily.) At first sight, however, the school may seem to be a consensus organisation. The conflicts are minimised and suppressed through a number of records and administrative regulations. What will happen when an open collective self-evaluation takes place in such an organisation? Most likely the fronts will quickly meet, and disagreement regarding perspectives and values arise. Due to its nature, school evaluation will be opposed to the prevailing organisational form, which may create insurmountable obstacles, if the actors do not recognise and understand this kind of antagonism.

Self-reflection will demand that new investments be made to protect the critical and analytic activity. The thinking and reflexive school is not equivalent to the Norwegian standard variant. A first and important step in the preparation of a systematic evaluation will therefore be to identify and recognise the school's distinct character as an organisation.

The school's history is important at this stage. Gaining knowledge of the school's role as grading machinery for attractive social assets is part of our homework. Equally, it belongs to the history homework to follow the school's manifest function as a ranking body at best following the Jesuit pedagogical credo for today's hidden, but very strong differentiating tasks. The official goal is to qualify students. Differentiating is the concealed goal (Fredholm, 1988). A successful school evaluation requires that we are able to identify both open and concealed arrangements and functions. The competent and professional school evaluation cannot accept simple superfluous evaluations. Critical questions about whose needs and interests today's school reflects, and in what manner the school maintains, produces or changes the prevailing distribution of power in society, should be a part of this work. Equally, it is natural that the participants of the evaluation process discuss what values are included in the curriculum. The school's practice must be seen as a social construction and not as a nature-given norm.

It is necessary, but not sufficient, to develop check lists and guidelines for school self-evaluation. In this work, we should look to England, where these kind of instruments have been used for several years (e.g. McMahon *et al.*, 1984). The so-called GRIDs project (Guidelines for Review and Internal Development in Schools) have been criticised by among others, Helen Simons, for basing its work on the assumption of a hierarchical, bureaucratic and harmonious school organisation.

The GRIDs project thus was not able to challenge the deeper structures in the school, and lead to a change in the existing situation. The GRIDs process failed to recognise the school's special character as a conflict organisation. The collective self-evaluation of a school is in the end a question of organising and handling the conflicts, which are necessarily stirred up and revealed through the evaluation process.

Experiences from the GRIDs project indicate that the top managers are the most content with the arrangements. This logical and systematic model to a certain degree has functioned as a tool in school development, but its weakness is the failure to engage teachers in the evaluation of fundamental teaching and learning processes. Peter Holly, who was associated with the project, concludes that the arrangement 'succeeds only in tinkering at the organisational edges' (Holly, 1984, p. 14).

Furthermore, Holly in an interesting manner ponders the relationship between real change and the institutionalisation of miscellaneous ideas and projects. Ironically, facts prove, that the easier the process of institutionalisation goes, the more difficult it is to obtain actual changes. With reference to GRIDs he points to the fact that in spite of the project seeming to be democratic one may with good reason question whether it functions more like a preserving and conservative influence in the process of change (ibid., p. 15).

Advice

I refer to what has been said previously, and to my own experiences as an adviser for a recently started development project within school evaluation in the upper secondary school. With this background, I would like to state three hopefully helpful points. The first one deals with making a thorough consideration of the matter, talking at considerable length about it, and then carefully beginning the work. The next one focuses on the necessity of reinforcing experiential learning, and the third has to do with the pupil's perspective.

The National Council for Upper Secondary Education (RVO) decided to test two new ideas in two of our counties (Finnmark and Hedmark). After approximately one year of preparatory work, the project was started. It contains two stages; full further training of external and internal teaching supervisors, and development work in two counties over a 3-year period. The roles of the different levels in school evaluation have been analysed and discussed thoroughly. The majority of the weight is placed on the individual school's self-evaluation. The final objective is to improve the school's ability as an organisation to fulfil its social function. During the first 3 years, the school authorities on the central and regional levels will support actively the schools' self-evaluation. In the preparatory stage, the participants have appreciated this and clearly expressed the need for a theoretical training programme and a careful stage by stage programme of development.

The capacity for experiential learning must be increased. This is my second piece of advice. Norwegian researchers have pointed out that experiential learning does not hold a strong position in our schools. The last official report on teacher training has experiential learning as one of its basic principles. Experience over time is not enough if you do not learn anything in your daily work. Methodology is an especially weak point. There is little or no knowledge or competence in the field 'qualitative methods'. Ethnography and ethnographical methods like job analysis, shadowing and keeping journals are only rarely heard of, and even fewer people regularly practise the methods. However, teachers and school managers seem to be catching on to the usefulness of these kind of tools in the evaluation work. Experiences from the named project in the upper secondary school also show that motivation is high for working with these methods. However, the schools lack tradition and facilities for these kinds of thinking and activities. The room for action must be expanded. Time and space are critical variables. It is therefore necessary to organise and re-organise the school environment. Some schools have had positive experiences with the establishment of subject-related and pedagogical fora, but the problem is of course that this activity must take place within social settings which are firmly established.

My last piece of advice concerns the pupils and the significance of strengthening their perspective in school evaluation. This reinforcement means two things; first, that the adult actors in the schools work more systematically and conscientiously at recognising the school's and the pupils' circumstances from the juvenile point of view, and secondly, that the pupils' participation status is strengthened.

The term 'responsible learning' has obtained a central position in writing and speech lately. It is said that pupils should be allowed to participate actively in the planning, implementation and evaluation of school work. The pupils are to be made accountable. The basic rules of participatory democracy are to apply to the young ones as well. The pupils' importance as a resource to school development is stressed. The pupils are not to be the parentheses of school society. We wish to change the pupil's role from a passive recipient of the school's prepared knowledge, to an active participator in the learning process.

At present there is much rhetoric about responsible learning, but all of us share the responsibility for turning this into a reality. The traditional pupil role is far too established in our minds, as well as in the expectations of the schools and society, for it to be changed overnight. However, we have started an important process that must be continued. Through large projects in the fields of organisational development and management, we have learned that the pupil perspective was neglected. This was later pointed out as a weakness.

The organisational theory only exceptionally grants pupils the status of a full member of the school community. There has been an unilateral stake on developing the adult environment. The business model can usually be seen in the background; the pupils are the raw material to be processed and refined. Pupils are the ignorant. They do not know their own good - yet. They must therefore be trained and brought up. Seen in this perspective, responsible learning becomes a 'to teach the young ones' responsibility. We have come so far, that more and more people regard this development as unhealthy, and desire to do something about it. I believe that the time has come to take the pupils and their perspective seriously in the new school evaluation programmes, that are now coming into life. We are dealing with a large and all too poorly utilised resource.

Learning prospers best when the pupils identify known and close interests that preoccupy them. School knowledge is not something you can stuff into empty spaces. The spaces are not at all empty! Pupils possess an abundance of everyday knowledge. The big task will be to coordinate the school's knowledge the pupils' knowledge. It is an important task to find out the knowledge that the pupils bring. However, there are barriers, of course. The pupil's perspective is welcomed by the democratically-minded teachers, and sooner or later will challenge the narrow-minded instrumental teachers. Such confrontations, however, cannot be avoided in a work where evaluation is to be an instrument for developing the school system.

Review

Decentralisation has given the individual school and the teaching profession new and tremendous challenges. The question is whether resources and skills are available to meet these challenges, and how we can best introduce balance into the system. Increasingly promoted decentralisation is based on school development, among other things. We desire to improve our school system. We desire to understand the meaning of true development.

'Trust' is a central term in a decentralised school system. Without trust towards the teaching profession, the decision-making authorities would less likely have given the individual school such a wide mandate, as they have received previously. However, some uncertainty has been spreading lately. This uncertainty is understandable in view of the attacks on schools, particularly from the right wing. Even though we know that critics have their own motives and are often unreasonable, the uncertainty is still present. The media's gloomy picture has also left its marks. Parents and teachers who have other and more positive experiences cannot argue much with the black-and-white thinking, which has manifested itself lately.

I claim that the trust in teachers must be re-established. So far, the schools have responded well to the new challenge that decentralisation presents. We need to identify what to change and what to strengthen. There is no reason for changing tracks again. A turn towards centralism would be a catastrophe for the school.

School evaluation, where the individual school consciously and systematically evaluates its activity, is in line with the development mandate it has been given. We need a steady hand in the times ahead of us. New evaluation arrangements will be given substantial support. The point must be to come up with an evaluation that supports the aims of and perspectives school development.

In my opinion, the main effort should be on the local level - at the individual school, when school evaluation is concerned. School self-evaluation will help to preserve quality. However, this does not mean that other levels in the system will not perform evaluations. The important thing is to facilitate a positive educational ecology. We must avoid a situation where evaluation measures at different levels base their work on different basic values, and thus counteract each other. There will always be a certain risk for such an imbalance. Last year's development seems to indicate a somewhat exaggerated drive for evaluation. In his paper for the conference, Kjell Eide critically illuminates new, comprehensive and national evaluation systems (Eide, 1989). This kind of criticism is essential at this stage. Minor adjustments here and there would be all right, but extensive systems of testing, quantitative measuring, indicator-based research, national inspector bodies, and so on, may prove negative instead of positive. We may get so preoccupied with measurements and tests, that we forget to evaluate the quality in those fields that cannot be measured, but will have to be the object of sound judgement. Factual knowledge to a certain degree may be measured and weighed and compared from one country to another. However, on a higher knowledge level, it is difficult to compare countries in this way of analyses, and it is probably without any value. Also, what good does it do if we win the European knowledge contest, if this process leads us away from society's more important goals for the school system?

We feel relatively safe in expressing confidence in a school self-evaluation that is coloured by insight and knowledge, and that will serve as an appropriate instrument in developing the school in the desired direction. We should therefore concentrate on this field. School self-evaluation can be supplemented, but never replaced by different kinds of external evaluation systems. If tests, controls, inspections and measurements take over the girder on which the school system rests, it will break.

References

Bjørndal, L. (1989), *School Evaluation in Norway: A Pilot Project in Upper Secondary Education*, Oslo: Rådet for videregående opplæring.

Elliot, J. (1979) 'The case for school self-evaluation', *Forum*, 22, 1, 23-25.

Fredholm, L. (1988), 'Praktik som barare av undervisningsinnehåll och form', *Acta Universitas Gothoburgensis*, Gøteborg Universitet.

Holly, P. (1984), 'The institutionalization of action research in schools', *Cambrigde Journal of Education*, 14, 2. 5-18.

Løvlie, L. (1984) *Det pedagogiske argument*, Oslo: Cappelen.

McMahon, A. *et al.* (1985), *Guidelines of Review and Internal Development in Schools*, Secondary School Handbook, Schools Council Publications, York: Longman.

NOU (1988) 32, For et lærerikt samfunn.

Polsby, N. (1979), 'Preface'. In Sharpe, L.J. (ed.) *Decentralist Trends in Western Democracies*, London: Page.

School evaluation, a basic paper. 1988. Rådet for videregående opplæring.

Simons, H. (1987), *Getting to Know Schools in a Democracy: The Politics and Process of Evaluation*, London: Falmer Press.

Stenhouse, L. (1975), *An Introduction to Curriculum Research and Development*, London: Heineman.

Tiller, T. (1986), *Den tenkende skolen. Om organisasjonsutvikling og aksjonslæring på skolens egne premisser*, Oslo: Universitetsforlaget.

Tiller, T. (1989), *Erfaringslæring. En utfordring i kompetanseoppbygging*, Hefte nr. 12 i serien Ledelse i skolen, Oslo.

Chapter 16

Fitting evaluation within the governance of education

Maurice Kogan

Many of the chapters in this book have been rightly concerned with the deeper significance of both decentralisation and evaluation. In particular, they point out the potential conflicts of values implicit in each of these apparently benign concepts. Weiler usefully links the notion of evaluation to that of legitimation. Others have gone further in pointing out potential pathologies that might attach to evaluation if, for example, it is used primarily as a means of control or even of censorship.

These reservations and anxieties are well worth taking on board, as long as they themselves are treated with the appropriate degree of scepticism. For example, it is not clear that legitimation is a bad thing. Do we prefer the use of non-legitimated power? Positivistic statements of social conditions and policies must indeed be taken for what they are. The information frame upon which they might be based can entail presuppositions about desirable policies, and to the extent that they come from official sources, or sources otherwise concerned to maintain existing positions of power, the data and assumptions will inevitably be tied up with particular perspectives on social reality. At the same time, there is danger in the kind of dour neo-Augustinianism that assumes that all governing and social relationships are inherently evil, that attempts to arrive at collective systems of control and accountability are necessarily part of the slave owners' conspiracy. The downside to critical sociology when it applies its sceptical eye to the attempts of politicians and administrators to make things work is that it can lead to an unnourishing form of reductionism and immobility. Practitioners and their clients need at least a common sense appraisal of what is going on. Over-critical approaches can lead to a cosy assumption that because no evaluation can be value free or free of the interests of those who make it, educational institutions and their employees should be left to do their own thing without too much concern for society's things.

In this chapter I try to share the problems being faced by Norwegian polity makers as they change from a highly centralised system, governed by rules, to one in which decentralisation becomes the operational norm. In the reformed structure evaluation will be the means of ensuring some link between decentralised schools and local authorities and national policies. Most specifically, I will, with the boldness born of ignorance of the Norwegian system, specifically suggest how evaluation can be fitted to the functions of the school, the local authority and the ministry, and indicate the knowledge needed for the performance of those functions, the sources of evaluation and the uses made of the knowledge and evaluation thus generated. I will also note how evaluation could and probably should fit into other aspects of an educational planning and allocative system.

Underlying assumptions

The following assumptions underlie the use of evaluation in the Norwegian decentralised educational system:

(a) the intention is to decentralise as far as is possible to individual schools and other institutions. These will be given 'a greater mandate for development work and innovation. This will carry with it, at the school level, a function of self-evaluation of their programmes';

(b) at the same time, there will be decentralisation to the counties (upper secondary education) and the communities (for the compulsory school). This will take the form particularly of a system of general grants covering the whole range of services administered by these two levels. The centre will give up its power to make detailed regulations and recommendations to the politically elected local authorities.

It is not clear, however, what the relationships between the local authorities and the schools will be in terms of development and control of the curriculum. In the last Mønsterplan it was the schools that were supposed to 'concretise the curriculum in a local plan'. This is a relationship that remains to be clarified;

(c) Parliament will retain overriding responsibility for the educational system. It will stipulate education's goals in legislation. But the laws will be 'frame laws' and not specific regulations. Parliament will decide educational budgets to be incorporated in general grants to local authorities. The Ministry will decide the national curriculum, but as already noted, it is local authorities and the schools that will convert it into action. This leaves open the issue of what the Ministry's role will be;

(d) evaluation will occupy several functions in the new scheme of things. As Lundgren points out, education needs to be legitimised; information about how the system is functioning would be a vital contribution to this. Such information will no longer emerge as a secondary product of the imposition of controls. It follows that other ways of evaluating the extent to which goals are being achieved, and making it available for purposes of critique, become more important;

(e) in principle, the national evaluation of the system will not be used for directly prescriptive purposes. Instead it will enable the national authorities to have adequate knowledge about the system for which they are accountable to Parliament. It will enable the Ministry of Education to make its case for resources on the basis of competent knowledge. It will enable the Ministry to ascertain how far present national objectives are being met end how far they need to be modified. And it will enable the Norwegian people as a whole to know what it is getting for its tax money. Evaluation will therefore contribute towards the ways in which society influences the work of the schools, but the means will be through modes of normative influence rather than through direct legal prescription.

In considering the nature of the system to be evaluated the issue arises, and is referred to in Lundgren's chapter (Chapter 3), whether policy making should proceed on rationalistic lines. A rationalistic system led by the centre is essentially one in which the ends of educational activity (or objectives or goals) are set by the centre which then attempts to ensure that they are met mainly through regulation and financial control. From then on, the evaluative task could be relatively easy because the goals incorporate the criteria against which activities at each level of the system can be assessed. A truly decentralised system, however, cannot proceed on the rational model. By definition, the goals are not pre-set but are to be determined by the primary actors in the field, namely the teachers. They will interact with their pupils within a world of knowledge and ideas founded upon professional perceptions of what people need to learn and also responding to local wishes and needs. The variability and unpredictability of the goals to be set, over so many schools, communities and counties, will he further complicated by the power that undoubtedly will rest with politicians at these local levels. Centralisation means coherence in goal setting; decentralisation aims at proliferation.

Decentralisation will be balanced by policy-making at the centre, which inevitably sets national goals. These are expressed through the Mønsterplan and through the budgets allowed to local authorities. A *structured decentralisation*, implying a carefully limited form of rationality, will therefore be necessary if two potentially conflicting ideals are to be met. They are the need for genuine growth of power, creativity and good work at the working levels of the system, and the need for the Norwegian people to be satisfied that certain national and social criteria such as equality, relationship to the needs of the economy, and individual development are well sustained in the nation's schools.

A framework for the system

Unless decentralisation is to be anarchic, which is not the Norwegian intention, and if it is to shed centralised prescription, it must be accompanied by sensitively worked out national influences over what the schools do. In effect, educational government will move from *prescription*, and the coercion implicit in it, to *normative* measures of control. This will require information and judgements relevant to knowing what is happening in education to come into the public domain. Decentralisation should not entail greater local privacy; on the contrary, it should lead to more openness. This normative requirement, however, can easily become devoid of meaning unless particular actions are associated with it. Moreover, as we have already noted, the structure within which information, judgements and persuasion can find their place will be complex because so many levels - the individual pupil and teacher, the school, the local authority and the central ministry - will each have a role to play in setting up the information and making judgements on it. At each level, too, there will be multiple judgements. It is unlikely, for example, that at the community level the politicians and the professional educators will, or should, share a similar perspective. However, both have an evaluative function. An open and pluralistic system will provide multiple evaluations from which choices can be made. There might then be a danger of evaluation overload. Experience and common sense may eventually lead to a reduction of effort.

This leaves us with three difficult technical problems. The first is to differentiate functions and evaluative activities at each level. The second is to fit evaluation into other governing activities including needs assessment and planning. The third is to determine how evaluation might be used.

The first problem: evaluation at the different levels

The nature of evaluation at the different levels will depend upon the functions of the different levels. It is possible to use some of the same information at all three levels, but only in the case of certain data. Much evaluation will be determined by the precise audience for it. Knowledge should be sought only if it is needed; it should therefore be linked to functions to be performed. Figure 16.1 attempts to give examples of the different kinds of knowledge that might be necessary at different levels. The suggestions contained in it are not intended to be definitive or prescriptive; they are examples only of the kind of analysis that might be useful:

- column 1 shows the main functions of the levels of schools, local authorities and ministry;

Figure 1 - Evaluation at the different levels: some preliminary possibilities

	1. Functions	2. Knowledge needed	3. Source of evaluation	4. Uses made of knowledge/evaluation
School	1. Interpretation of Mønsterplan 2. Development of local curriculum 3. Creating teaching and learning processes 4. Relationships with parents 5. Relationships with other social services 6. Evaluate itself and publish its evaluation to the local authority and community 7. Development of curriculum and school life on basis of pupils' perspectives 8. Self-development of teachers	1. Records of individual pupils' development 2. Knowledge of pupils' social backgrounds 3. Assessment of teacher performance 4. Knowledge of general social and economic circumstances affecting pupils: 'needs analysis' 5. Pupil knowledge and assessment of school 6. Knowledge of school's development as an institution of evaluation.	1. teachers assessments of pupils 2. External tests of pupils 3. Needs assessments of areas provided by local authority 4. Judgements made on the school by parents' councils, individual parents, other school-related professionals (social workers, careers officers and the like) 5. Judgements made on the school by local authority 6. Pupils's assessments 7. Critical assessment of criteria	1. To adjust local curriculum 2. To reappraise and modify relationships with pupils and parents 3. To make reports to local authority and client groups (school councils 4. To make case for resources to local authority 5. For teacher self-development 6. Organisational development of school and local authority
Local authority	1. Decide proportion of general grant to be used for education 2. Allocate finances and other resources to schools 3. Provide buildings, equipment, etc. to schools 4. Ensure that schools provide adequate education according to the Mønsterplan 5. Ensure that schools adapt Mønsterplan to local needs 6. Provide support to schools through in-service training, advice, etc. 7. Engage in needs assessment, strategic and operational	1. Educational outcomes of schools' work 2. Schools' relationships with community and clients 3. Needs of population, both social and economic 4. Condition of schools resources (buildings, staffing, etc.) 5. Level of professional development in-service training in schools 6. Quality of self-evaluation made by the school	1. Own statistical work on school outcomes 2. Qualitative assessment of education being given in the schools, made by own staff, or inspectors or advisers including regional directors 3. Reports made by schools on programmes and outcomes educational and managerial	1. To create an assessment of needs of area 2. To create educational plan for area 3. To decide on allocation of resources to education and its institutions 4. To create appropriate in-service training, both

	planning connecting education to other services 8. Evaluate schools' and teachers' performance			
Ministry	1. Create national goals for education in relationship to goals determined by government and Parliament 2. Allocate resources to local authorities 3. Determine 'hypothecations' contained in general grant to local authorities 4. Create adequate quantitative data systems about the functioning of the education system 5. Evaluate the work of local authorities and of schools to ensure connections with other social and economic policies 6. Ensure that local authorities and schools make their own evaluations 7. Collate results of evaluations at other levels 8. Ensure that education relates adequately to other public sector functions, e.g. the economy and employment	1. Assessment of pupil achievement throughout the country (through light sampling) 2. Qualitative assessment of the working of decentralisation at both schools and local authority level 3. Assessment of data on social outcomes (e.g. equality) of education 4. Assessment of data on economic outcomes (flow of qualified manpower) of education 5. Collate assessments of educational outcomes from employment organisation	1. National surveys of samples of pupils' achievement 2. Longitudinal data about school and pupil achievement, and access to different forms of employment 3. Qualitative data provided by regional directors, countries, communities and schools themselves 4. Research, both quantitative and qualitative, about changing nature of schooling 5. Social and labour market data about educational outcomes	1. To make public reports on the state of education throughout the country 2. To justify work of education system to parliament and the Norwegian people 3. To consider modifications to Mønsterplan over time 4. To monitor the extent to which existing laws affecting education are appropriate 5. To determine allocations made to different local authorities

- column 2 shows the kind of knowledge needed for them to achieve their roles;
- column 3 shows the possible sources of the knowledge; and
- column 4 shows the uses to which the knowledge might be put.

The second problem: evaluation and the assessment of needs

The second problem is fitting education into other governing functions. Evaluation should be one element only of a sophisticated system in which schools and education authorities reflect upon what they are doing, on how to do it, on the results that they achieve, and on the basis of that analysis move back to decide what they should do next. Figure 16.2 links evaluation not only with policy-making but also with assessment of needs, planning, resource allocation and development and delivery of service. In such a cycle of operational planning the categories need not be exclusively hard and quantitative. Many of the most important judgements will be subjective and in words rather than in figures, although we must recognise that 'words are fat and figures are thin'.

It may be helpful to elaborate a little more what is meant by needs assessment. Unless there is knowledge about needs to be met it is difficult

Figure 16.2 - The operational planning cycle

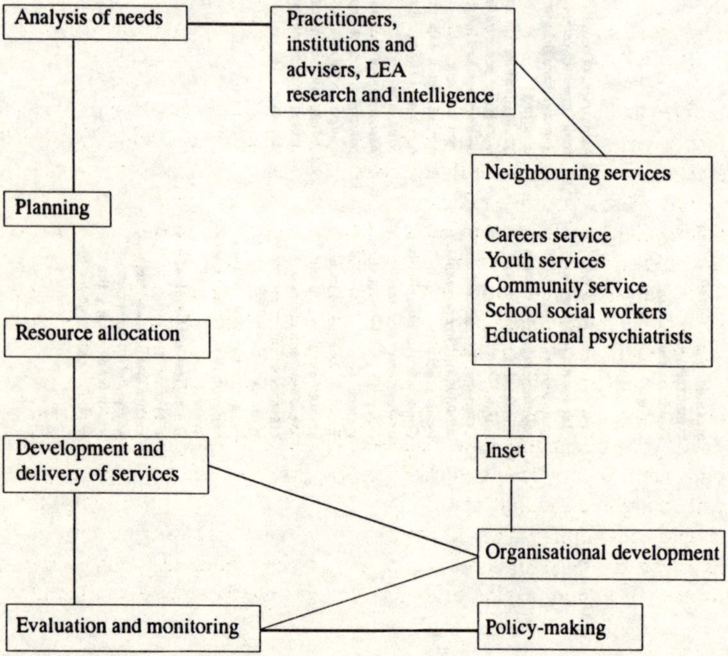

Figure 16.3 - Reviewing needs assessment for 16- to 19-year-olds

Data to be collected*

By schools

Existing courses and student numbers
Perceived demands & needs of students, e.g. academic, vocational or social
Student destinations
Employers' needs and demand
Planned changes in process
Needs institutions cannot meet
Institutional priorities

Similar inputs from:

Careers service
Youth service
School social work service
Educational psychologists
Special needs

By local authorities

Needs being met by present
Provisions
Information on employers' needs
Local or national factors
Affecting changes in provision
Statement of priorities

Unmet needs to be assessed:

Part-time students; non-participants small employers to be assessed through:

Surveys
Careers service
Pastoral systems
Visits to employers
Analysis of school records
Outreach work
Industrial liaison officers

* Adapted from Whitaker, T. and Packwood, T., *Needs Assessment in Post-16 Education*, Falmer Press, 1988.

to form a view of desirable objectives and to evaluate the extent to which they have been met. An analysis of needs could provide a base upon which teachers could determine their curricula in the light of clients' wants. It would make it possible to determine the courses for which there is a need and demand and the best institutions to offer them within a local authority. It would enable priorities to be set, and resources to be allocated rationally. The analysis would apply to different levels and parts of the education system, including those parts not provided by schools themselves, such as school welfare and psychological services and careers services.

The content would vary according to the age and phase. As far as the children in the compulsory school are concerned, the analysis could be devoted to elucidating how the contents of the Mønsterplan, as modified by schools locally, can be developed for different groups of pupils. This would involve thought about how far a local authority and its schools should help pupils with particular abilities and needs including those from deprived socioeconomic backgrounds, or with particular needs deriving from their ethnic origins or from other family characteristics. Children

Figure 16.4 - Examples of sources of evaluation and monitoring

Evaluative data	**Sources**
Professional judgements	
Judgements on the work of schools and teachers, based on regular visits observation and records	Advisers-Inspectors
Judgements on the work of schools and teachers, derived from school councils reports.	School Councils
Judgements on the work of schools and teachers made from perspectives of educational psychology, school social work and careers services.	Professionals in relevant services
Self-evaluation of school by staff	Heads & staff
Self-evaluation of school by School Council	School Council
Quantitative data (educational)	
Performance in national tests	R&I (Research and Intelligence in Ministry & Local Authorities)
Performance in secondary school and other examinations	R&I
Staff activities (quantitative)	
Turnover rates of staff; capacity to attract staff	Advisers R&I
Participation in Inset	Advisers
Appraisal of teachers' performance	Heads & Local Authorities
Educational outcomes (quantitative)	
Take up rate of courses (post 16 mainly)	R&I
First destination statistics	Careers
Problem indicators	
Truancy rates	R&I
Numbers of pupils seen by school social workers and education psychologists.	SSW & EP
School and community milieu (qualitative)	
Relations between staff and governing body	Advisers & LA
Relations between staff and parents	Advisers
Financial management data	
Judgements on competence with which delegated money is being administered.	Ministry
Quantitative data on degree of over/underspend, competence of data collection, etc.	

with special educational needs would be another group that would require a different analysis.

Figure 16.3 (based upon work in the UK by Whitaker and Packwood, 1988) gives the example of needs assessment for 16- to 19-year-olds who are quite similar to those to be found in the Norwegian upper secondary school. It shows the kind of data that might be collected by schools and by local authorities.

Multiple sources of evaluative data

There are several potential sources of evaluation and monitoring of schools. Figure 16.4 is a list drawn up (but slightly modified) for UK purposes that will show the multiplicity of sources that might be considered appropriate.

Making use of multiple kinds of data

As Lundgren's chapter (Chapter 3) shows, depending wholly upon quantitative data would be unsatisfactory. Such data depict either the costs of education (inputs) or narrowly defined outputs in terms of measured performance. But some of the quantitative data listed in Figure 16.4, if used sensitively, can give clues not simply to outcomes but also raise questions about the quality of what is going on in the school. Why is there, for example, a rapid turnover of staff in one school or constant staff absenteeism? 'Hard' data on pupil absence rates need to be interpreted carefully. They can mean a demoralised and poor school or they can mean that an excellent school is having to cope with pupils with serious family and social problems. But these questions might not be raised at all unless data are available and used. The matching, however, of quantitative and qualitative data is a difficult task that cannot be shirked. The following points are relevant:

(a) quantitative data can provide one base for evaluation, and securing them should be a first task. They cannot, however, he used by themselves in order to make decisions about what to do next, whether that be providing more in-service training or offering blame or praise to a school. They are unlikely to embody sufficient weighting for the context in which a school is working, and are often ambiguous. Quantitative data can act as a 'tin opener', that is to say, they can at least lead to the raising of key questions. And, of course, some data, although crudely quantitative, may be sufficiently indicative in their own right to be usable;

(b) it follows that quantitative data should be scrutinised against qualitative judgements. The problem in Norway is that local administration may not have the capacity to create and collate qualitative judgements.

Where these are made elsewhere, as in the UK, large numbers of both national and local authority inspectors and advisers are available to perform the task. In Norway it may be possible to consider the following:

(i) local authority administrators should be selected for their educational as well as their administrative experience and should thus be able to make such evaluations;

(ii) the regional directors whose role is now less certain than hitherto could make evaluations;

(iii) heads of schools, preferably from outside the local authority itself, could evaluate the work of their colleagues. This is, after all, the pattern applied to university research, and peer review of this kind has many advantages;

(iv) evaluation made by professionals near but not of the school might also be used. Educational psychologists, school social workers and careers officers are often able to form a view of the competence of a school at least in certain respects and are certainly concerned;

(v) training in a range of evaluative modes should be available.

If, however, local authority or regional administrators make the evaluations, their status should be defined. Are the evaluations the property of the school or will they lead to action by the local authority? Are they 'summative or 'formative'?

Making evaluation and decentralisation work

To move from a system in which prescription gives way to normative influence operating largely through multiple forms of information will require enormous shifts in behaviour and attitudes. The dangers are obvious. Decentralisation may not mean more freedom to a local school if either those in political control, or clients, or, indeed, a head or a dominant group of teachers choose to be restrictive rather than open. A further danger in the kind of proposals made by the OECD examiners is that of the overwhelming weight of information to be absorbed and used. It was Nabokov who wrote of the 'vertigo of facts', which, he declared, made him dizzy and sick. However, of course, enormous numbers of facts are already collected. The important thing is not to have information but to make it work for those who need it. Essentially evaluation is creating data so that worthwhile judgements can be made. They become worthwhile if they contribute towards efficiency, greater democratic participation in the running of education, and fairness between those who provide it and those who receive it, and between different recipient groups.

It is not possible to specify the optimum level of information from a distance. Authorities at the different levels will have to make their first approximations and quickly correct for errors of omission or too much commission. Throughout, common sense rather than technology should prevail. Collecting data can be expensive in the light of the return one would get from it. *In principle, evaluation should not be made at all unless those making or requiring the evaluation are sure how they are going to benefit from it.* Evaluation can be used in order to help teachers and administrators improve their own performance. It would thus feed in, perhaps, to in-service training or into active adjustment or management of teaching procedures or the like. It can be used for purposes of management control so that, for example, a local authority may need to evaluate because it is not certain about the standards of what the people in the community are receiving. Or it can be used in order to make sensible allocations of resources to the different groups who need them. It would be astonishing if in any democratic system good information, delivered clearly and transparently to those affected by education, were not needed.

The contributors

Kjell Eide is trained as an economist. He spent ten years on research policy in Norway, before serving three years as the head of the educational planning activities of the OECD. He then became General Director of the Department for Research an Planning in the Norwegian Ministry of Education. After twenty years in the position, he is now Science Adviser to the Ministry of Cultural and Scientific Affairs. He has for many years served as the Norwegian representative to OECD's Education Committee and CERI, including functions as chairman and vice-chairman.

Sigbrit Franke-Wikberg is a professor of education at the University of Umeå in Sweden. For twenty years she has been doing theoretical and empirical research on educational evaluation and she has been leader of several research projects on evaluation encompassing all school levels. She has been the dean of the faculty of social sciences and is now acting as the vice president of the University of Umeå.

Marit Granheim is the project manager for the EMIL project, administered by the Norwegian Research Council for Applied Social Sciences. She is presently on leave from her position in the Royal Norwegian Ministry of Education where her area of responsibility is research and development work in primary, secondary and upper secondary education.

Ernest R. House is Professor of Education and Director of the Laboratory for Policy Studies in the School of Education, University of Colorado at Boulder. He has worked on numerous evaluations and policy studies for various government agencies. His latest book is *Jesse Jackson and the Politics of Charisma: The Rise and Fall of the PUSH/Exel Program*.

Maurice Kogan is Professor of Government and Social Administration at Brunel University and is presently acting as the University's Vice-Chancellor. He is the author of many works on the government of education including *Education Accountability* (1988), *Evaluating Higher Education* (1989) and (with other authors) *The Use of Performance Indicators in Higher Education* (1988). He has been an OECD examiner in studies of American R & D, and Norwegian and Swedish education.

Steinar Kvale is a Professor of Educational Psychology and Director of the Center of Qualitative Research at the University of Aarhus, and adjunct faculty at the Saybrook Institute, San Francisco. He graduated at the University of Oslo. His main research areas are evaluation and qualitative methodology.

Jon Lauglo is Director of Research, Programme of Research on Education, Norwegian Research Council for Science and the Humanities. At the time of writing this paper he was a lecturer at the University of London Institute of Education where he taught policy studies and planning and management in the Department of International and Comparative Education.

Ulf P. Lundgren is Professor at the Stockholm Institute of Education and head of the Research Department for Policy Analysis and Studies of Cultural Reproduction. He worked as expert for the Minister of Education in Sweden and in Portugal, and has been expert to the council of Europe. He was one of the members of the OECD team reviewing educational policy in Norway.

Thomas S. Popkewitz is Professor in the Department of Curriculum and Instruction at the University of Wisconsin-Madison. His work is concerned with the social and political implications of educational research, reform and teacher education. He is currently writing a book on issues of power and knowledge in educational reform.

Gary Sykes is an assistant professor of education at Michigan State University, where he also serves on the staff of the Holmes Group, a consortium of research universities pursuing a reform agenda in teacher education. He conducts research through the Center for Policy Research in Education, and his interests include policy effects on teachers and teaching, teacher education, and the assessment of teaching. Dr Sykes receives his doctoral degree in the Design and Evaluation Programs from Stanford University.

Tom Tiller is a Professor at the University of Tromsø - the most northern university in the world. His research has covered studies of local educational cultures and how educational knowledge is formed in practice.

Lise Vislie is a professor at the Institute for Educational Research, University of Oslo. Professor Vislie has been expert to the OECD/CERI Project on the education of the handicapped adolescent. She has been a member of the Norwegian Council for Social Science Research since 1985, and is presently the Chair Person of the Council.

Erik Wallin is a Professor of Education at Uppsala University, Sweden. He is Dean of the Faculty of Social Sciences at the same University. He has worked as an expert to the Minister of Education in Sweden and to the National Board of Education. He has also functioned as an expert to the Council of Europe and to OECD/CERI.

Ingemar Wedman is Professor of Education at the University of Umeå, Sweden. He has specialised in educational measurement (and to some extent in research on exercise and sports). He has been a post-doctoral fellow at the Division of Educational Psychology, Measurement and Statistics and Iowa Testing Programs, University of Iowa, USA during 1975-1976 and is now a Professor of Education and Educational Measurement, and Dean of Faculty for the Social Sciences at the University of Umeå. He is a member of several federal research organisations and runs a number of research projects in the field of educational measurement.

Hans N. Weiler is a Professor of Education and Political Science at Stanford University. He has been the Director of the International Institute for Educational Planning (IIEP) in Paris and a consultant on educational policy to a number of national governments and international organizations. His most recent books are *Educational Planning* and *Social Change and Comparative Policy Analysis: Learning from Experience* (with Meinolf Dierekes and Ariane Antal).

Index